# MEOW MEOW

Celebrating
30 Years of Publishing
in India

# MEOW MEOW

## THE INCREDIBLE TRUE STORY OF
## BABY PATANKAR

### SRINATH RAO

HarperCollins *Publishers* India

First published in India by HarperCollins *Publishers* 2023
4th Floor, Tower A, Building No. 10, DLF Cyber City,
DLF Phase II, Gurugram, Haryana – 122002
www.harpercollins.co.in

2 4 6 8 10 9 7 5 3 1

Copyright © Srinath Rao 2023

P-ISBN: 978-93-5629-587-2
E-ISBN: 978-93-5629-588-9

The views and opinions expressed in this book are the author's own and the facts are as reported by him, and the publishers are not in any way liable for the same.

Srinath Rao asserts the moral right
to be identified as the author of this work.

All rights reserved. No part of this publication may be reproduced, stored in a retrieval system, or transmitted, in any form or by any means, electronic, mechanical, photocopying, recording or otherwise, without the prior permission of the publishers.

Typeset in 11.5/15 Sabon LT Std at
Manipal Technologies Limited, Manipal

Printed and bound at
Thomson Press (India) Ltd

This book is produced from independently certified FSC® paper
to ensure responsible forest management.

*When my brothers and I were in school, our grandfather gifted us personalized copies of* Jack and the Beanstalk, *with us kids written in as the heroes. It was the first time either of us had seen our names printed in a book.*

*This one is for you, Nanaji.*

## Cast of Characters

- The Psychonaut; call centre manager
- Acid and Tracksuit; drug peddlers
- Don Vito Dada; former inspector, Anti Narcotics Cell, Mumbai Police Crime Branch
- Vijay Surve; Don Vito Dada's friend and informant
- Madhukar Shingte; police constable, Mumbai Police
- Shashikala 'Baby' Patankar; alleged drug dealer
- Girish Patankar; Baby's older son
- Satish Patankar; Baby's younger son
- Dipti Patankar; Girish's wife
- Sarika Patankar; Satish's wife
- Arjun Mazgaonkar; Baby's younger brother
- Kisan Mazgaonkar; Baby's older brother
- Bharti Mazgaonkar; Kisan's wife

- Shatrughna Mazgaonkar alias Badshah Peer; Baby's older brother–taxi driver, alleged drug dealer and self-proclaimed godman
- Baliram 'Ballu' Pujari; Baby's right-hand man
- Inspector Ashok Dhawale; in-charge Anti Narcotics Cell Worli unit
- Reshma Dawood; Girish's second wife
- Madan Singh; the Patankar family driver
- Divakar Shelke; inspector in-charge, Anti Narcotics Cell Worli unit
- Suhas Gokhale; senior inspector, Anti Narcotics Cell, Azad Maidan unit
- Yashwant Parte; police constable, Bureau of Immigration, Mumbai international airport
- Sudhakar Sarang; sub-inspector, Mumbai Police
- Gautam Gaikwad; suspended police inspector, Maharashtra Police
- Jyotiram Mane; police constable, Anti Extortion Cell, Mumbai Police Crime Branch
- Dharmaraj Kalokhe; police constable, Marine Drive police station, Mumbai
- Gyan Manikkam Samuel; former India Post employee and alleged drug peddler
- Paulraj Padaiyatchi; customs clearance agent at Air Cargo Complex, Mumbai, and police informant
- Rafiq Bam; police informant
- Sameer Wankhede; superintendent of police, National Investigation Agency
- Baidabai Veer; Dharmaraj Kalokhe's sister
- Popat Veer; Baidabai's husband
- Anusuya Kalokhe; Dharmaraj's mother
- Jagannath Pawar; Dharmaraj's neighbour

## Cast of Characters

- Namdeo Chavan; deputy commissioner of police, Anti Narcotics Cell
- K.M.M. Prasanna; additional commissioner of police, Mumbai Police Crime Branch
- Atulchandra Kulkarni; joint commissioner of police, Mumbai Police Crime Branch
- Rakesh Maria; Mumbai police commissioner
- Abhinav Deshmukh; superintendent of police, Satara district
- Inspector Ashok Shelke; in-charge of Khandala police station, Satara district
- Inspector Padmakar Ghanvat; chief of Local Crime Branch, Satara Police
- Deepak Humbre; deputy superintendent of police, Wai Division, Satara Police
- Pravin Chinchalkar; senior inspector, Marine Drive police station, Mumbai
- Sachin Dhayalkar; Girish's friend
- Naresh Pardeshi; Girish's business partner
- Inspector Vijay Darekar; the investigation officer at Marine Drive police station
- Rachna Singh; Girish's third wife
- Senior Inspector Avdhut Chavan; in-charge of Unit I, Mumbai Police Crime Branch
- Inspector Rajesh Kasare; the investigation officer at Unit I
- Naveen Chomal; Dharmaraj Kalokhe's lawyer
- Jayesh Wani; lawyer and Chomal's junior
- Ayaz Khan; defence lawyer specializing in narcotics offences and Gokhale's lawyer
- N.N. Gavankar; senior advocate and Baby's lawyer
- Varun Kumar Tiwari and Nityanand Thevar; drivers in Mumbai
- Vikas Puri; businessman and Tiwari's employer

# Prologue

## *Mephedrone arrives in Mumbai after being chased out of Europe*

Which fictional journalist could credibly make it as a crime reporter in the real world? Neither Clark Kent nor Peter Parker. They're constantly distracted from their jobs by having to save the world!

Neither Tintin, Lois Lane nor Seema Sohni (Sridevi in *Mr. India*). They flout the cardinal rule of reporting: never become the story. Also, you can't take your pet to work, heels are an inadvisable choice of footwear, and a source can be anonymous but not invisible.

Photographers Sudhir Mishra (Ravi Baswani) and Vinod Chopra (Naseeruddin Shah) in *Jaane Bhi Do Yaaro* are shoo-ins. *Delhi Belly*'s Nitin (Kunaal Roy Kapur) shows promise.

All three share an unwavering dedication to their work, the ability to lighten morbid situations with a joke and utter disregard for danger.

So to answer the question, not too many.

Any number and combination of disaster and death, misery and misfortune, scandal and sleaze may occupy a crime reporter's day. But, the interlude between big stories can be excruciatingly dull. You *need* something to happen.

Which brings up a major grouse.

Our heroes always seem to be working on the 'Biggest Story of Their Lives'. Fortuitously or through sheer dumb luck, they stumble upon, unmask or are chosen to report sensational stories of violence and greed. There isn't a single uneventful day, no tedious assignment.

A reporter doesn't get to choose the story. The story doesn't choose the reporter either. As a rule, a big story breaks at the moment of peak inconvenience—uncannily at the end of the working day or minutes into a late-night movie.

Then, there is this unconscionable obsession with murder. Murder stories reside at the top of the food chain, but the candidates at the bottom are just as worthy of a look. Take, for example, a story about drugs.

But drug stories don't often dominate the news cycle as murder stories do. Not unless the principal actor is, well, the offspring of a superstar actor. Despite our strangely cosy word association with cocaine and heroin or our culturally approved use of weed, the focus of a drug story isn't always on the drug in question.

A drug story isn't a story if it doesn't shock, scare or amuse. No one cares about a regular drug story. Neither the cop, the editor nor the sub-editor at the desk. Regular drug stories are simply space fillers. At most a five-minute hack job.

But every once in a while, a drug story emerges that demands more than a cursory effort. A story straight out of 'Ripley's Believe It or Not'. Life is never quite the same after a story like that hits.

In 2015, Meow Meow was that kind of a story.

For nearly eight years I wrote about mephedrone alias Meow Meow alias MD and its pervasive presence in Mumbai, but never once saw it with my own eyes.

Now I know what you're thinking: how hard could it be? Crime reporters have easy access to dodgy situations and people all the time, right?

Sure. But this isn't the same as sitting across the table from a pistol or knife or axe at a press conference or feeling the coarse strap of a *satyashodhka patta* in the detectives' room.

Curiosity crosses over into the realm of a potential criminal offence when you ask a contact to show what mephedrone looks like.

And yet, I couldn't write a book about a drug without some first-hand knowledge. So before venturing into a territory I had consciously avoided for this long, I set myself one ground rule: No tasting. Under no circumstances. Not even a pinch.

But before engaging my senses with mephedrone I needed to know what it had to do with cats.

The substance was first discovered in 1929 by the French chemist Saem de Burnaga Sanchez during his experiments on the Khat plant (*Catha edulis*).[1] Khat leaves have been either chewed or brewed into a tea by indigenous communities in the Arabian Peninsula and Eastern Africa for generations.

Australia's Alcohol and Drug Foundation describes Khat leaves as having a 'mild aroma and an astringent, faintly sweet taste'[2]. Depending on the amount consumed, it leaves a consumer feeling euphoric, talkative, energetic, social, alert and with improved concentration. At the same time, consumers note an increased heartbeat, rapid breathing, higher body temperature and blood pressure, and uncontrollable sweat.[3]

Except to the expert eye and unless you taste or smell it, mephedrone is nearly indistinguishable from salt, monosodium glutamate—the indescribably savoury taste agent found in Mumbai's street food staple Chinese Bhel—and its distant cousin cocaine. Just like cocaine, mephedrone acts as a nervous system stimulant by increasing the levels of the neurotransmitter dopamine—a chemical that conveys messages from the rest of the human body to the brain. Dopamine is more easily recognized as the 'happy hormone', playing an important role in how we experience pleasure. Stimulants like mephedrone alter the balance of dopamine, shooting it up to levels where a person actively chases risky but rewarding or pleasure-seeking activities like drug use. Mephedrone is an addiction-causing drug that impairs the brain's ability to stop its use after a point. This also means that the user needs larger and larger quantities of the drug to receive the same level of pleasure or 'kick' from it. This is what makes mephedrone especially dangerous—once hooked, a user's consumption of this drug rises rapidly.

While isolating these compounds, de Burnaga Sanchez also managed to derive a synthetic cathinone—4-methyl methcathinone—which he named mephedrone in his paper 'Sur un homologue de l'ephedrine', published in 1929 in the *Bulletin de la Societe Chimique de France*. After this publication, mephedrone finds no mention anywhere apart from the odd medical journal.

The credit for rediscovering mephedrone almost a century later lies with an Israeli chemist who likes to be identified only by the moniker Dr Zee. In his home country, Khat is pronounced 'Qat', and the plant is a known snack among Israeli citizens of Yemeni origin.

Dr Zee investigated Qat for his employers at a private agricultural products firm in the early 2000s while seeking a solution to protect crops from pests in Israel.[4] Dr Zee also had his private supply of Qat leaves from a bush in his garden, which he liked chewing on. In 2003, he was reported to have sold 700 kg of mephedrone pills intended for human consumption after devising a process for their production.[5]

Mephedrone was marketed in Israel as Hagigat, which comes from the Hebrew word 'Hagiga', meaning celebration or party. Soon, convenience stores and pharmacies sold Hagigat as '100% natural and without chemicals', a cheap and legal alternative to cocaine and ecstasy, and as a sexual stimulant. Hagigat lived up to its name and quickly became a best-selling product at retail stores.

So newspapers set out to investigate. Writing in *Haaretz*, the journalist Idit Avrahami described a wedding party in a central Israeli town where the bartender mixed Hagigat capsules in the guests' drinks.[6]

Avrahami had followed up an account by *The Guardian* journalist Conal Urquhart, of just how crucial legal drugs like Hagigat were to a good night out in Tel Aviv's nightclubs. After taking a Hagigat capsule, a club-goer said:

The music is now flowing through my body. I look around the bar indulgently. This is a great night. Now I feel more than warm, almost sensuous. I need to stroke something, anything. The feeling remains with me for the next couple of hours. Eventually I feel a sense of anxiety and the warmth decreases. I feel impatient, and I need another drink or maybe just another Hagigat.[7]

There are accounts of club-goers snorting Hagigat on tables or in the privacy of nightclub restrooms and participating in orgies for hours. Serious instances of side effects were also reported, such as the cases of the twenty-eight-year-old woman who collapsed at a wedding with extremely high blood pressure levels and the twenty-two-year-old man who was unable to move and broke into a sweat after popping two Hagigat pills at a party.

Israel became the first country in the world to ban the drug, mephedrone.

Mephedrone's next two stops were Europe and the USA. The suppliers were Chinese laboratories that reverse engineered Dr Zee's production method.[8]

The drug surfaced in the UK as 'plant food' in 2007. Research papers attribute the English street name M-Cat to an abbreviation of mephedrone's wordy chemical name. After all, 4-methylmethcathinone doesn't slip off the tongue as easily. The leap to Meow Meow is fairly predictable, as one British scientific review article likened mephedrone's odour to cat urine.

Mephedrone use was first reported in India in 2013, naturally in its financial capital, Mumbai. As in Europe, it was advertised here as doing everything that cocaine did but at a tenth of the price.

At the average neighbourhood *paanwala* in Mumbai, it lay camouflaged among his bottles of *chuna*. Say the magic word and fork over Rs 200 and he packed you a one-gram *pudi* [packet].

Meow Meow was new, it was fun. It gave users a surge of energy; it was as good for a night-long jagrata or party as it was for last-minute exam-eve cramming.

But most importantly, it was legal.

# 1

*Sometime in 2014*
*Seven Bungalows, Mumbai*
*2.30 a.m.*

From the tip of his pinkie finger to its first crease—as far as lines went, the Psychonaut had seen and done way longer than the tiny-ass one set in front of him. On one of the Psychonaut's palms sat a mobile phone and on its screen, a thin streak of dull white powder like a crudely drawn crease on a cricket pitch lay still, waiting. The faces of three boys, bathed in the amber glow of a streetlamp, were trained on the Psychonaut's. His brother, unsure but at ease, hung back.

There had been no forewarning when the Psychonaut and his brother had set out from home half an hour ago. They'd planned to smoke a quick joint with their friends and head back before their parents got too mad.

The brothers had parked their motorbike at the entrance to Gautam Lane, a narrow street with uniformity on its left flank—Gautam Nivas, Gautam Apartments and Gautam View—and incongruity on the right.

Their friends waited on bikes parked outside a shuttered scrap dealer's shop. There was little sound except for the boys' chatter. Beyond them, JP Road was troubled only by the occasional sputter of a passing vehicle—the *paav bhaji tawa* at Blue Park Pure Veg across the road had gone silent at least four hours ago, the metro train pillars had stopped quaking at midnight, and the waves crashing at Versova beach were too far away to reach their ears but close enough to prick their noses with a salty-fishy-sewage-y spray.

'Idhar aa na bro [Come here, bro]. I want you to try something.' One of the boys called to the Psychonaut. He held out a piddly line on his mobile phone.

The Psychonaut knew exactly what he was looking at. For months he had heard murmurings of the new poor-man's coke. A drug like no other. An urban legend with a silly name.

'What is it?' he asked.

'Try it first,' the friend said.

But it wasn't like the Psychonaut to dive nose-first into a substance he knew nothing about. Once he had outgrown the frenzied quest for stimulation that marked his teenage years, each experiment with a narcotic or psychoactive agent had been a carefully researched and considered decision. A child's curiosity coupled with a scientist's sense of caution. It was never one for the other.

This night, he did not have enough information on what he was being asked to sample. The internet had warned him that the drug could be dangerous, but it also hinted at an unsurpassable experience.

His gut pushed away at his indecision and goaded him to try it. Just once. He had done MDMA—the King of Amphetamines. He had nothing to fear. He swooped in.

The powder set fire to his nose as it was sucked forcefully in. It tunnelled its way up the sinuses and shot straight towards the brain. In a snap, the chemical reached its destination and burst into a powerful neural explosion. It made the Psychonaut's head throb in pain the same way that a large bite of ice cream does. An urge to sneeze came over him and passed. Already, his heart was beating with a newly acquired ferociousness, almost straining to rip out of his shirt and restrained only by his ribcage. The chemical assimilated into his body and was travelling to all corners of his body.

He lit a cigarette to calm himself down.

The soothing touch of nicotine helped him focus, to watch for signs of the chemical taking effect. Suddenly he felt no urge to yawn. He eyes no longer drooped in the half-awake state of this in-between hour. He spoke to his companions but did not notice the words. He tingled with the tiniest stirrings of cheerfulness. He waited and waited for a sign, any sign, until it was time to go.

His brother kicked the bike to life and waited for the Psychonaut to hop on. But the Psychonaut had no desire to be a passive passenger or go home. He felt a happiness, whose origin he could not trace to a natural source, that flooded him with a feverish energy and compelled him to run.

He shot out into an empty JP Road and turned right, shoes slapping concrete in a thunderous tattoo and hair flopping wildly on a chemically altered head. Caught by surprise but by no means worried, his brother rode after him.

'Stop running and get on the bike!' the brother pleaded.

The Psychonaut ignored him. The brother opted for a close follow, eyes peeled for obstacles.

'Where are we going?' he asked.

'Juhu beach,' the Psychonaut said, unsure of where the answer had come from but convinced that it was where he needed to be.

In the days that followed, the Psychonaut would try to put into words that sense of pure happiness that seemed to have taken up permanent lodgings in his body.

But now, the Psychonaut could not resist the urge to tell everyone whom he loved that he loved them. He started by telling his brother, who either resembled a running instructor observing his ward or a biker who couldn't decide if it was worth knocking down the lunatic ahead of him.

The Psychonaut needed his phone to administer the other 'I love you dude(s)'. Some twenty minutes later, exhausted but ecstatic, the Psychonaut rang his mother to tell her what he had done, and for the first time in his life, to tell her that he loved her.

'It's three in the morning! *Ghari ye!* [Come home now!]'

'I'm at Juhu Beach, Mom.'

But his mother didn't care. 'Come home right now!' she ordered.

Next, he dialled his best friend, the man who had initiated him into mind-altering substances some years ago, with acid.

The best friend sounded concerned. 'I hope you've not called up anyone else. Just get home. You're under the influence. I hope you've not called up your family,' he said.

'I called up my mom. I jacked off to everybody I know bro,' the Psychonaut said.

With some of the happiness seeping away now and tiredness taking its place, his final phone call was to the friend he had met at Gautam Lane less than an hour ago. He had to thank him and tell him that he had had a great time.

'We'll meet in the morning and chill some more bro,' the friend said.

'Sure bro,' the Psychonaut said, but only half-heartedly. There was nothing else to do and no more lines to be had. The Psychonaut let his brother take him home.

## A *few weeks earlier*

At work, the Psychonaut was required to be, and for a while was, the face of virtue. He liked working in HR, just not managing engineers in technology companies. He'd left one behind to join a call centre on Ghodbunder Road in Thane. He felt at home on a call centre floor, where he was both supervisor and overlord, a friend and confidant to his employees, an overseer and enforcer for his bosses. The mix of people drawn to working in a call centre and the reasons that compelled young men and women from Mumbai's northern reaches to spend their nights servicing the needs of aged Australian citizens fascinated him. The Psychonaut took an ethnographer's delight in his work.

It was while sharing the occasional post-work joint with his new colleagues each afternoon that the Psychonaut noticed how prevalent drug use was among call takers desperate to stave off drowsiness. The hours on the floor and smoke breaks in his first two weeks helped the Psychonaut discover a small drug ecosystem in the office—a couple of dealers who sold to colleagues and a larger number of others who, like him, sourced their stash from elsewhere. It stood to reason then, that on most nights, any one of his colleagues might be loaded.

In his third week there, the Psychonaut was pulled aside one night by a worried senior manager. She had noticed a pattern of truancy in the last two months among employees who had earlier always been on time and rarely reported sick. The absentees would always fail to report to work after a long weekend. More worryingly, she told him, their phone conversations with customers had taken a strange new tone.

The Psychonaut's junior colleagues were trained to end their phone calls within three minutes. The senior manager, however, had observed that these employees were chatting endlessly with the customers, like best friends on the home landline phone on a school night. It was weird.

The Psychonaut listened in to some of these calls. The first thing he noticed was that these employees had veered so far from the prepared script that they had begun to sound like friendly nurses to lonely senior citizens situated thousands of kilometres away. The other thing that caught his attention was a stuttering, slurred speech. They were not the voices of experienced call centre employees who had rested adequately before working the graveyard shift.

'Slurring sounds like they're intoxicated no?' the Psychonaut asked his manager.

'*Aisa hi kuch lag raha hai* [That's what it seems like],' she said.

But it was not enough evidence to act upon.

Then one night, evidence showed up for work up to two hours late.

The floor went silent as the employee's team leader confronted him.

'You took the office transport, didn't you? Where were you for two hours?'

The Psychonaut watched as the employee stumbled through his explanation. He noted how dry the man's lips were, how his eyes bulged, and how the words shot out of his mouth and collapsed upon each other in an unintelligible heap. He caught some incoherent mumbling about loitering in the office parking lot.

Soon, a crowd had formed around the cornered man. One of them whispered to the Psychonaut. '*Arre, yeh toh line karke aaya hai* [This guy has snorted a line].'

'Line?' the Psychonaut asked aloud. He hadn't marked the man out as a cocaine user.

The employee was pulled aside and ordered to open his locker. His team leader searched his backpack, removing a mobile phone, keys and a tiny plastic bag filled with long white rice-like crystals. To the Psychonaut, it looked like at least four grand worth of coke, just about a gram in all. A colleague said that it looked like Ajinomoto.[9]

The Psychonaut and his fellow managers were legally bound to inform their client company and the police that a suspected drug and a drug user had been found on company premises. But they could sidestep their obligation if the employee resigned.

His desk was empty the next day.

Over the coming weeks, the Psychonaut noticed the same dilated pupils, dry mouths and a jerky, nervous manner in many other colleagues. But even to his trained eyes, they showed no obvious signs of intoxication. The floor was buzzing with activity during hours when the occasional nap between calls was acceptable.

Finally, in the parking lot one afternoon after work, as the Psychonaut and a colleague shared a parting joint, he asked what the crystals in the locker were.

'*Bhai, woh to Meow Meow tha* [That was Meow Meow],' the friend said. The Psychonaut hadn't heard of it.

'*Yeh sab log Meow Meow kar rahe hain. Yeh log coke woke nahi kar rahe hain. Inke paas coke ke paise nahi hain. Ekdum sasta nasha hai Meow Meow* [All these people are doing Meow Meow, not cocaine. They can't afford cocaine. Meow Meow is cheaper].'

Days after his sprint to Juhu beach, the Psychonaut began snorting lines with colleagues in the parking lot. The fact that he knew nothing about the chemical he was inhaling scared him, but that awareness did not stop him from doing more of it. For the first time in his brief lifetime of usage, he had abandoned his rule of allowing himself a calculated experience.

He had slid frighteningly quickly from researching every single LSD blotter he did to shoving ever larger quantities of a mystery chemical up his nostrils.

He was in freefall now.

Before Meow Meow, he had not known dependence to any substance. He had always sourced from and consumed in the company of a small circle of close friends who had initiated him into drug use. It was with them that he had first experimented with LSD. Far from satiating his curiosity, his first acid trip made the Psychonaut hungry for similar experiences. He recorded detailed voice notes of each trip. Weeks later, when a trip had become a distant memory, he would pull out an entry from the dope depository on his phone and step through a portal to the past.

He'd fall back into the same room, the same clothes and the same company. Doing those lines again sent uncontrollable palpitations through his heart. His nose itched for another.

But even so, his usage had more in common with a beer enthusiast who samples every brew on the tasting tray and not so much with the alcoholic who chugs by the litre with the intention of blacking out.

Before long, he found a reliable Meow Meow dealer in the eastern suburbs through one of his acid friends. He especially enjoyed his dealer's sales pitch, delivered in a mix of Hindi, Marathi and convent-school English. The accent was hard to place but could only originate from the tongue of a Mumbai native. The dealer called his product 'chawal'—the Hindi word for rice.

'*Ley ley bro. Rush accha hai. Lamba lamba daana hai* [Take it bro. The rush is great. The crystals are long]. Onset is heavy,' the dealer had said during the first meeting. That was the mark of a good product.

'*Wahi toh chahiye* [That's exactly what I want],' the Psychonaut said. Every meeting induced in him equal parts thrill and fear.

The dealer was careful, almost paranoid in his caution. Unlike other pushers who worked their territories with tiny plastic pouches of their product wedged in multiple pockets and bodily orifices, the Psychonaut's dealer would take him to the man placed above him in the dope chain.

They arranged to meet on a busy road after dark. The dealer slipped into the front passenger seat of the Psychonaut's car and directed him to a quiet spot away from homes, roads, passers-by and streetlights. At a distance close enough—the Psychonaut could not clearly make out the man's face from the car—the dealer asked him to stop the car.

'Wait in the car,' the dealer said, pocketing the Psychonaut's cash.

He returned seconds later and ordered the Psychonaut to drive. The dealer charged extra for the rendezvous but the Psychonaut always found the price worth the risk. It was a safe experience.

But quality product wasn't always easy to come by. Because there was no time to inspect what he'd purchased, the Psychonaut would sometimes find his stash either composed entirely of a fine yellowish powder, methylone, or crushed glass that left him with a lacerated nostril.

Inconsistent supply would at times force the Psychonaut to seek out other dealers and risk scoring out in the open. His acid friends had told him to look for a middle-aged woman in Wadala who spoke Hindi with a thick Tamil accent. She wasn't hard to find.

Amma, as her customers called her, did not encourage talk. One simply handed over the cash and walked away with a plastic packet extracted from the depths of her saree. There was no lingering.

But just like his dealer's man in the shadows, the Psychonaut detected a steadily deteriorating quality in Amma's supply before long. So, the next time he walked to the dark corner where Amma operated, he instantly broke both her rules of transaction.

'*Yeh kya hai? Yeh toh Meow Meow jaisa nahi dikh raha hai. Jo last time diya tha yeh wahi hai kya?* [What is this? It doesn't look like Meow Meow. Is this the same thing you gave me the last time?]'

Amma was not pleased. '*Baby ka maal hai lawde! Zyaada baat mat kar* [This is Baby's dope, you fucker! Don't run your mouth],' she barked.

The Psychonaut felt a foolish question rise to his tongue but held back.

When he returned to his dealer the next time and complained about how crappy his supply had become, he received the same cryptic response.

'*Bro yeh baby ka maal hai. Doubt nahi karne ka* [Bro, this is Baby's dope. Do not doubt it].'

Baby, he said with the condescending patience of one teaching the alphabet to a toddler, controls the Meow Meow market in the island city.

'*Colaba se leke Mahim tak,* [From Colaba to Mahim],' he said, 'she has a strong network of trustworthy boys.'

Another pusher who hid behind a cute mononym, thought the Psychonaut.

A maxim in the Mumbai Police goes thus: 'A man who volunteers to work in the traffic department is either greedy or foolish.'

No one willingly signs up for a job requiring field personnel to witness and punish people displaying some of the worst possible behaviour that a human being can exhibit. When it's not hopelessly flagging down speeding and possibly drunk maniacs on Marine Drive at one in the morning—knowing that one of them could smash through the barricades any second—it is having to stick their noses close to the faces of dozens of drivers with questionable oral hygiene. It is no different in the contiguous towns of Thane and Mira-Bhayander to the north-east and west, respectively. Only the scenery changes; the faces may not.

A traffic blockade or nakabandi is the police department's steady money-maker, a cash cow that is either missing a helmet, speeding, drunk or doesn't have a driver's licence. In the pre-Covid-19 and pre-breathalyser age, detecting a whiff of alcohol on a driver's breath meant having to establish a dentist's proximity to a person who would sooner run you over than pay a fine and have his vehicle impounded.

The traffic police are trained to spot tell-tale signs even before having to examine the stench. The nervous ones execute a sudden U-turn in the middle of the road and flee at the sight of barricades. The overconfident ones tend to overcompensate with an entire packet of mint, chewing gum, mouth freshener or gutkha.

In early 2014, there were some unexplained blips on the radar. Field traffic police personnel posted at Ghodbunder Road nakabandis began sending in reports of bikers displaying unusual behaviour. The men had a restless manner about them. They seemed to be high on something, but nothing that constables at the barricades could identify. Reports from different stretches of the road had similar observations: the bikers had dilated pupils, something white and sticky clung to their nose-hair and a faint smell of urine emitted from their faces. These were not enough signs of criminal behaviour.

Even the Psychonaut and his colleagues, in their heightened states, had noticed the split second longer that they were now being scrutinized at nakabandis, the policemen glancing carefully at their faces and shrivelling their noses as though trapped in a toilet.

The men's loo of the Psychonaut's office was crowded at 2 p.m. every day as scores of users picked their nostrils clean and bathed in perfume. They would joke saying, *'Perfume ka smell itna aayega ki cops ke naak ke baal hi jal jayengey!* [The smell of perfume is so strong; it would burn the nostril hair of the cops!]'

The only time the Psychonaut ran into a nakabandi minutes after snorting a line, the police spotted his wide-open eyes staring into the mid-day sun and pulled him aside.

'*Yaane amali padarth kela aahey. Yacha nakaat check karu ya* [He is high. Check his nostrils],' one of them said. But the Psychonaut had already carefully wiped himself clean. They had to let him go.

Even as he reckoned with his own habit, the Psychonaut watched Meow Meow use in the office explode to epidemic proportions. His fellow managers found employees going off in pairs on unusually long breaks, and it wasn't just those who were dating their co-workers.

In between calls they snuck off to a patch of wood behind the building or an empty meeting room or a deserted lobby. Even the common stairwell. And all done with bare minimum concealment.

Like the three monkeys, management blocked everything out. Even when embarrassed security guards brought CCTV footage. Eruptions of fornication at the workplace were fine as long as productivity wasn't hit. The drug-fuelled copulation at the call centre continued.

Then one night, the sounds echoed down the stairwell to a call centre four storeys below. The police dropped by the complex to investigate a complaint of an active prostitution ring. Management *had* to pull out of its collective denial now.

Sheepish explanations followed: 'Our employees have gone wild,' management told the police.

There was no mention of Meow Meow, the employee who was made to quit or the stash in his cupboard. The police found nothing to investigate. Management got away with a censure.

Soon, the Psychonaut was summoned by his senior manager.

'I don't understand what is happening. You've come from corporate HR. You know the rules, you know the laws, you take charge,' she told him.

The organization could have faced an audit from its client for failing to report drug use and neglecting to enforce a drug testing policy. The best case scenario for management was a hefty fine. The worst was too frightening to consider. It was easier and cheaper to cut the offenders loose.

Overnight, the Psychonaut laid off 120 employees. He'd smoked joints and done lines with some of them and shared rides to work with others. There was a time and place for sentiment and guilt. But this wasn't it.

He had miraculously escaped. Now he had to leave before management discovered that he was buried just as nose-deep into Meow Meow as the employees he had fired.

The Psychonaut had been experimenting with filmmaking to stave off the ennui of nearly a decade in HR. A fledgling film production company offered a way out of Ghodbunder

Road. The job offer ensured two degrees of separation from his past. The catch was a new city with new beginnings and new friends. The reward was a possible remedy for his growing addiction.

The interview was an invitation to 'chill' with the company's founders and employees at a hillside bungalow a couple of hours' drive away from Mumbai one weekend. The Psychonaut took a friend along. At the bungalow, they found a dozen twenty- to thirty-year-olds massed around a table piled high with what looked like eight grams of Meow Meow. The Psychonaut's test, it seemed, would be to join in.

On the way out the next morning, the Psychonaut and his friend noticed that the table had been polished clean of all traces of the white powder. Between them, they'd snorted an entire gram—a huge dose by their usual standards, and they needed to rest over the weekend to recover.

But sleep was fitful and interrupted by brain zaps—painful bursts of electrical shock in the brain that shook their bodies awake like puppets twitching on a string. They awoke with their jaws bound tightly with an invisible clamp and their senses overwhelmed with weariness. The Psychonaut had read enough about the chemical composition of Meow Meow to know exactly what it was doing to his body: it had given him such intense pleasure the previous night that it had depleted his stock of dopamine, the body's mood regulator, leaving behind an anxious, depressed and terrified husk.

He had fucked up.

Throughout that week, the Psychonaut received panicked text messages from his new friends, who had been strangers just days before. They had overdosed and couldn't handle the downer. No one knew how long it would last. They swapped stories of spending entire days being depressed and nights feeling regret, jolted awake every time their eyes shut. Kept awake by their own bodies, the Psychonaut and his friend spent their nights sobbing by Powai Lake. Something was broken inside, and neither of them knew how to fix it.

By the end of that week, the Psychonaut's body healed. He felt better, closer to his old self. As soon as the bosses at the film production company had recovered from their trips, they offered him the job.

The Psychonaut's dealer had run out of ways and words to show his gratitude.

Scoring drugs is a plain business transaction. The party most likely to feel grateful is the one doing the scoring. This was different. A thousand thank you(s) felt grossly inadequate. Not when the new colleagues were buying 50 grams every month and putting his kids through school.

The dealer was always just a phone call away, always ready to hop into a taxi for a three-hour trip. For the first time in his life, he could blow two grand on a taxi ride. Pretty soon, he started making trips unprompted.

'I'm the area bro,' he'd say. 'Call me if you need anything.'

The colleagues were floored. Both by the man and his product. On the rare occasions when it didn't hit, there bore no hard feelings.

The Psychonaut wasn't as chuffed with the move. Now that he was here, his bosses wouldn't just give him the cinematographer's position. Hunger and ambition did not equal education and experience. Hooking them up with a reliable dealer didn't count.

It helped then that he was an autodidact, that his appetite for information was unquenchable. But so was his colleagues' appetite for Meow Meow.

Like clockwork, half of the office partied on the last weekend of every month.

Over three, sometimes four days, they snorted through eight grams of the dealer's finest.

A disturbing pattern set it. For the first time, the Psychonaut's habit had begun to affect his work and his relationship with his family. He spent the first two weeks of every month recovering from a marathon binge. In the third week he was sufficiently focused to work on a project. And the last week rushed past in furious anticipation of the next party. When a month ended, he found himself back on the top step of the Penrose Stairs.[10]

Taking weekends off to visit his family didn't help. On the drive to Mumbai, he'd flare up without warning. The drug would turn a mild temper into a hulking monster ready to erupt at fellow drivers and pedestrians alike at the slightest provocation. One weekend back at his parents' home, he punched and smashed the television screen after an argument. He'd return to work feeling hateful. To keep himself from teetering over, he'd do a line and block the world out.

The absence of noticeable physical side effects had given the Psychonaut and his colleagues a sense of invincibility. There was not enough scientific research dedicated to documenting how Meow Meow damaged the mind and body. It made one of his colleagues, who guzzled lines like a dumper truck, dangerously overconfident. The man snorted twice as much as anyone else every month and revived himself with a cocktail of water and multivitamins. At the rate he was going, there was no way his body could keep up. Sooner or later, the man was sure to croak, and the Psychonaut didn't want to be there when that happened.[11] He tapped out and submitted to therapy.

Ever since he'd cleared his class tenth examination in 2002, the Psychonaut had not known a single year without an addiction. It had begun that year with gutkha. He was enrolled in a Marathi-medium school in the river-side ghetto town of Mumbra, north of Mumbai. The progression to tobacco, marijuana and alcohol was organic.

He was in his twenties when the family moved to the western suburb of Andheri East in the big city. The move gave him a toehold on the ladder to respectability and social mobility. Bollywood waited on the other side of the railway tracks.

In Andheri East, he discovered a self-professed group of psychedelics. These guys experimented with anything they could score. The idea was to taste, test, depart temporarily from their ordinary lives and compare notes. Not to wind up shrivelled, deranged and lying on a bed of newspapers below Byculla bridge.

That first night in Seven Bungalows, he ran like Archimedes, discoverer of the key to happiness.

Gradually, he began to shed his caution. Meow Meow drove away the very idea of protest.

Nothing else brought on that tidal wave of joy on whose surface he could float for hours without going under. He stopped seeking happiness elsewhere. Without intending to, he had become a *nashedi* (addict).

In a far corner of his brain, where his ability to repel temptation lay buried, his exhausted synapses pulsed feebly with a single message: no line will ever feel as good as the first one. In a world of paper planes, Meow Meow was a nuclear warhead. Not even the King of Amphetamines matched it for sheer destructive power. He was throwing away a promising career for the sake of a quest destined to end in frustration.

It was time he stopped running.

# 2

One March afternoon, I sat in a drab police office listening, for the second time in three months, to a strange retelling of the greatest mob movie ever made. That a cop who had spent most of his career chasing gangsters and terrorists should cite *The Godfather* as the reason for him becoming a policeman is a fairly predictable origin story. This is especially fascinating when you factor in that growing up, he idolized a local larger-than-life hoodlum and was the only one among his friends not to stray to the dark side.

First in Marathi and then in English, this middle-aged man with his swept-back dyed black hair and thin moustache was doing a passable Don Vito Corleone impression. It helped that his voice had a natural bark-like quality to it.

I couldn't match his devotion to the subject. But I also didn't want him to know that I hadn't watched the film fully. So, I fell back to my role as an enthusiastic listener. It never fails.

With frequent nods, short bursts of laughter in all the right places, and a strategically-placed 'yeah!', 'what are you saying!', 'and then what happened?', and 'I don't believe it!', I've emerged from countless situations both as an impressive audience and without appearing to be an ignorant chump about things I'm expected to know as a crime reporter.

I waited for him to run through his stock of favourite dialogues so I could gently change the subject to shoptalk. I wanted to know about his role, back when he served in the Mumbai Police's Anti-Narcotics Cell (ANC), in setting into motion a chain of curious events six years previously. At the centre of the storm was a drug whose name no one seemed able to get right.

Don Vito Dada beat me to it. 'When I joined the ANC, mephedrone was still new. It was legal; people were falling sick, and we needed to act. Some users said it was like *amrut*, like nectar. I was curious and thought of trying some myself …'

But his high blood pressure and the thought of his family made him abandon that idea. There is a proverb in Marathi, *Vishachi pariksha kashala*, which essentially means, why fool around with poison?

Someone else would have to fool around with it instead. He found a volunteer in a friend of nearly thirty years.

One evening in 2014, he invited the friend to stay over. The wife and kids were away—the perfect opportunity to attempt an experiment that finds no mention in police records.

It took me some seconds before I found my lost tongue.

'Sir, *aap mazaak kar rahe ho na?* [You're joking right?]'

This sort of yarn should trigger the bullshit-meter—a piece of advice given by Rajkamal Jha, the Editor-in-Chief of *The Indian Express*, on my first day of journalism school. Mine was honking and blaring itself hoarse in my head.

I was still reeling when I left sometime later. But I just *had* to know how true this story was and asked the cop later that evening if his friend would agree to meet me.

The only study on mephedrone in India I knew about at that time was one on the consumption habits of users conducted by postgraduate students at Grant Government Medical College and Sir Jamsetjee Jeejeebhoy Group of Hospitals in South Mumbai. The other demographical research had come from interviews with students, clubbers and addicts in Europe. I hadn't thought of another category of people with easy access to mephedrone, its sellers and consumers—cops on the narcotics beat.

So a week later, I sat across the table from the cop and his friend, Vijay Surve, at a restaurant in south Mumbai with *paav*, needlessly spicy omelette, and milky *chai* laid out between us.

'There is nothing I wouldn't do for him,' Surve said, answering my first question. 'Of course I was scared when sir told me what he needed me to do. But he had explained to me what I should expect.'

Surve was the ideal candidate. Skin as rosy as the pink full-sleeved shirt covering his wiry forty-one-year-old frame. A slight roundness about the middle. The only clue to unhealthy habits was in the tell-tale brownish tint of his teeth.

The cop was the ideal observer. He was as well acquainted with sober Surve as with drunk Surve.

That evening, the cop brought home a bottle of whiskey and one gram of high-grade Meow seized from a peddler. He poured out a measure of whiskey each.

A few minutes later—Surve was sufficiently relaxed at the time—the cop poured a second drink into Surve's glass and mixed approximately half a gram of mephedrone into it. Then, he watched Surve drink it.

With no discernible changes in Surve's behaviour once he had drained his glass, the cop waited fifteen minutes before mixing the rest of the mephedrone into another peg of whiskey.

Through the night, the cop kept one eye on the clock and another on Surve. Every half hour he asked Surve how he was doing and every half hour Surve said, '*Mast lag raha hai!* [I feel great!]' And, he meant it.

At nearly 2 a.m., Surve was still wide awake and alert. 'From the inside I felt the freshness of just having brushed my teeth and taken a bath,' he said.

Surve's face told a very different tale. I asked the cop to show me what it had looked like. He trained a deathly Amrish Puri glare at me and hung his jaw limp loose like jelly melting in the sun.

Surve felt time slow down. His friend's voice seemed to echo as though the words had been yelled from across a valley and reached his ears after an age. When he opened his mouth to respond, his vocal chords seemed sedated.

'I had never seen Vijay like that before. In any case, I wouldn't have been able to explain this to anyone so we just stayed put,' he told me.

He made Surve lie down in his bedroom, believing that a supine position would eventually cure him.

But Surve could not sleep. His eyelids blinked but did not drop.

'*Kaisa lag raha hai*, Vijay?' the cop asked.

'*Mast lag raha hai*, sir,' Surve said.

No sign of drowsiness.

The cop was too worried to sleep. As an added precaution, he bolted Surve's bedroom door shut.

'Suppose he got up and ran out of the house? I could not risk that,' he told me.

At 4 a.m., he checked on Surve again.

'BEHENCHOD KAISA LAG RAHA HAI?'

Still awake, Surve said, '*Mast lag raha hai.*'

Surve got no rest that night. His lungs were constricting. His thoughts turned increasingly frantic and clouded over with worry. He lay restlessly on the bed until the cop roused him at 9 a.m. and forced some breakfast down his throat. The cop watched over Surve for two more hours and convinced that he was better, allowed him to leave and take a train home to Khopoli, a town more than 70 km from Mumbai.

'I kept calling him every thirty minutes until he had reached home. What if he fell out of the train? How would I have explained that?' he said.

At home, the feeling of restlessness did not leave Surve. Throughout the day he was fidgety. He had impulsively walked to a friend's home but returned within minutes.

'I could not keep still,' he told me.

It was only late in the evening, almost a whole day later, that he began to feel sleepy. The next morning, his heart no longer raced, the tightness in his chest had eased and when he opened his mouth, the words didn't ooze out in ultra-slow motion. He was fine.

He was also done with mephedrone.

For the next two days, the cop questioned Surve closely, pressing him to remember every detail. The cop's verdict? 'I'm not convinced by mephedrone,' he told me at the end of lunch. 'The feeling of being high is fake.'

# 3

On a humid afternoon, some days before that lunch with Don Vito Dada and Vijay Surve, I stood in a quiet lane leading off the Worli Sea Face holding a ziplock baggie in my sweaty palm. Facing me were two men: one dressed in a black shirt with the top three buttons undone and acid-washed jeans; the other track-suited, scowling, scarred, and nearly bald. We were only four buildings away from the observatory windows of Isha Ambani's mansion.

For months I had tried desperately to hear from people involved in the business side of mephedrone. I'd pictured meeting them somewhere a little private, not out in the open on a billionaires' row. I didn't know then that the guys I was pursuing for an interview were protégés of a woman called Baby who lived on top of a hill in Worli. Dropping her name impressed the first guy. The other one glowered, if possible, with added menace.

'You can keep it if you want bro. Taste it, study it. But if you plan to throw it away, give it back to me now,' said the black shirt man—let's call him Acid.

The unsmiling one, let's call him Tracksuit, quizzed me on mephedrone. I rattled off the loss of appetite, insomnia and nosebleeds. At the mention of nosebleeds, Tracksuit sneered.

'Everything you just said was wrong. You only get nosebleeds if MD is mixed with crushed glass,' he said. I would have argued but the scars and welts covering Tracksuit's face and arms warned me against it.

Tracksuit wanted to leave, but Acid pleaded with him to stay for fifteen minutes. In return, Tracksuit scowled some more. 'I'm leaving in fifteen minutes. *Mereko kaam hai* [I have work to do]. I'm not getting paid to do this.'

But first we had to get out of such a public place. We rode deeper into the lane and emerged on RG Thadani Marg, where the boys parked by the pavement. Acid disassembled his phone. Hidden in the battery cavity was another baggie. A smaller baggie was folded inside. From his wallet, he pulled out a debit card and a ten-rupee currency note rolled into a thin pipe. He emptied the baggie onto the glass panel of his phone and crushed and ground the white crystals with his card. Then, he patted it into two neat lines. Tracksuit glanced around the road for any spotters, saw that there were none and exhaled forcefully. Then, he took the currency note from Acid, held it under one nostril and snorted one line in one smooth motion. He handed back the note, tapped his nostrils twice and sat on his bike. No reaction and certainly no nosebleed.

Once Acid had snorted the second line and put the phone and note away, he wanted to know if I could meet them later that night. 'I'll call you,' he said.

I hung around while Acid and Tracksuit got ready to leave. Tracksuit had to make a stop at home before heading to his 'kaam'. He wiped his nostrils with a handkerchief, but I could see a few strands of white still clinging to his nose hair. He tilted his head back and made Acid look up his nose to see if he was clean. '*Arre ghar pe mummy dekhegi toh chillayegi na? Unko pata chalta hai agar main snort karke aaya toh* [My mother can tell when I've snorted a line. If she finds out, she's going to yell at me],' he explained, smiling for the first time since I'd showed up. He dug the handkerchief into his nostrils for a second time and gave them a vigorous rubbing. This time he did a better job.

'*Clean aahe, chal aata* [You're clean. Let's go],' Acid said.

Acid and Tracksuit rode to RG Thadani Marg around half past midnight on a sports bike. Acid looked friendly and was carrying a backpack. Tracksuit simply glared.

In the daytime, the tree-lined lane had been virtually deserted but for the security guards ambling outside building gates and taxi drivers snoozing in their parked cars. No one had paid us any attention. But now, when Acid and Tracksuit returned, a couple was out on a midnight stroll; a few groups of young men and women stood smoking in the shadows. The still air smelt distinctly of marijuana smoke. Very little traffic passed through except for bikers taking a short-cut to the Sea Face. It was not a quiet place to talk.

'Find us somewhere to crash in Koliwada,' Acid begged Tracksuit, 'we can't stay here.'

Tracksuit shrugged indifferently. '*Bagh mitra* [look friend], that's not my problem. Once I get home, my mother will not let me leave again,' he said.

'Bro don't do this. You want us to sit on the *maidan* all night?' Acid said. Tracksuit wouldn't commit. In his head, Acid had resolved that he and I were going to Koliwada. At the maidan, we'd wait, hope for Tracksuit to sneak away from his mother.

The more Acid pleaded the angrier Tracksuit became. He boiled over when Acid asked for the bike.

'*Mi hyaala gheun zaato* [I'll take him along with me],' he said.

Tracksuit shot another glare at me. I looked away. So much for not getting involved. Slowly, eyes still locked on me, he dismounted the bike.

'So I'll see you at three?' Acid asked, handing Tracksuit cab fare.

'I'm not making any promises,' Tracksuit said.

Acid rode north, down Sir Pochkhanwalla Road, zipped down its slope and only came to a halt on the Sea Face when the Indian Navy base, INS Trata came into sight. He went past the base with its friendly warning to shoot photographers, Cleveland Bunder and its snoozing fishing boats, the Indian Coast Guard Regional HQ (West) and finally into Koliwada. Solid blocks of salty, fishy and excrement tinged air bade me welcome into the fishing village.

Snaking through unlit lanes hemmed in by shanties, we emerged into an open ground. A water pump room and gym were situated close to the *maidan*. Men hung around the *maidan*, either talking on their phones or chatting in groups.

Acid parked along a row of scooters and motorbikes outside a home with a lit window and an open provision shop. He walked up to a man buying a cigarette and brought him over to where I was waiting. Acid's companion was his oldest friend. They had been in school together. 'And now he is my best customer,' he joked.

Acid's friend, whom we shall refer to as Office Boy, was earnest, with none of Tracksuit's grouchiness. He went quiet when Acid told him who I was and what I wanted to know. He wouldn't answer any questions.

'I have a wife and kid now. I've cut down on MD after marriage. I only do a few lines sometimes with this guy,' he said. Meanwhile, Acid had dug out a plastic baggie from his phone to do just that.

'*Yeh ley* [Take this],' Acid said, passing his phone and a 'snorter' to Office Boy once he had finished cutting two lines. Office Boy guided the note across the glass surface and handed the phone and note back to Acid. Office Boy then told me of the day he had first tried mephedrone.

'I don't remember the exact year but I know it was during Ganesh Chaturthi. I had a friend working in an office in the building next to mine. One day, he called me at work and asked if I wanted to try a new drug. He said it was unlike anything he had done before. I was curious. So, I told him that I would meet him during lunch break.'

Sometime later, Office Boy returned to work feeling energized, with no signs of post-lunch lethargy. 'I was able to focus on work much better after I returned. But I couldn't do more than one task at a time. And I was also very irritable throughout the day,' he said.

Luckily, his family was away, and Office Boy had the house to himself that evening. But then the friend called again. 'He told me to come over and do some more MD,' he said. He had just sobered up after a quiet few hours at home but couldn't refuse his friend's offer.

That night, it was well past two when Office Boy left. He had felt the same rush as the previous afternoon. As he was walking home, he spotted a woman who seemed to be a little too well-dressed to be visiting a slum at that hour. He wanted to speak to her but did not know how to strike up a conversation naturally. Then, he noticed that she was smoking a cigarette. So, he fished one out of his pants pocket and asked her for a lighter.

Office Boy suspected, but couldn't think of an inoffensive way of asking if she was a sex worker. Even as his brain formed a question, words blurted out of his mouth.

'What are you doing here so late?' he said.

A harmless inquiry. 'Going to see a client,' she said.

'The sort of client you're going to sleep with?' Office Boy said. The question had popped out before he could bite down on his tongue. He felt a slap coming.

'But she said yes,' he told me.

Emboldened by the drug, he had asked the woman if she would have sex with him too. The woman did not; she had an appointment to keep.

Office Boy did not give up. All he had to offer in exchange was a line of MD. Did she accept payment in highly addictive drugs or in cash only?

'At first, she did not want to try it but I kept persisting,' he said.

Eventually, hoping he would leave her alone afterwards, she agreed.

'She liked it so much that she came home with me—.'

Acid cut in to explain, 'MD makes girls horny.'

Once home, Office Boy suffered an erectile disappearance. The woman did not have all night. She blew him. On her way out, she left a Rs 500 note for the line.

'Too much can also make a guy go soft,' Acid explained.

Office Boy did two more lines with Acid before insisting that he absolutely had to go home. His wife was waiting up. But before leaving he answered the question I had asked him an hour back.

'The MD available in the market right now does not compare with Baby's. She sold the best *maal*,' he said.

It was past 3 a.m. when Tracksuit finally answered his phone. He had found us a place: a first-floor room behind a bus stop. Tracksuit ushered us in. Two tiny windows admitted just enough air to breathe in. It was impossibly stuffy inside and sweat poured down our backs. The night's 'snorter' was a crisp fifty-rupee note. Acid had rolled it so thin that the Father of the Nation disappeared and only a sliver of its bright blue margin and the last of three Pillars of Ashoka were visible.

Acid rang a customer who should have arrived an hour ago. 'How long will he take?' Tracksuit asked.

'He's at a party. He said that he is leaving now,' Acid replied. Tracksuit's perma-scowl deepened.

An hour and dozen phone calls later, the customer finally rolled in at 5 a.m. He was in his early forties and dressed in a black dress shirt with buttons opened to show off a waxed chest, denims, and a pair of slippers that encased two sets of exquisitely formed toenails. The customer, Acid informed me, was an exclusive cocaine user who did mephedrone only occasionally.

Toenails greeted the dealers and sank into a chair. He pulled out two iPhones from his jeans pocket—one black and one white. He'd come to stock up for a Holi party next week.

'How much?' Tracksuit asked.

'Five grams should be enough. *Pan bagh mitra, maal full asla pahijey aani hit karayla pahijey* [But look friend, the packet better be full and should give a good hit].'

The boys were hurt. Each of their packets weighed between 850 and 900 grams. 'I pack them myself,' Tracksuit said.

Acid cut three lines on the lid of a steel water drum. Toenails used a new two-hundred-rupee note and snorted his line with a fit of violent coughing and a loud clearing of his throat. Then, he went back to his black iPhone.

A few minutes later, his white phone buzzed. He spoke in urgent, worried tones and stepped outside. Soon, we heard the screech of tyres and seconds later, Toenails returned with a man wearing a similarly expensive white dress shirt, dark blue pants and black Louis Vuitton moccasins. In between furiously chewing gutkha with his mouth open, Moccasins swore. A lot.

'I'm going to fuck the guy who fucked with you!' he yelled. Toenails had a hard time restraining his friend, who looked like he might put his fist through the closest wall.

'I want some MD!' Moccasins barked. Without a word, Tracksuit handed him a packet. Moccasins paid for it and left, keeping up a string of abuses even as Toenails tried to talk him out of whatever he was about to do. They argued on the landing inaudibly. I couldn't catch their words despite straining to hear them, but the sound of their feet pounding down the stairs was loud and clear. A few seconds later, we heard the car pull away. Toenails returned alone and went back to his phone.

I could see that Toenails was logged into a betting app. He kept alternating between tennis matches, a cricket match and Roulette.

The roulette wheel and the ball spun in a casino on Toenails' phone. When both the wheel and the ball stopped spinning, a number flashed on the phone screen and Toenails let out a loud groan. 'I lost 20,000.'

'Rupees? Like actual money?' Acid asked.

'Haan,' Toenails replied. He spun again. This time he won Rs 25,000. He shut the roulette window and switched to tennis, where he had money hanging on the fate of two matches in progress halfway around the world—Anastasija Sevastova vs Cori Gauff and Chris 'O'Connell vs João Sousa at the Miami Open.

'How are you betting on tennis?' asked a bewildered Acid.

Eyes glued to the screen, Toenails explained: 'I place simultaneous bets on a win and loss for both players, depending on the odds. No matter who wins, I make some money.'

Both matches were far from completion, so Toenails switched to cricket. Toenails had laid down Rs 30,000 on the third One-Day International match between New Zealand and Bangladesh in Wellington. He hadn't just bet on the outcome but also on the projected score every five overs. His dejection grew deeper with every over bowled. Devon Conway and Daryl Mitchell were crossing his five over hurdles with ease. Bangladesh's bowlers couldn't defend any of Toenails' targets. With the air of a man who lost some and won some every night but always came back, Toenails stopped watching.

He switched to another window. This one took him to Greyhound races in Australia. Two tables popped up on the screen: the racers' names and the odds. He ignored the first one. In present company, he wasn't going to attempt saying them aloud. This was his first time, he told us, betting on the dogs. He wouldn't say how much.

He picked one with the best odds and an unpronounceable name. It won. He had another go and to his own surprise, won again. He scrolled down the tables a third time and found a dog whose name he *could* pronounce. Improbably, he scored a hattrick. He logged off. Quit while you're still winning. He wasn't done though.

'Is there any football being played right now?' he asked the room at large.

---

Sometime later, a baby-faced twenty-something boy with massive hands and a grip like a pair of pliers knocked on the door. He was Tracksuit's cousin and had been out looking for him.

'Does your mother know you're not home?' Tracksuit asked.

'I told her I'm going to the toilet,' the cousin replied.

Tracksuit ordered his cousin to fetch water, Thums Up and cigarettes.

'I don't have any money,' the cousin said. Toenails handed him his 'snorter'.

'Who is the kid?' he asked, once the door had shut.

'He's my younger cousin. He's good at cooking and at giving massages,' Tracksuit said. It was more a sales pitch than an introduction. Toenails looked interested.

Meanwhile, Acid was still sweating. 'Can I switch on the fan? Please?' he asked. Tracksuit silenced him with a glare.

Acid busied himself with cutting three more lines. This time he asked me if I wanted to try.

'No, thanks,' I said.

Tracksuit's cousin returned. Toenails put away his phone.

'I need a cook at my party next week. What can you make?' he said.

'My mom says I make good mutton biryani and pork vindaloo,' the cousin said. Toenails nodded, asked some follow-up questions but didn't commit to hiring him.

Toenails then noticed the boy's hands. 'I have knots in my back. Can you massage them?'

'I don't have a lot of experience,' the cousin said, 'I've only massaged my dad and uncles.'

Toenails was insistent. 'Why don't you start now? If you're good, you can come home with me and give me a proper massage. I'll pay you,' he said.

The boy got to work, kneading Toenails' left arm, stretching his fingers and cracking his knuckles before moving to his back. Toenails made no sound of bodily tension being released. He was too absorbed in his phone. When the boy moved to the right arm, Toenails moved his phone to his left hand. He turned his head the same way, ignoring his masseur.

Ten minutes later, the boy finished.

'Come home with me. I'll pay you Rs 250 to massage my back,' Toenails said. The boy looked at Tracksuit, who nodded his approval.

Acid pleaded with Tracksuit for permission to switch on the fan. Tracksuit finally gave in.

'Fine, but turn it away from me,' he said. Acid pounced on the switchboard.

Sunlight had begun filtering in through the windows and door when Toenails got up to leave. The silent wakefulness of the slum outside had been replaced with the sounds of honking buses and people stirring out of their homes. Tracksuit locked up and headed home to face his mother.

Toenails sat the boy on his bike and rode off. Acid asked me to come with him to deliver Toenails' stash of mephedrone. En route, he had to make another stop.

I find riding on a bike in normal conditions in Mumbai mortifying. Riding on a sports bike with a man who had spent the last twenty-four hours shoving a mountain of mephedrone up his nose was terror times ten. As Acid casually made phone calls and sent and read text messages while weaving through traffic and dodging drain covers, manhole covers and potholes, I wrapped one hand around a small strip of leather at the front of the passenger seat and the other over the flimsy left rear indicator. There was nothing else to cling on to.

We stopped inside an apartment building in Parel. The security guard on duty made no effort to ask who we were or where we were going.

'Keep it running,' Acid said, tossing me the keys and punching the elevator button. I didn't know what to do with them.

'I'll wait for you here,' I said. He was back five minutes later.

At what seemed to me was twice the speed, double the recklessness of before and half the time he'd spent upstairs, Acid rode to Toenails' place in Dadar.

We parked in another apartment complex. This one had four-storey blocks spread neatly around a large manicured garden. Toenails had warned us not to ring his doorbell. So we waited at the foot of the staircase leading to his floor while Acid rang Toenail's phone. Toenails emerged shirtless and covered in oil. Tracksuit's exhausted cousin trailed in his wake.

'*Mitra, maal strong asnaar na?* [Will the stuff be strong?]' Toenails asked.

'Try it,' Acid said.

He spread out three lines on his phone. Both he and Tracksuit's cousin snorted their lines without fuss while Toenails let out another hacking cough and shook his head.

It was past ten in the morning. Beyond the staircase was a narrow corridor that looked out into the adjacent apartment block. We were no more than ten feet away from the nearest door and in imminent danger of being discovered by someone climbing up or down the stairs. The men made no effort to speak softly or hasten their business. No resident chose that time to leave their home and take the stairs.

Toenails paid the boy, but not the promised amount.

'You could have done better. Come back when you get some training,' Toenails said, handing him an oil-stained hundred-rupee note.

Acid cut another line.

'It's not hitting me,' Toenails grumbled.

'It will. Trust me,' Acid said, 'you're my best client.'

He cut another three lines. Toenails borrowed the hundred-rupee note he had given the boy and dragged it across Acid's phone display. The boy turned the note the other way to snort his line before putting it away. Acid held the phone up to his face, leaned in and skimmed his nose across the line. He tapped each nostril and smiled.

'This is one of my special skills,' he said.

Toenails paid Acid Rs 7,500 for five grams of mephedrone. Then, we left.

I asked Acid if he wanted something to eat. He made a face.

'Don't talk about food now bro,' he said. By then, I was barely able to stifle my yawning. This seemed to tick him off even more.

Before we parted ways, Acid asked if I planned to meet the woman who introduced him to mephedrone a decade ago.

I did. Did he have any tips?

'There are younger people selling now. Baby and her family are finished,' he said.

That wasn't all. 'Don't fuck around with Baby bro. She is a dangerous person.'

# 4

*Sometime in 2011*

The legendary Hindi cop drama *CID* gives drug testing a bad name. Rules and procedures do not apply to ACP Pradyuman. He never has to carefully seal, label and sign a seized drug or fill out a mundane chemical analysis form and cover letter or send them along with a constable to the Directorate of Forensic Science Laboratories (DFSL) in Santacruz East. No, ACP Pradyuman has it too easy. He gets to watch the foolhardy Dr R.P. Salunkhe use the tip of his tongue to identify mysterious substances.

The DFSL's strict protocols governing drug testing do not make for captivating television. Scientists do not accidentally get high.

The lab also doesn't entertain requests from the police that an analysis be kept off the books. Don't they read the Do's & Don't's on the way in? But every once in a while, when the police bring in a puzzling new oddity, the lab makes an exception.

One day, police constable Madhukar Shingte, a veteran of the Mumbai Police's Anti Narcotics Cell, brought a plastic ziplock baggie the size of his thumb to the lab from Siddharth Nagar hill in Worli.

'Tell me what these white crystals are,' he told the chemical analyser, 'and keep it quiet.'

In a lab which bears no resemblance to Dr Salunkhe's, scientists ran at least four different tests to examine the molecular structure, change in colour and molecular mass of the substance. The crystals could easily be cocaine, ephedrine, MDMA or plain talcum powder. The only way to make sure was to examine the substance under a microscope, expose it to ultraviolet light, dissolve it in either chloroform or methanol and spin it in a centrifuge.

A few weeks later, the results were in: the substance was neither cocaine nor ephedrine nor MDMA nor talcum powder. It was 4-methylmethcathinone, better known as mephedrone. How the bath salt had come to Mumbai was not a question for the forensic scientists to ponder. Mephedrone was not classified as a controlled substance under the Narcotic Drugs and Psychotropic Substances (NDPS) Act. There was nothing illegal in Shingte's baggie. The scientists asked him to collect the rest of his sample.

Shingte took news of the all-clear back to the hill.

Baby was pleased. Nothing stopped her now.

---

Shashikala Pandurang Mazgaonkar was born on 14 November 1963 after five boys—Vasant, Kisan, Bharat,

Shatrughna and Arjun. So everyone called her Baby. The pet name stuck to her ever since.[12]

Her father, Pandurang, drove a taxi and her mother, Kesharbai, tended to the home. The Mazgaonkar family was one of many non-Koli families who had made the fishing village of Worli Koliwada in central Mumbai their home. With his meagre earnings, Pandurang could only afford a hutment by the sea.

The Worli Koliwada of a half-century ago lacked minimal civic infrastructure. There was no public toilet to serve the locality and residents relieved themselves on the rocky sea shore.

For a woman, it was a scary place to live. Aside from the sheer physical discomfort and indignity of only being able to access this open-air toilet in the dark, women faced the added peril of being sexually harassed and assaulted by groups of men on the way to and from relieving themselves.

The aftermath of one of these sickeningly routine incidents would rip apart the Mazgaonkar family.

On the evening of 27 July 1974, Vasant's wife Urmila rushed to the seashore. A teenage Shatrughna was her escort. His job was to keep an eye out for sexual predators and one man in particular—Marian John Carvalho. But on the way, Carvalho and his cronies accosted them. They molested Urmila and beat up Shatrughna when he stood up to them.

Seeing his wife and brother bloodied and bruised when they returned home later, Vasant swore to retaliate. Such an outrage could not go unpunished. The three elder brothers grabbed sickles and sticks, charged at Carvalho and hacked him down.[13]

Vasant, Kisan and Shatrughna were booked by the Dadar police station for committing murder. The police also picked up Bharat—a minor at that time—and allegedly assaulted him in custody. While his older brothers were jailed, Bharat was released and returned home covered in bruises. Though still very young, Baby noticed how Bharat was never the same afterwards. Within days of being freed, the depressed teenager set himself on fire.

The shock of seeing three sons behind bars and another dead in such quick succession killed Baby's mother. Her father passed away two months later. The orphaned girl grew to hate the police.

Left to fend for themselves, the two youngest siblings were briefly cared for by their mother's relatives and brought to live in their native village in Khandala taluka, in the western Maharashtra district of Satara. But with no opportunities to support themselves in the village, Arjun and Baby returned to Worli Koliwada, dropped out of school and looked for work. Arjun found a job at a garage while Baby sold bottles of milk early every morning and worked as a housemaid the rest of the day. For a while, she also sat at a fish stall for a Koli family.

At fifteen, her mother's family arranged her marriage with Ramesh Kamlakar Patankar of Satara's Patan taluka.

Ramesh was a taxi driver and an alcoholic. His drinking meant that Baby did the heavy-lifting, pulling in shifts at textile mills in Worli. Her job was to inspect reams of cloth rolling out of a pair of massive steel rollers for stray threads. She had only a few seconds to sew the threads back into place before the cloth was piled into bundles ready to be shipped out. For nine hours a day, six days a week, Baby would inspect and clear four to five 150-metre-long bundles. At the end of the month, she was paid Rs 400. It was back-breaking work, but Baby was good at it. She liked the job and had a good eye for catching the smallest defect.

She had to be good. Workers in textiles mills in the 1980s had little protection from sudden termination. The fiery trade union leader Datta Samant was out to change that. He agitated for better pay and working conditions and a safety net. At the time when Samant led lakhs of workers in a strike in 1982, Baby was employed at Sadhna Mills. It was the fourth and by far the smallest mill she had worked at. Mill owners responded by sacking their protesting employees and downing shutters for good.

Baby's biggest fear was suddenly realized. Unlike scores of her neighbours and colleagues who had farmland to fall back on, Baby had nowhere to go. She found temporary work as a midwife in a hospital.

One day in 1995, Ramesh collapsed, clutching his chest. He had suffered a fatal heart attack. He left behind two young sons—Girish and Satish.

Soon after, Baby and her youngest brother, Arjun, left Worli Koliwada behind to make a fresh start with their young families. They chose a hill located just off Acharya Atre Chowk, better known as Worli Naka, but not out of choice. Worli's tonier neighbourhoods—the Sea Face, Worli Hill Road, Sir Pochkhanwalla Road—and even its lower middle-class BDD Chawls were out of the question. So, a hill flanked by Dr Annie Besant Road and BG Kher Road in the heart of Worli was their only option.

Rent for a tiny shanty at the foot of the hill was two hundred rupees. Baby was barely able to make rent most months and had little left afterwards. A kindly neighbour advised the young widow to build her own home at the top of the hill.

The summit of Siddharth Nagar was bare for a reason. Thick vegetation grew untamed and undisturbed and concealed rats the size of small kittens. The settlers on the hill had confined themselves largely to its base but space was beginning to run short. Baby would have to face the rats.

Excluded by the city's formal housing market, the siblings joined dozens of other families in clearing shrubs, rocks and mud by hand and assembling bare shelters with bamboo poles and aluminium sheets.[14]

On 14 November 1985, the day Baby turned twenty-two, India's first law to regulate and penalise the cultivation, manufacture, sale and consumption of drugs came into force after being rushed through Parliament. To Baby, who had by this time stopped selling milk and washing people's homes to push brown sugar,[15] this law would have felt like being gifted a pair of handcuffs.

The alleged instigator was Baliram Pujari, the brother of Kisan's wife Bharti and a compulsive user and peddler of *charas*—a narcotic drug made from live cannabis leaves. Baby's sons called him Ballu mama. Kisan had been living as a free man in Worli Koliwada after jumping parole in 1977. He had found the time to marry and would remain untraced for the next three decades.

Ballu set up both Bharti and Baby as peddlers of brown sugar, named for the dark colour of low-grade heroin.

The origins of women dealing drugs or operating illegal liquor dens in Mumbai's slums are rooted in necessity. In the 1980s, they tended to attract lesser attention from the police than their male peers. It was no different for Bharti and Baby. Both also needed an extra income. Through connections with dealers in Worli, Tardeo and Victoria

Terminus—since renamed Chhatrapati Shivaji Maharaj Terminus—Ballu procured one gram packets of brown sugar and *ganja* wrapped in coarse paper, which Baby and Bharti hawked on the streets for two rupees each.

Less than a decade into her new career, another act of violence would mark the Mazgaonkar–Patankar family out as serial troublemakers in the eyes of their neighbours and the police.

When Bharti's charred body was found in her home in 1993, her young sons, Manish and Vivek, were home alone and the prime suspect, her husband Kisan, was missing. The police suspected that Kisan had driven Bharti to set herself aflame after subjecting her to unbearable abuse.

Bharti's sons suspected that their father and aunt had conspired to kill her.[16] It was also revealed that for years Baby had been informed by peddlers that Bharti would often allegedly pose as Baby to corner newer customers. Baby had warned her sister-in-law on countless occasions to back off.

At Dadar police station, the investigation was assigned to a sub-inspector named Gautam Gaikwad. Though Gaikwad became acquainted with members of Kisan's family owing to the many rounds of questioning to ascertain what had happened to Bharti, he was never able to trace Kisan. Once Gaikwad was transferred two years later, the investigation went into cold storage. Bharti's death would remain a mystery.

Baby was not charged by the police, and now found herself free of one competitor.

# 5

The view from the summit of Siddharth Nagar made it obvious to anyone living there that the rest of Worli had left it behind. While Worli built modern homes with roofs which didn't leak in the rains, bought cars and air-conditioners and took the family out for roast pork in oyster sauce and honey noodles served with vanilla ice cream at Flora, Siddharth Nagar, trapped like a fairy-tale hill inside a snow globe, watched on enviously.

On the eastern skyline, never the same two months running, tower after new tower gave Siddharth Nagar the finger: *fuck you, you filthy hill people and stay where you are thank you very much.*

To the west, aerial empires rose from the graves of century-old *bhavans* on Worli Hill and the Sea Face like so many weeds. To the boys and girls doing their homework on the hilltop garden, the towers seemed to blot out of the sun. Every new floor snatched away a wisp of the Sea Face breeze which fluttered the children's hair and toyed with the leaves of their books until the scaffolds came off and the air in the garden grew still.

Worli had wilfully excluded the people of Siddharth Nagar, kept its boot pressed on their throats and rubbed its diamond rings in their noses. And yet, Worli needed these people. Worli needed them to clean their toilets, watch its children, drive its cars and keep guard at night.

Worli left the children in the garden with three choices— get angry, get high or get out. The child who chose the middle path, numbed by *charas,* burgled homes in the hill, nicking anything he could lay his hands on. Lightbulbs. Trousers drying on clotheslines. Even door knobs.

Occasionally, when he became too serious a menace to ignore, his family trussed him up and locked him indoors. Forcing a *charsi* [drug user] to go cold turkey is to invite trouble. This one responded by breaking free of his bonds on the second day and set his house on fire.

The angry boy snuck into homes at night. Door knobs were of no use to him. He stole cash or gold to live Siddharth Nagar's version of *la buena vida*: an entire weekend of teen patti, booze, girls and dance bars.

Siddharth Nagar was not a safe place to live.

It was only a matter of time before the epidemic of theft struck Baby's home.

Despite her hatred for the police, the young widow had to turn to them for help when her home was burgled in 1996. Baby did not lose much but the break-in convinced her that she couldn't live in a slum forever. Not if she wanted her sons to remain in school. Pushing *ganja* and brown sugar, Baby was working towards an express ticket out of Siddharth

Nagar. But without a man to provide for her and look after her sons, she felt helpless.

At Worli police station, plainclothes detectives were assigned to look into the burglary. Among them was a promising young detective named Dharmaraj Baburao Kalokhe, an unsmiling, pensive presence. Yes, his perfectly pressed shirts were, even for a cop, a tad too severely tucked in. And yes, it was impossible to imagine him as anything other than the stern police *dada* who mothers claimed took away naughty children. But by 1996, as his six-year-long stint in Worli came to an end, there was no doubting Kalokhe's reputation as a reliable sleuth.

For the second time in three years, the police took an interest in Baby's life. On this occasion, it was on her and not so much the case that the cop had an eye. Investigating the theft gave Kalokhe a perfect, legitimate reason to visit Baby as many times as he wanted. His arrival cast a forcefield around her home, one that no starving *charsi* or angry thief could breach. In Kalokhe, Baby found a companion, a man she needed to talk to, the kind of straight-talking father figure she hoped would keep her boys from ever straying. Single and smitten, Baby fell for him.

Kalokhe had much more to consider, specifically a wife and two children and a flat at the police quarters in Grant Road. Like his colleagues, he knew that Baby was a peddler, knew what corners of Worli she worked and knew that the next time his boss ordered him to purge drug peddlers, she would have to be on or near the top of his list. When the call came, would he slap on the handcuffs or make like the three monkeys? Commit to Baby and he risked committing not just adultery but also aiding the sale of drugs.

A few months after Baby reported the theft, Kalokhe shut down the inquiry—the one his conscience had initiated. From this point on, he would be two-faced Dharma.

The couple exchanged garlands and rings one morning at Mahalaxmi Temple. On the seventh circuit of the pyre Kalokhe violated Section 26 (2) of the Maharashtra Civil Services (Conduct) Rules, 1979: no government servant, having a spouse living, shall enter into, or contract, a marriage with any person.

Marriage to a policeman brought Baby a modicum of stability but not societal acceptance. Word had spread that Baby was now a police *patni* (wife). This was one twist Siddharth Nagar's grapevine hadn't seen coming. To Siddharth Nagar she was still '*gard* (brown sugar) *powder waali* Baby *tai* (sister)'. The *tai* wasn't meant affectionately.

While people talked, Baby worked. Migrants and destitute families were pouring in to Siddharth Nagar every day. They needed a place to stay from where the municipality wouldn't chase them away. So, they all gravitated to the hilltop where there were no municipality taxes to pay or government officials asking for ownership papers. As Baby watched the slopes of her hill disappear beneath blue tarpaulin sheets, it occurred to her that she could profit. She didn't own the hill. She just had to act like she did. Siddharth Nagar was repulsed by Baby *tai*. Now it would learn to fear Baby *tai*. This was her hill.

She was not Siddharth Nagar's first squatter. But no one had perfected the art of turning patches of the hill into ready-to-move shacks quite like she had. Hers was the leisurely construction operation of a landowner. Not of some stealthy sneak thief. She assembled a house in five stages: first came a skeleton of bamboo poles, then an aluminium roof above, then walls and flooring and finally, to render its occupant eviction-proof, an electricity meter.

At the end of every stage, Baby disappeared for days and left the site unguarded, as if daring the authorities to pull it down while her back was turned.

As space on the hill began to run out, Baby leased and sold dozens of homes in a market where she was both realtor and landlady. Fixed price. No bargaining please. Siddharth Nagar learned, begrudgingly, to respect Baby *tai*.

Attention from the police, the unpleasant sort every entrepreneur operating illegally dreads, was coming. Baby could feel it. She had a plan—a trade-off she hoped would protect her investment.

### The pink cabin

It is hard not to sight a policeman or run past a police office in Worli. A complex of dilapidated apartment buildings, which retains its colonial title of Worli Police Camp, exists on one leafy side of Sir Pochkhanwalla Road. It houses police constables and officers. On the other side are the offices of the traffic police, armed police, the police mess, the Maharashtra State Police Housing Corporation and the Maharashtra Anti-Corruption Bureau.

Downhill and on the other side of two clandestine stairway passageways is the Worli police station and a modern apartment block for senior police officers. Across the road and past rows of boys hunched under the halogen streetlamps of *Abhyas Galli*—meaning 'study street'—are the

Bombay Development Department (BDD) chawls. Set into these three-to-four storey buildings, where flats the size of hutments are piled like so many bunk beds, are more homes for the constabulary. On the ground floor of one chawl building are the offices of the Worli Traffic Police Station and the central Mumbai outpost of the Mumbai police's drug enforcement department, the ANC.

The rows of parked tow trucks and a signboard clearly advertise the presence of the traffic police station. There is, however, nothing to indicate that the ANC occupies the very first room to the left. Outside, plainclothes policemen who seem to try to pass off as ordinary civilians spend most of the day discouraging visitors from stepping past the threshold. '*Aagey jao. Traffic chowki agley room mein hai* [Move on, the traffic police station is the next room],' they say.

Inside what would be the sole room in a chawl-home can be seen wooden desks, red and white plastic chairs, stainless steel and wooden cupboards overflowing with stacks of paper. Most of the wall on the right side is covered by a large pinkish pane of translucent glass behind which the contours of an inner cabin are faintly visible. The door leading inwards to the sanctum of the in-charge police inspector is kept cracked open an inch.

Another door on the far side of the room leads to a smaller inner room identical to the first in features and fittings. Occasionally, a forlorn man sits on the floor at the foot of one table, his eyes either drooped in defeat or alive and alert depending on how much trouble he's in and what hope he harbours of escaping it.

The only other people who enter the ANC office willingly are other cops, people with complaints to file, reporters and informers. Baby belonged to the last category of visitors, and in the late 1990s and 2000s she had put a number of people on the floor of this last room.

Baby didn't visit the ANC out of some sense of duty as a responsible citizen or to clean Worli's streets off drug pushers. In return for informing on drug deals, the ANC left her alone. With every deal that Baby helped thwart and every pusher she grassed on, she systematically cleared her turf of rival operators.

A successful bust also meant a cash reward, equivalent to five-to-ten per cent of the value of the contraband.

The ANC had, to be fair, tried its damnedest to catch Baby in possession of a drug, any drug. Not once had it succeeded. Storming the hill, however stealthily, had proved nearly impossible. To the practiced eyes of locals in Siddharth Nagar, policemen stood out even in everyday clothes, something about their watchful expressions and purposeful strides gave them away. Spotters at both entrances to the hill relayed word to the top and by the time the ANC reached Baby's doorstep, she had climbed down the other side.[17]

When the ANC did reach her home undetected, there was nothing to find. Baby had exercised adequate precautions, bullying and terrorizing her next-door neighbours into hiding some of her stash in their rooms. They had no option but to comply.

Under the NDPS Act, unless you proved drug possession on a person arresting them was meaningless. Baby had been taking notes. She never carried a stash if she could help it.

Calling a truce was the ANC's only option.

Once a month in the late 1990s, Baby visited the man in the glass-fronted cabin. Its occupant then was an officer named Ashok Dhawale, who would later distinguish himself as a serial transgressor. She also dropped by the ANC's headquarters on the first floor of Cuffe Parade police station and occasionally proved useful to a young police sub-inspector named Suhas Gokhale, the department's rising star.

By the turn of the century, a gram of *ganja* sold for fifty bucks, and Baby was estimated to be making at least five thousand a week from *ganja* alone. For Dhawale, the real value lay in peddlers who dealt commercial quantities of brown sugar. Not every bust yielded large enough quantities to justify filing a case. But while his subordinates often dumped small seizures, Dhawale sold it back to peddlers like Baby at market price, threatening to frame her if she refused.

One subordinate, the second-generation police constable Yashwant Parte did not approve of Dhawale and Baby's methods. And while he had no choice but to obey Dhawale's orders, he privately urged Baby to quit peddling. But she had no time for his sermons.

The arrangement ended abruptly with less than three months gone in 2001 when Baby's collaborators were transferred out. It was a routine transfer, not the result of a misdemeanour.

Baby was, by now, no mere peddler. She brokered deals with heroin suppliers in Madhya Pradesh and Rajasthan in person. Couriers brought consignments to Mumbai by bus or train. Once she checked and packed the *maal*, she had a network of boys working the streets. Other peddlers bought from her too.

The new guys at Worli ANC didn't uphold the truce. But they wouldn't break the law to bring Baby in. They'd either bring her in the right way or not at all.

All that changed in the morning on 21 March, when the inspector in charge of the unit met his superior officer for a routine briefing before proceeding on a month's leave the next day. It was his daughter's wedding.

'I need you to register a case before you go on leave,' the boss said.

'But sir, we are still working on the case we filed last week. How will we register another one at such short notice?' the inspector asked.

'I don't want to hear excuses. I will cancel your leave unless you file a case today!' the boss said.

Back the unit, the dejected inspector broke the news to his subordinates. They had the same question. 'Call Baby,' he instructed them. It was the boss' orders.

Baby answered the summons with an inkling of what was to come. Up until now, most of the unit had kept her at arm's length.

She was asked to wait in the first room. Inside the cabin, a constable had assembled the following items: a filled First Information Report proforma, typewritten witness reports and 30 grams of heroin retrieved from the evidence storeroom. All that remained was for the inspector to sign the papers.

This wasn't the way he'd imagined putting Baby away. But orders were orders.

Baby spent that night in the lockup. The next morning, she was produced in court and remanded to judicial custody. Byculla District Women's Jail would be her home for the next eight months.

Her case came up for trial unusually quickly. The prosecution's case, argued half-heartedly and involving unreliable evidence, never stood a chance. She was free by November. But behind bars, Baby feared that she'd lost her carefully cultivated protection from the local police.

It was time she took Parte's words seriously.

# 6

Parte was right. She had made enough money from pushing brown sugar. Now it was time to leave the *jhopad patti*—the slum—for good. Baby bought an apartment in Gorai in Mumbai's northern extremities; another one in Palghar district further north; a two *guntha* plot in Savantwadi, Sindhudurg District; a home in Ghorpadi, Pune city; and a bungalow near the Malavali railway station in Pune district, which she named *Aai*, meaning mother.

She had also tried to do right by her brothers. She purchased a house for Arjun in Savla village in Panvel and briefly paid for his son Upendra's education. She even informally adopted Nishigandha, the daughter of her jailed brother Kisan.

Baby spent most of her time in Siddharth Nagar, where she now owned seven homes. Ballu stayed in one, and two others were set aside for when her sons would marry.[18]

Girish and Satish were proving to be constant troublemakers. They had never approved of the means their mother used to provide for them, or of Kalokhe kaka. Throughout his teens, Girish had violent arguments with his mother.

He hated her work, never warmed up to Kalokhe and resented his near-constant presence. He made his feelings clear every time Baby and Kalokhe set off on a holiday, which was quite often. Girish gave her countless ultimatums. But they had little effect. Baby did not stick to her promises too long.

When it came to her boys' education, though, Baby's commitment never wavered. To her eternal disappointment, however, the only distinction they ever achieved was in making trouble.

Girish switched three schools by the time he was fifteen. He spent most of his time on the cricket field and developed into a moderately talented wicket-keeper. He wasn't good enough to make it past Worli's maidans. When he failed his Class X exams, Baby banished him to Gorai to live with his uncle Kisan.

Once he finally cleared the exams, he enrolled at the Esplanade Junior College of Commerce and Science in Kandivali West. To no one's surprise, least of all Baby's, he took three years to clear his Class XII exam. It was also at this college that he met his wife.

Dipti Patel came from a Gujarati family of modest means in Kandivali. Girish, who was four years her senior, sneaked her home every chance he got. They dated in secret until Dipti's growing belly became impossible to conceal. The families had little choice but to organize a hasty wedding. That day in 2003 was pure agony for Dipti's parents. Once the last gulab jamuns were topped off and Dipti departed for her new home, they cut off all ties with her.

Now that he had a wife to provide for and a child on the way, Girish took on the profession of his grandfather, father and uncle. He worked for a businesswoman in Parel as her part-time personal driver but didn't last long at the job. Baby, who lived a few rooms away, was forced to provide for the couple.

In September 2003, Dipti gave birth to a boy. He was named Saurabh. Far from bringing the family some much-needed cheer, the arrival of Baby's first grandchild only added to the simmering animosity between Girish and her. Girish was unhappy with his allowance, leading to friction between mother and son.

Girish dropped out of college in early 2004 to work as a shoe salesman at Atria Mall in Worli. He quit in six months to study for his Class XII exams. It paid off.

In the next academic year, he enrolled in the Bachelor of Legislative Law course at Rizvi Law College in Bandra West. A chance of becoming an educated professional was within his grasp. He didn't take it.

The longer Girish stayed unemployed and dependent on Baby for survival, the tension between them grew worse. Money dominated every disagreement. After a particularly nasty argument in 2005, he moved out with Dipti and Saurabh. They didn't go too far. The room they moved to was also on the hill and *also* owned by Baby.

On 17 March 2005, Girish and Dipti had their second child. They named her Sayali. Girish could not afford to study with two children to feed. Once more, he dropped out and began working as a driver.

Living away from Baby did not help his marriage. Girish had been spending most of his time in the adjoining slum of Prem Nagar with Reshma Dawood, a Class 9 dropout and house maid. Word of Girish's adultery soon travelled to Siddharth Nagar and reached Baby's and Dipti's ears. The two women rarely saw eye to eye. Now they had found common ground.

In no time, they rushed to Reshma's home and before her stunned parents and brother, unleashed a flood of abuses. Baby's ill-repute as *gard-waali Baby tai* preceded her. The last thing that respectable families in Prem Nagar wanted was Baby charging at their doorstep like an enraged bull. An angry Baby was a very, very dangerous Baby. For Reshma's parents, caught unawares and battered by Baby's crude tongue, the fact that their daughter was seeing a married man was bad enough. The fact that the man was Baby's son made her sin unpardonable. A *raada* [quarrel] with Baby naturally brought all of Prem Nagar rushing to watch.

Baby came at the Dawoods with all the destructive force of a cyclone. She left them in utter ruination, the family name torn to shreds in front of a packed audience. She had called their daughter names never spoken in their home before. So they took the only acceptable course of action.

They kicked her out.

Reshma turned to the only person who could help her. In open defiance of his wife and mother, Girish rented a room for Reshma in Prem Nagar. A mutinous wife did not prevent Girish from lavishing time and money on Reshma. Like a man with both feet planted on two blocks of melting ice, Girish's prospects of a stable marriage with Dipti and peaceful cohabitation with Reshma were sinking.

Girish and Reshma's relationship hadn't had a solid foundation to begin with, and not surprisingly, cracks appeared remarkably quickly once Reshma became dependent on Girish. The fighting began soon enough, even though Girish would try to get away to be with Reshma as much as he could. Soon, he began to hit her. Every time Girish raised his hand, Reshma rushed crying to her parents' home and pleaded with her mother to take her in. Some days later, a remorseful Girish showed up begging forgiveness and persuaded Reshma to return. A wedding in 2007 only briefly interrupted this cycle. Nothing changed for Reshma. She would never be a part of her husband's family.

Girish did visit her in the hospital when she gave birth to their son but from then on, he was, at best, a Sunday dad.

Reshma never discovered how Girish managed to provide for her. He evaded every question about what he did for a living. He only admitted to Baby being a pusher and flatly denied working with her.

After her father passed away of a chronic illness in 2010, Reshma moved back to her parents' home. Girish had not come good on promises to buy her a home.

Satish fared no better. In 2005, he fell in love with a girl called Sarika Singh. He met her during his frequents visits to Kisan's other home in Borivali East, a northern Mumbai suburb. Incidentally, Sarika too was a student at Esplanade College. When neither family consented to the union, the couple eloped and married in a civil ceremony at the metropolitan magistrate's court in Bandra on 15 May 2005.

Sarika's father Ramesh Singh filed a case of abduction, forcing the couple to flee to Baby's home in Ghorpadi. They stayed hidden for a year. Baby sent them money at regular intervals. Whenever that ran out, Satish worked odd jobs.

Satish and Sarika had a son in April 2006 and with his birth, found the courage to return to Mumbai. Baby gave them the room she'd reserved for Satish in Siddharth Nagar. Ramesh Singh forgave his daughter and reluctantly accepted his son-in-law.

## Looks like cocaine

With both her sons under eye now, Baby started a transport business, which she named after Saurabh, her first grandchild. In 2009, she purchased a Maruti Swift Dzire car and installed Satish as its driver. The next year, she bought a Tata Manza car and designated Girish as the driver. She rented both cars to the Income Tax Department for Rs 29,000 each. Every month, she gave them a third of the rent as allowance. They drank away a good chunk of that. In 2011, she fired them and hired other drivers in their place. The boys spent too much time of their time in bars and too little at work.

Baby had also resumed selling *ganja* after a break of four years, teaming up with her older brother Shatrughna, whose own transport business was a front for peddling *ganja* and *charas*. After serving his life sentence for murder, Shatrughna had returned to Worli and got a driver's licence. Like his father, he began driving a taxi. He shared Baby's fierce piety and renamed himself Badshah Peer, one among countless 'godmen' who claimed to solve life's many problems and advertised his services in posters on local trains. The siblings established a large drug-peddling network across south and central Mumbai. But when ANC's field unit in Ghatkopar, eastern Mumbai, arrested Shatrughna, Baby once again found herself the sole proprietor of the family business.

Baby attended all of Shatrughna's hearings in court. She was always accompanied by Kalokhe, a man Shatrughna did not like. Every time Shatrughna cornered Baby, she stonewalled his questions. Eventually, she admitted that Kalokhe was her 'mister' and helped her procure brown sugar.

Up until this time, Baby was buying back brown sugar from Ashok Dhawale at extortionate rates. By 2011, Dhawale was a Deputy Superintendent of Police in the Protection of Civil Rights Department of the Maharashtra Police. Only four years previously, he had been dismissed from the force after being arrested in the eastern suburb of Vikhroli for smuggling liquor in a police vehicle.[19] Once the court acquitted him and the department reinstated him, Dhawale resumed his coercive arrangement with Baby. Her friends in the police advised her to turn in Dhawale.

Baby arranged to meet Dhawale in Worli on 22 February 2011. Undercover officers from the crime branch and the ANC watched Dhawale arrive at the rendezvous in a police jeep driven by an unidentified male. They waited and watched while a bag extracted from the jeep changed hands. The moment it was in Baby's possession, they swooped in. The haul was one dirty cop, 1.5 kg of heroin and a suspected drug peddler behind the wheel of the jeep.[20] Oh, and one relieved informant. The reward made Dhawale's capture even sweeter.

Months later, Shatrughna returned home on bail. While serving time in Arthur Road Central Jail, he befriended Gyan

Manikkam Samuel, a twice-sacked India Post employee with a nose for finding trouble.

The first time, Samuel had lost his job in 2000 for allegedly stealing gold from a parcel. Three years and a trial later, he was acquitted. India Post reinstated him and transferred him to Nagpur.

In 2008, he was reassigned to the Nariman Point Post Office in south Mumbai. That year he met a fellow parishioner in Wadala named Paulraj Padaiyatchi, who incidentally had roots in Samuel's village in Tamil Nadu.

Padaiyatchi ran an operation similar to Baby's at Mumbai's Air Cargo Complex in Sahar village. On the one hand, he smuggled drugs abroad through a network of crooked complex employees. On the other, he passed on information on these very activities to the Narcotics Control Bureau [NCB].

In Samuel, Padaiyatchi saw another potential addition to his network. Samuel, resolved to avoid trouble, refused. Padaiyatchi waited him out. Principles weren't going to feed the Samuel household for too long or put his son through college. Even so, Samuel's resistance lasted a year.

The job was simple. Twenty-five kg of methamphetamine manufactured in a factory in Punjab were on their way to Mumbai in an SUV. Its final destination was Cambodia. Padaiyatchi needed a man he could trust to meet the transporters, give them a pre-decided code word, '*pachees*' [twenty-five], pick up the meth and dispatch it to Cambodia through air cargo. There was a decent commission in it for Samuel.

Padaiyatchi had selected the secluded, altitudinous lane between the Oberoi Mall in Goregaon for the meet. With a hill on one flank and the loading docks of the mall on the other, it was a safe spot to carry out business unobserved. The unlit pavement below the hill seemed to invite cars to park abreast it.

Padaiyatchi's final instruction to Samuel was this: find a taxi driver who wouldn't ask too many questions.

If all went according to plan on 8 June 2009, the taxi would drive Samuel from Wadala to Goregaon, halt momentarily while he received and loaded two pieces of luggage from an SUV and shook hands with the strangers and return him home.

All Padaiyatchi needed from Samuel, as he set off that evening, was the registration number of the taxi.

But Samuel, inexplicably, chickened out. He fed the taxi driver the instructions and sent Padaiyatchi the registration number, omitting to mention the inconsequential detail that he wasn't riding in it.

Neither the men from Punjab nor the taxi driver were to know that half an hour before their rendezvous, the NCB had scoped out the lane. An anonymous informant had furnished the agency with precise information: at 8.45 p.m., look out for an SUV with a Punjab registration transporting approximately 25 kg of methamphetamine and a local *kaali peeli* taxi. The informant had also given the NCB registration numbers of both cars.

The taxi driver arrived at five minutes past the allotted time, the SUV ten minutes later. Hands shaken and code word confirmed, three men disembarked from the SUV and loaded a large carton and a maroon coloured trolley bag into the boot of the taxi. The NCB team emerged from the shadows to surround the cars before they could pull away.

The taxi driver returned to Wadala that night, just not with the cargo Samuel had expected. He was back in jail.

This time, he would stay for eleven months, fueled by a desire for vengeance. Everything about that night screamed set-up.

Meeting Shatrughna was the sole bright spot of that year. They stayed in touch once they were freed.

Back once more at Baby's side, Shatrughna broached the idea of branching out in dealing synthetic drugs. He'd studied the market and his one-line summary was this: kids in Mumbai are experimenting with chemicals and can't tell one white powder from the other.

In short, ka-ching.

'We'll start with something simple, like ketamine,' he told Baby, 'I know a guy. I met him in jail.'

Samuel was torn. On the one hand, he wanted to inflict serious harm on Padaiyatchi. On the other hand, there was easy money to be made supplying ketamine to Shatrughna—an order only Padaiyatchi could fulfil. Samuel hit pause on his revenge mission.

Samuel and Shatrughna met in Parel.

'Try it and tell me what you think,' Samuel said.

Shatrughna snorted the packet clean in less than a week. This was good stuff, seriously good stuff, precisely the stuff he had in mind. But was it ketamine? He couldn't tell. Samuel could.

'I want more,' he told Samuel. 'Bring another sample to my sister's home.'

Kalokhe was in the next room, listening, when Samuel visited Siddharth Nagar.

'This is MD,' he said, handing Baby a small plastic packet. The word meant nothing to Baby. The contents of the packet weren't making a strong first impression on her. As she lifted a pinch to her face, she smelled the early morning piss-soaked Worli sea shore of her childhood. In her experience, a promising new product should not possess the odour of a public toilet.

Baby's wrinkled nose prompted Samuel to give her his pitch: MD is stronger than cocaine, it is cheap and it is completely legal. Baby wasn't floored. She preferred her herbs, and personal prejudices aside, coke's *el cheapo* cousin just wasn't her game.

As a matter of courtesy, Baby asked Samuel to leave the sample behind. She was curious, tempted even, to give synthetics a try. Shatrughna gave a glowing user review and ordinarily, that would have been enough. But she needed more information. A full name to begin with. Samuel's word alone would not do.

She rang constable Shingte, her old contact at Worli ANC, for a favour. If the sample cleared forensics, she would take the plunge. If not, she would point Shingte in Samuel's direction.

# 7

The most plausible explanation for the name Worli is in its first syllable. 'Wor' or 'var', which in Marathi means 'up', stemming from the island's position above or to the north of Bombay island.[21]

Historians over time have discarded theories that suggested the name originated from the Marathi words for banyan tree (*vad*) and village (*ali*), referencing a village of once-abundant banyan trees on the island. There was also insufficient evidence to support the other theory that the name arose from a blessing, or 'var' in Marathi, believed to be granted to the island by Goddess Mahalaxmi.[22]

Worli, the northernmost of the seven islands, was cut off from Malabar Hill by what the British called the Great Breach—a mass of water which at high tide 'poured with all the fury and the pleasure of an Arabian Colt'.[23] Flooding a hollow basin of land between the islands of Parel and Bombay, the sea drowned an estimated 4,000 acres of good land. The British had named the submerged land the Flats. Twice a day, the sea would retreat to leave behind a sprawling swamp matted with coconut leaves on which nothing grew but marshy vegetation. Strung across the Great Breach were the remains of a stone embankment, the first attempt to hold back the sea, dating to a time before the Portuguese colonized the islands.

The British East India Company was desperate to turn the Flats into profitable farmland. At first, the Company's motivations in reclaiming the Flats were driven more by securing its territory against attacks from the Portuguese and Dutch and 'to make the island self-supporting in crops and pasture'.[24]

Concerns over health came later. But it hadn't escaped the notice of the Company that the swamps might provide classic breeding grounds to the malarial mosquito. The Company also attributed the alarming mortality among its employees every monsoon to diseases arising from the 'pestilential vapours' stewing in the Flats.

Charles Boone, the Governor of Bombay between 1716 and 1720, is credited with planning the first sea-wall across the Great Breach. The causeway was to run in a straight line and subsume a spit of rock which now houses the tomb of the fourteenth-century Sufi saint Haji Ali Shah Bukhari. But the sea would not bend to the will either of British engineers or native contractors and the first attempt was abandoned after the waves repeatedly smashed through the wall.[25] Work on the sea-wall stopped for nearly a decade.

The present semi-circular shape of the causeway is believed to have its origins in the legend of a contractor named Ramji Shivji Prabhu and a dream he had one night. The goddesses Mahalaxmi, Mahakali and Mahasaraswati visited him in this dream and promised to remove all obstacles to the construction of the sea-wall if he offered to build it and in the process, recover their idols submerged in Worli creek and construct a shrine for them on the mainland. A local lore told of how repeated persecution visited upon Goddess Mahalaxmi and the Hindu populace of the seven islands by the Emperor Qutb-ud-din Mubarak Shah (1316–1320) of the Khilji dynasty had forced her to leap into the creek and stay hidden there until the islands were rid of his tyranny.

Prabhu did as commanded and when his divers found the idols in the place he had dreamt about, he requested the Company for land on a rocky outcropping in present-day Mahalaxmi—a short walk away from the Haji Ali *dargah*—to build a temple. With the goddesses appeased, the sea did not interrupt Prabhu's efforts at damming the Great Breach.[26] The enterprise cost the Company upwards of Rs 1 lakh.[27]

The new temple was also situated close to a shrine dedicated to Ma Hajiyani, believed to be the saint's sister—the shrine is now housed in a blue-domed mausoleum which overlooks Worli bay from its rocky outpost a few metres to the north of Haji Ali *dargah*.

Both siblings are believed to have travelled to India from present-day Uzbekistan with the intention of propagating Islam and to have settled in Bombay. When the siblings passed away during a sea voyage, their followers buried them at the sites where their bodies washed ashore.[28]

The damming of the Great Breach gave rise to a saying in the growing city that 'under British rule Mama Hajiyani (Mother Pilgrim) and Mahalakshmi have joined hands, or in other words, that the old animosity between Musalman saints and Hindu gods has disappeared'.[29]

Prabhu's sea-wall did not fully succeed in draining the Flats. Writing in 1754 in his *Voyage to the East Indies*, the British traveller, writer and Company employee John Henry Grose observed that, 'about two miles out of town towards the middle of the island the sea had so gained upon it with its irruption that it almost divided the island in two, and made the roads impassable. The causeway (vellard) is about a quarter of a mile in length and of considerable breadth; but there is one gross fault remarked in it, that being bending near its middle, the architect has opposed to the sea a re-entering angle instead of a salient one. In the meantime there lies within the breach a considerable body of water that has a free communication with the sea, as it appears by its ebbing and flowing, and is probably but the wholesomer for it.'[30]

Plans for a permanent solution to keep the sea at bay were firmed up during the tenure of Governor William Hornby (1771–84). And though Hornby had left Bombay by the time the embankment was completed, it was named Hornby Vellard, after 'vellado', the Portuguese word for embankment. The naming was in commemoration of Hornby's contribution to the engineering project that foreshadowed the bridging together of the seven islands.

The Company was quick to reclaim elevated portions of the newly liberated land for farming. As Bombay expanded northwards, the island's natives and migrants built the first homes in the present-day localities of Bhuleshwar, Mandvi and Umarkhadi.[31]

Bombay owes the very soil it walks on to the 'noxious vapours' that roiled the delicate constitutions of early British settlers and administrators in the late 1600s. Every time a coconut palm leaf descended or was blown to the ground, it stayed there until the sea swallowed it up as it did all other dying plant matter. Over several millennia, this decaying mush formed a rich topsoil over the islands. The Koli fishing community, Bombay's original inhabitants, fertilized the bases of their precious toddy palm trees with rotting fish—an excellent manure that tinged the wind blowing across the islands with an odour the British found unbearable.

This practice earned Bombay the eccentric distinction of being built largely on a base of rotten fish and coconut palm leaves, distinguishing itself from Calcutta (the shifting black mud of a tidal estuary), central London (rice gravel), Leningrad (marsh) and New York City (rock).

The Company's court of directors, alarmed at the short lifespan of employees dispatched to serve in these backwaters, prohibited the Kolis' practice of fertilizing the soil—also called buckwashing—in 1708.

The Company noticed another 'unwholesome' practice on Worli island, that is of the production of catgut.[32] Before present-day synthetic polymers, catgut—a tough cord produced from sheep intestine—was used as surgical sutures.

Then Bombay Police Commissioner S.M. Edwardes used stomach-churning graphic language to describe the process of catgut manufacture. According to him:

> The intestines of sheep, as soon as they are purchased from the butchers, are put into a vessel containing water and are cleaned externally by the intestine cleaners. The dung etc. is removed by them by drawing them through the fingers. They are next drawn over the rib of a sheep, which removes the fat and dirt and thins them. The cleaned intestines are then sold to a merchant called

from his trade a *tantgurra*. The *tantgurra* soaks them in water for three days and then scrapes them with an iron scraper known as a *jora*. After three days he soaks them in the sap of the *rui* tree (*Calatropis gigantea*), which makes them firm and strong. The intestines are by this time reduced to about 1/3rd of an inch in size. They are finally put on a wheel and twisted into a cord, which is afterwards dried and sold as *tant* (catgut).[33]

Unsavoury sights and smells persisted in Baby's Worli in the mid-1800s when the first cotton textile mills were built on the island. Before the Great Breach was dammed, Love Grove was a grassy hillock at the mouth of Worli creek cut off from the rest of the city. *The Gazetteer of Bombay City and Island Volume I* recorded that the promontory gained its name 'having formerly been selected as the grand resort of newly married couples during the honeymoon'.[34] The seclusion it offered to the love-struck was compared with the Arabian desert.[35]

The sea wall made Love Grove accessible by road. And, with the road came drains and sewers. The Bombay Municipal Corporation selected the hillock to build a pumping station to drain rainwater from the low-lying Flats back into the sea, depriving Love Grove of its 'romantic associations by sewers, drains, pumping stations and other accessories of the worst smell in Bombay'.[36]

By 1911, no traces remained in Love Grove of its eponymous history.

When the Government of Bombay are again searching for someone whom the King may delight to honour, we hope they will single out the individual in the service of the Bombay Corporation who is responsible for our street nomenclature. Apparently he prefers to blush unseen, for no one knows who he is, but he is a genius of the highest order. One of his gems is the delectable title of a small lane near Girgaum, which used to rejoice in the distinct appellation of 'Night Soil Depot Lane'. That is a nice savoury and suggestive address heading but more recently this gentleman has gone a step farther. Realizing that the bumpy lane past the Pumping Station, which is the despair of motorists and an olfactory outrage on every passer-by, should not remain undistinguished, he has christened it 'Worli Love Grove Pumping Station Road'. It is a pity that so much bright ingenuity should stop short here, and as the descriptive art is to be cultivated in our street nomenclature, we suggest a few alternative titles to the Commissioner. What could be more appropriate than 'Road to the Ten Thousand Unnecessary Stinks', for any new thoroughfare in the neighbourhood of Love Grove?[37]

Squatting at the end of the city limits, Worli was not considered prime real estate as the twentieth century beckoned. The northernmost of the Bombay Municipal Corporation's seven administrative wards, Worli and Mahim had the lowest rents in Bombay. On average, a chawl was available for rent at 1 rupee 3 annas in 1898–90 and 3 rupees in 1908–09; a one-storey home for Rs 50 in 1898–90 and Rs 70 in 1908–09; and a ground floor bungalow for Rs 65 in 1898–90 and Rs 81 in 1908–09.[38] One moved to Worli if they found living in Bombay, Colaba, Mazgaon and Sewri islands beyond their means.

*Give a man an inch ...*

Like every great city in history, Mumbai has been cruel to its less fortunate. No one knew that better than Baby. In December 1985, Prime Minister Rajiv Gandhi visited Bombay to celebrate the centenary of the founding of the Indian National Congress. Pained to see large numbers of the city's estimated nine million people living in slum tenements topped with blue sheet metal roofs, Gandhi gifted the city a grant of one hundred crore rupees to improve their housing situation.[39]

The Worli Koliwada of Baby's youth could have done with some of the prime minister's largesse. Bombay, modernizing at a furious pace, pushed the Kolis to the margins, stripping away the pride of performing a centuries-old profession and turning their sea into the city's sewage pit. The sea would have to provide more than just fish if the Kolis were to continue living as they always had.

And provide it did.

The village's isolation from the rest of the city had made it an ideal conduit for smuggling rings operating secretly to send Video Cassette Recorders (VCRs), music systems, watches, cloth and all manner of imported goods into the mainland. The promontory on which a Portuguese-era fort stood as a sentinel provided ideal cover for boats to launch out into the sea in the darkness and recover caches of goods dumped in the water by overseas smugglers wrapped up in fishing nets or attached to buoys. Young Koli men saw in smuggling a quick and steady income that an entire day tending to the nets and battling the elements could not.

Every August, the Kolis in Worli, like their brethren up and down the western coast, mark Narali Poornima as the most significant holiday of the year. Dressed in traditional finery, fisher folk offer coconuts and prayers to the sea in anticipation of the start of another fishing season. The offerings are made in exchange for the men's protection and their safe return every day.

During the closing decades of the twentieth century, mechanized fishing boats were yet to reach Mumbai's fishing community. Fishing was back-breaking work teeming with risk. The reward for braving the sagar, or the sea, every day was navsagar, meaning alcohol, at the day's end. Smuggling was a way out of these labours and promised profits. Unlike fishing, there was also no danger of returning home with empty nets.

Little change was discernible on the surface. The needs of the village were administered by its nine chiefs or 'Patels', who formed the village council, authorized to hear and resolve disputes among villagers. Even after democracy, elected representatives, land laws, roads and the police came to the village, these village patels retained their inherited titles but lost most of their historical authority. Villagers were still required to approach the council first, but anyone who wasn't satisfied with its decision was free to approach the police and the courts.

Far from the claustrophobia of the present day, very little land was actually occupied by houses in the village. Families were massed close to the shore in wooden homes built on raised platforms to keep the sea from flooding their verandas during high tide. Some families had built indoor toilets while the rest of the village used the rocky shore to relieve themselves. Women went while it was dark and took along umbrellas as a measure of added privacy.

Roads brought traders, markets and intra-city migrants eager for work and a place to live. The village, where families had carved up land as private fish drying yards, still had plenty of it to spare. But as the old Marathi proverb goes—*bhatala dili osri ana bhat haat pay pasri* [give a man an inch and he'll take a yard], once the hospitable Kolis allowed migrants to settle on their land, they never left. Some prescient members of the community began selling plots to ever-increasing droves of homeless people, and the village took its first steps to becoming the slum it is today.

In a changing village, the patels' sway was diminishing. Smugglers were enticing the young in each home, Koli and non-Koli alike, with promises of luxury. And nothing advertised the change better than the smuggler himself, who strutted about the village white-shirted, white-trousered and white-slipper-ed like an albino peacock looking to attract a mate. He *wanted* to stand out.

Smuggling brought with it organized crime and targeted murders to a village that had thus far only known drunken brawls among neighbours and quarrels between competing fisher folk.

Rival smugglers took each other out in broad daylight; their bright white clothes made them easy targets. Gangs tied up their victims in layers of cloth and smashed their skulls on the ground. Men like Marian John Carvalho molested women in a village where Koli women bedecked with several grams of gold jewellery used to go about their work unharmed. The shore was made unpassable at night by moonshiners operating with impunity. Even the police feared entering the village and rarely ventured to the fort. The foolhardy ones who did were often shoved off the rocks and into the sea by lurking smugglers.

Nearly every non-Koli household had a family member employed in the mills. Datta Samant, the trade union leader who led a one-and-a-half-year-long strike against mill owners, was a regular visitor to the office of Manishankar Kavathe, the Communist Party of India's nine-time municipal councillor for Worli Koliwada. Kavathe brought streetlights in the area and public toilets for women.

Samant led agitations for a wage increase for over 2.5 lakh workers employed at sixty mills. But when mill owners remained unmoved, Samant had to call off the eighteen-month-long strike and admit defeat. More than 75,000 workers lost their jobs when the strike ended in failure in July 1983. Thousands of mill workers, including those in Worli Koliwada, returned to their villages in rural Maharashtra. Those who stayed behind struggled to keep their boys away from the temptation of gangs, smuggling and easy money. Many families educated their children, saw that they got respectable jobs and stayed out of trouble.

Some others, like Baby's, did not.

# 8

A feel-good news broke in Mumbai on 15 February 2014. The Indian Police Service (IPS) officer Rakesh Maria, who had attained legendary status as a detective, was announced the Commissioner of Mumbai Police.

'It was like a dream come true,'[40] Maria told journalists in his first-floor office at the police headquarters in Crawford Market that morning.

It was the story of a hometown boy come good, a boy from Bandra who loved basketball and detective stories.

The Maharashtra government had picked Maria for the job over seniors and batchmates in the service and now, he was expected to deliver. Like every incumbent before him, Maria was also posed the staple question reserved for the new commissioner: 'What do you count as your biggest challenges?'

Unlike his immediate predecessor Satyapal Singh, who had embarrassed himself and the department nearly every time he spoke in public, Maria was a seasoned veteran of the police press conference. All through 2013, Singh had offered a glimpse of what he and his future colleagues in the Bharatiya Janata Party (BJP) would sound like on election campaign trail the coming summer. *Mid-Day* had branded him Mumbai's 'Top Khap'.[41]

Maria never made the news for a faux pas. With a news sense keener than some editors, he delivered newsy quotes effortlessly. In private, Maria, was reserved.[42] At press conferences though, he could be loquacious. The day-one presser was all about delivering crowd-pleasing platitudes and dodging verbal landmines. His response was suitably unremarkable. He vowed a 'zero tolerance to street crime'.[43]

In his first meeting with his subordinates, Maria ordered them to take drug users off the streets. He did not want to see any junkies snorting, injecting or pushing at playgrounds, abandoned buildings or derelict mill compounds. By the end of February, the police had rounded up four hundred alleged drug users.[44] Within a month of his taking charge, Maria's men put away 1,512 alleged drug users in 944 cases.[45] Not all of them went to jail. In most cases, the seizures were so miniscule that magistrates simply fined them and let them go. That was the law.

Maria's focus on cutting off street-level consumption made little difference to the city's vast drug supply chain. It only took addicts in need of rehabilitation away from their corners temporarily and gave women, children and the elderly the fleeting impression that the streets were safe. The fact that drug users were walking free hours after arrest with just the slight inconvenience of losing their stash made the numbers behind Maria's push to clean up the city seem less impressive.

As of 11 March 2014, the police had confiscated 62 kg of ganja, 1.7 kg of ephedrine, 1.25 kg of charas, 17 grams of cocaine, 14 grams of amphetamine and not a single gram of Meow Meow. The white powder and the persons pushing it were on the right side of the law.

Angry letters poured in from citizens all over the city urging Maria to act. He couldn't admit that the police's hands were tied. It didn't mean they were completely helpless. Maria asked Sadanand Date, his new Joint Commissioner of the Crime Branch to write to the NCB about the urgent situation in Mumbai. The NCB was authorized to initiate the procedure to classify the drug as a controlled substance under the NDPS Act. It was a question of making a persuasive case before the agency.

But even as he waited for the cogs of bureaucracy to roll, Maria still needed to find an answer within the law to counter Meow Meow. The public's faith in the police and in his leadership could quickly evaporate if he didn't.

At the press conference on the first day, he'd talked up the need to go back to the 'basics of policing'.[46] He had followed that up by installing signboards at every police station which read:

A complainant is the most important person in our police station. He is not an interruption to our work, he is the purpose of it. He is not an outsider for our station, he is a part of it. We are not doing a favour by serving him, he is doing a favour by giving us an opportunity to do so.

What served the complainant best was getting Meow Meow off the street. And, so, Maria found a makeshift solution.

Henceforth, the police would prosecute peddlers of Meow Meow under Section 328 of the Indian Penal Code, invoked most commonly against food caterers and suppliers in instances of mass food poisoning. Its definition was vague enough to cover the sale of a new legal drug since it punished any person who administered a 'poison or any stupefying, intoxicating or unwholesome drug, or other thing with intent to cause hurt'.

It was intended as a stop-gap measure.

And it was either that or hoping that New Delhi, of its own volition, would act post haste. Maria was aware that the courts were unlikely to agree with his interpretation of the law. But he *had* to come good on his vow.

*Vada paav run*

After pushing for almost thirty years it took the near-death of her partner, Ballu, for Baby to stop. Doctors gave the emaciated drug addict, now in his sixties, little chance of pulling through. A lifetime of smoking weed and injecting heroin had laid waste Ballu's body. Baby prayed for Ballu to survive and when he did, her desire to push Meow Meow vanished. What her customers did with her product, Baby didn't give a toss about. But Ballu had given her a frightening reminder.

In those halcyon lawless years, Baby's product was acknowledged as the best in the Greater Mumbai area. Users came from as far as Bhandup in the east and the town of Vasai in the north to score personally from her, always losing themselves in the maze of houses on the hill on the first trip.

Like with every good dealer, the first packet was free. Once was never enough for a potential new customer. He came back to her, longing for more. Every time. After, inevitably, he went broke, Baby made him a proposition: work for me if you want to keep scoring. Most users jumped at the chance. Then too, there were no free handouts. Baby's peddler-addicts paid Rs 500 a pop.

Baby ran a referral system, like Uber, to reward existing customers with a free gram if they brought friends along. That is how Acid and Tracksuit went from being broke students to peddlers on a sports bike.

While Baby, Ballu and Shatrughna sourced, cut and packed the product, boys like Acid and Tracksuit introduced it to circles and places Baby could not have penetrated herself. Her name became a mark of guarantee, the ISI mark for Meow Meow. One snort compelled users to make the pilgrimage to the hill, no matter the distance and the risks. Contemporaries had set up shop in other parts of the city, but none could match Baby either for her product, her dedicated set of customers or for the geographical reach of her operation. None of them could expand beyond their own fiefs and not one of them could become for Meow Meow what Baby had: a synonym, byword and hushed code rolled into one.

Baby had struck up a reliable business relationship with Samuel. There was no looking back after the all-clear from forensics. An advantage of being Baby's exclusive supplier was gaining her trust. So much so, that in 2013, Baby loaned him Rs 5 lakh at a liberal 2.5 per cent rate of interest.

Baby had relapsed after Ballu's recovery but that year, she decided to quit her yo-yo-ing and retire. Kalokhe wouldn't let her. They were safe, he insisted, for as long as Meow Meow stayed in the legal grey zone. The law would take months, if not years, to catch up. 'We won't get caught,' he said.

Who, after all, would suspect a cop?

Baby wasn't convinced. Kalokhe's greed and naivety would bring them down. She didn't intend going back to jail. She had kept trouble at bay using all her cunning and by exercising restraint. Her partner, on the other hand, was asking her to run a stock clearance sale.

'We have to sell more while we still can,' Kalokhe said. Baby refused. She fought back. She tried to make him see reason. In the end, she gave in to his obstinacy.

In March 2014, as Maria ordered a purge of drug peddlers, Baby and Kalokhe set out for Pune one morning in a hired car to meet with Samuel. The meet was arranged at Joshi Vadewale *vada paav* shop at Tathewade village on the Mumbai–Pune Highway. Baby had the driver park close to the restaurant and waited in the car while Kalokhe stood at a cigarette shop close by.

Baby and Samuel had perfected this routine over the past three years.

Casual observers at Joshi Vadewale would detect nothing out of place in a woman receiving a piece of luggage at a roadside restaurant. Barely exchanging a word, Baby drove off to the bungalow where she opened the 25-kg travel bags in the privacy of her bedroom.

Their rendezvous had actually got off to a terrible start. The first two consignments were bad. Baby could tell by sight and smell that the crystals were not Meow Meow. She ordered Samuel back to Joshi Vadewale and hurled the bags back at him. Samuel was forced to dump 40 kg of contraband into a river.

This morning, like always, Samuel made his way to Pune and arranged for Padaiyatchi to pick him up in a Tata Indica car a few kilometres away from Tathewade. Two travel bags sat in the trunk. Padaiyatchi was accompanied by two other men: Varun Tiwari and Nityanand Thevar, both employees of Rukhma Industries, a pharmaceuticals company in the north Maharashtra district of Jalgaon.

At Joshi Vadewale, Baby saw Samuel pull up in a car with three other men she did not recognize. The men transferred the bags to the trunk of Baby's car and drove off. There was no time for Baby to open the bags and inspect her purchase. She hadn't brought any money either. Samuel had asked Baby to hand over the cash to his wife in Mumbai. Once it was safe, Kalokhe joined Baby and together, they went off to the bungalow in Malavali. The same evening, they returned to Mumbai.

At a pre-arranged time, a few days later, Baby met a younger woman in a run-down restaurant outside Wadala railway station and handed her an envelope of cash. Samuel's wife thought this was something to do with his loan. On the way home, Baby promised herself that this was the last time.

But one consignment was not enough for Kalokhe. Baby fought back. But for all the effect her arguments had, she might as well have been yelling at a brick wall.

Baby made two more trips to Pune in May and June, with slight variations. Satish drove her in their Maruti Swift Dzire. Instead of Joshi Vadewale, they stopped at Rohit Vadewale next door. Baby sent Satish indoors and remained in the car.

When they returned home one evening in June from the third trip, Sarika served them an ultimatum: this is the last time Satish drives you to Pune.

In August, Baby and Kalokhe drove to the bungalow to inspect their contraband: six bags and 150 kg of mephedrone stored in a ground-floor bedroom. They packed the bags in cardboard boxes and locked the room. From time to time,

Baby and Kalokhe opened up the bags and brought small quantities of Meow Meow to Siddharth Nagar. Leaving the rest guarded only by two watchmen made Baby nervous but she had no other choice.

Baby's meetings with Samuel at Joshi Vadewale ended in September when the Mumbai sessions court cancelled his bail. He surrendered in court and was taken away to Arthur Road Jail. He hadn't even begun paying back the loan.

The year only got worse for Baby. In November, the police picked up Ballu for allegedly selling Meow Meow to a youth in Dharavi: another scalp in Maria's clean-up drive.

Baby lost her right hand. Satish wasn't available anymore and she was growing tired of Kalokhe's demands. In the space of a year, he had gone from pleading, insisting that she give Samuel a call, to threatening her if she didn't. There was also something in the way Kalokhe looked at and spoke to her daughters-in-law that disturbed her.

In December, she bought another car, a Toyota Innova, and hired Madan Singh, a forty-year-old migrant from Uttarakhand as its full-time driver. Singh had been earning Rs 10,000 a month as a tourist car driver and sleeping inside the office of a travel company across the road from Siddharth Nagar for the past year. Baby gave him a raise, a room in Siddharth Nagar and designated him the family driver, which meant that like everyone else, he would have to call her Mummy.

Five days a week, he dropped Baby's grandchildren to and from school. He drove Baby, her sons and daughters-in-law to the market, on errands and to the bungalow. Rumours about Baby had reached Singh in his first few weeks in Siddharth Nagar. Before the month was out, he discovered that they weren't just idle gossip.

One late December morning, Singh brought the car around to the Nipponzan Myohoji Buddhist Temple, which abuts the entrance to Siddharth Nagar on Annie Besant Road. At 9 a.m., Baby arrived accompanied by a neatly dressed man Singh had not seen before. The stranger's mouth, Singh noted, was set into as severely a straight line as the fold of his tucked-in shirt. They sat in the back.

At the toll plaza in Vashi leading out of Mumbai, the man asked Singh to put his wallet away and flashed an identity card. The toll booth attendant waved them on. *He's a cop*, Singh thought. *What is mummy doing with a cop?*

Singh reached the bungalow by noon. Baby and Kalokhe stayed indoors for a while and were ready to leave after lunch. Every weekend that month, Singh drove Baby and Kalokhe to the bungalow. He never once paid toll. It wasn't his place to ask questions.

The security situation at the bungalow also had Kalokhe worried. He proposed moving the contraband to a safer location. One at a time, he took the bags to his mother's home in Kanheri village, Satara, in a state transport bus.

'Why can't you just take the car?' Baby asked him the first time.

'The police might search private cars. But they won't search a bus,' he said.

At home, Kalokhe stuffed the bags into three thick white plastic gunny sacks. He piled the sacks into a large plastic barrel in the living room. *There are chemicals in them*, he warned his mother, Anusuya, *so stay away*. She didn't know what that meant.

*Time's up*

In Worli, Baby's days of comfort were about to end. Madan Singh wasn't the only man with a new job that December. Two streets away, there was a new man in charge of the ANC: Inspector Divakar Shelke, a gruff-voiced former Deputy of Maria during his stints in the Crime Branch and the Maharashtra Anti-Terrorism Squad.

Shelke had brought down and put away the ageing gangster Arun Gawli after successfully tying him to the murder of a municipal councillor in 2007. He had investigated murders, gangland violence and terror attacks. But now that Maria had sat him in the pink-glassed cabin on the wrong side of Worli, Shelke was not happy. When he had asked Maria to be retained in the crime branch, this was not what he had meant. Drugs, and people who pushed them, repulsed him.

Mechanically and with the air of one steeling himself for an unpleasant task, Shelke asked his deputies for a list of prominent drug dealers in the jurisdiction. When Constable Shingte handed him the list, Shelke's heart sank further. There were several women on that list and not a single woman in his unit. Shelke took this quandary to Maria, with the intention of leveraging his way out of the ANC. The next morning, three women police constables reported for duty. There was no getting away for Shelke.

Along with the list, Shingte brought news on that first day, that a woman named Baby Patankar was waiting outside. Shelke had read about her in the list and heard of her connections with his unit and about Dhawale. He forbade his men from acting on any information that Baby passed. They would only be doing her a favour. Shelke also issued a clear warning: stop taking money from her.

Baby was still waiting.

'Tell her to leave,' he told Shingte.

Shelke used his first month to scope out Baby's home and familiarize himself with the entrances and exits to Siddharth Nagar. When he made his move, he did not want to give Baby a single avenue of escape.

And so, in a story similar to the FIR filed against Ballu a month previously in Dharavi, Baby was booked at Worli police station on 30 December 2014, under Section 328 of the Indian Penal Code for allegedly selling Meow Meow to two underage boys. That was the easy part.

Baby wasn't home when officers from the ANC and Worli police station reached her home that evening. Sarika answered the door. There were two others at home—Arjun's son Upendra Mazgaonkar, who had come down from Panvel, hoping to borrow his aunt's car for a trip to Goa, and Kisan's teenage daughter Nishigandha. The police took Sarika and Upendra away and booked them for allegedly poisoning Worli's youth by acting as Baby's accomplices. Baby, who was staying in her bungalow at that time, was dumbstruck when Nishigandha called her. She didn't return home that day.

After thirteen years, the heat was back on.

# 9

The police had expected to smoke Baby out of hiding by putting her daughter-in-law and nephew away. They placed her home, sons and peddlers under surveillance and monitored their phone calls. Sooner or later she had to show up. Surely, she wouldn't leave two close family members to take the fall!

But none of the usual tricks seemed to work. Baby had disappeared. Shelke hammered into the investigating officer at Worli police station that locating Baby ought to be his number one priority.

'Don't wait till she applies in court for anticipatory bail,' he had said.

Between alternating twelve-hour-long day and night shifts, patrolling the jurisdiction, noting down complaints in the station house and running at least half a dozen cases on the side, the investigating officer had no time to focus solely on Baby's whereabouts. But the harried sub-inspector wasn't too worried: sooner or later, every crook comes up for air. There is only so much squeeze on their family they can endure. Except, Baby was lying low in a place he would never imagine. Nothing in his training had prepared him to consider such a possibility.

Baby switched off her phone and spent the first week of the new year at the bungalow. Kalokhe got to work immediately, whisking Nishigandha away to Malavali as soon as he was able to. They couldn't stay there long though.

Someone in the family was bound to crack and tell the police where to look. They would have to move quickly and to a place the investigating officer wouldn't think of checking. He shifted Baby and Nishigandha to a guest house on Marine Drive. Until he found somewhere safer, this would do as a temporary hidey-hole.

Kalokhe had to think as the resourceful partner of a cornered woman—with useful friends in south Mumbai, and not as a detective. He was now posted at Marine Drive police station in Churchgate as a head constable. He was one of three Mill Specials, intelligence-gatherers who were first deployed in the 1980s to spy on Datta Samant's textile mill employees union and collect and report information of strikes beforehand. Now, Kalokhe kept a watch on anything out of the ordinary in his jurisdiction, particularly at the Vidhan Sabha, the latticed state legislature building in Nariman Point and Mantralaya, the seat of the Maharashtra state administration.

Kalokhe worked his connections.

There was one man who could help—Rajiv Shah, a generic drugs manufacturer and Marine Drive resident. Shah's father Kesarichand had been a member of the erstwhile Bombay

Cricket Association (BCA), since renamed the Mumbai Cricket Association.

In 1972, the BCA began constructing a new cricket stadium and sea-facing club house one street away from his home. The club house included sports and recreation facilities and twenty-five rooms for members in need of temporary lodgings and to house squads contesting Ranji Trophy matches at the stadium. Both projects were completed in 1974. The new cricket stadium was named after S.K. Wankhede, the BCA president who planned its construction. The clubhouse was named Garware Club House.

In 2011, the BCA renovated boarding and lodging facilities of the club house. Sixty-three rooms came up in a new glass-fronted building that also housed its administrative offices. Members could now reserve vacant rooms at the club house for themselves or their guests as long as they were available. Luckily, the hotel was never completely booked out. Members were known to limit access to these exclusive rooms to people they knew well. Casual acquaintances of club members and strangers were rarely known to stay there.

As one of the founding members of the club house, Kesarichand had seats reserved on match-days in the Garware Pavilion of Wankhede stadium.

Kesarichand and his family could enjoy meals at the club house restaurant, swim in its pool, play a variety of indoor games in its sports rooms, and rent rooms in the hotel. Rajiv Shah became a full member of the club in 1987 when he turned eighteen and succeeded his father on the club's managing committee when he passed away in 2006.

Today, some of Mumbai's most prominent real estate developers, businesspersons and lawyers are members of the managing committee. It is clubs like Garware, Bombay

Gymkhana, Breach Candy and Willingdon that give some moneyed south Mumbai families their infamous snoot and an outsized influence in the running of the city. Ordinary membership to Garware Club House, assuming you know an existing member, costs a measly Rs 25 lakh—life membership is double that amount.

Shah was also an influential member of the south Mumbai Jain community and trustee of Shwetambar Jain Temple, located down the road from his home on F Road, Marine Drive. One of his duties as a trustee was to apply for and seek permission from the police to hold public celebrations and processions of Jain festivals. He had become well acquainted with Kalokhe during the course of his visits to Marine Drive police station. Kalokhe would often go the extra mile in his duties by keeping a watch on the community's street processions. Over the years, that had earned Kalokhe a lot of goodwill with Shah for his courteousness. Kalokhe recognized Shah as a powerful civilian contact who might prove helpful someday.

That day was 19 January 2015.

On the phone, Kalokhe told Shah that his sister and niece were visiting Mumbai and needed a place to stay. Were there any rooms available at the club house? Shah checked immediately.

An ordinary club house member would have to drive down to the club house reception, give the manager his membership number, fill out a form and provide identification documents of his guests before being allotted a room. But a member of the managing committee could get the job done on the phone.

'I'll fill the form later,' Shah told the manager, 'add the bill to my monthly tab.'

Shah didn't ask Kalokhe for the names of his sister and niece but when they arrived at the front desk, the manager wrote them down on the club house register alongside Shah's membership number.

Baby and Nishigandha checked into room 401, a 200-square-foot apartment with twin beds and a flat screen television at Rs 5,000 a night. Salty breeze wafted through two facing windows. One gave a perfect vantage point of the blazing green turf of the Mumbai Hockey Association stadium. Another overlooked the club house swimming pool.

The sea was at their doorstep and Kalokhe's workplace a pleasant 1-km-long walk down the promenade. Along the way was the city's best biscuit ice-cream parlour. The fugitive from the law was living on Marine-fucking-Drive!

Baby, however, was too distracted to enjoy herself. Her mind went back to her heated exchange with Kalokhe a month ago. Kalokhe had taken over Ballu's corners and customers and wanted Baby to buy more product from Samuel. He needed the money to buy a plot of land in Pune.

'Call Samuel,' he'd insisted.

She'd pleaded with him to quit selling and to get rid of the stash. 'I'll go to the police if you don't,' she'd warned him.

But Kalokhe had laughed off her threat.

'Just see what happens if you do. I'll make sure that you and Satish go to jail,' he'd said. In the end, she had no choice but to call Samuel. But Samuel was in jail.

Baby could not relax. Had Kalokhe set her up like he had threatened to?

While Baby stewed in her hotel room, Kalokhe contacted her lawyer, N.N. Gavankar, and instructed him to file an anticipatory bail application on her behalf at the Bombay

City Civil and Sessions Court. The police opposed her application once they got wind of it.

Baby and Nishigandha sulked indoors for three days. On the eve of checking out, a teenager and his worried father walked into Manickpur police station in Vasai town some 70 km away. He had caught his son stealing money. The father noticed that the boy had become unexplainably sickly and even for a teenager, unusually irritable. The previous October, he had passed out at home.

The doctor who treated the boy suspected that he was doing drugs. Drug peddlers on the way to school had got the boy addicted to Meow Meow, the father told the police. The boy had been cleaning his father's wallet to buy a gram for Rs 600. The father had confronted the peddlers and begged them to stop hurting his son. But they waved him away. Do what you want, they'd dared him.

The next afternoon, while Baby and Nishigandha returned to Siddharth Nagar, plainclothes policemen trapped two drug peddlers in a park in Vasai. The ill teenager identified them as the men he had been scoring from. One of the peddlers, a former bookie at the Mahalaxmi Racecourse in central Mumbai, claimed that he had been scoring from Baby at the discounted price of Rs 1,500 a gram. In Vasai, he preyed on kids walking to school. He had last scored from Baby two days back, he claimed.

Once again, Kalokhe got to work. Before the police from Vasai could come knocking, he applied for anticipatory bail for Baby at the Sessions Court in Thane. He called in another favour—this time from Jayesh Wani, a former journalist with the Marathi news broadcaster Jai Maharashtra who was now training as a criminal lawyer. A portly man in his late thirties, Wani had been working as a junior advocate in the south Mumbai chambers of Naveen Chomal, then a largely anonymous criminal lawyer who disliked taking on narcotics offences. Kalokhe had been a useful source for Wani in his reporting days. Wani persuaded his boss to take on the case.

On 22 January 2015, the Sessions Court in Mumbai overruled objections filed by the Worli police station and granted Baby protection from arrest. Sarika spent ten days in jail before a judge granted her bail. Upendra stayed inside for two months.

But for now, Baby was safe.

A relieved Kalokhe rang Rajiv Shah to thank him and ask about the hotel room tariff. Shah told him. Kalokhe didn't make any offer to pay him and the two men didn't speak again. In March, the club house billed Shah for three days and two nights at the hotel.

*Get him!*

For the second time in as many months, Kalokhe had bailed Baby out. But she was convinced that it was, in fact, he that got her into trouble in the first place.

*He's after my money,* she thought. Baby had been consumed by that fear ever since the fight in December.

*He wants me out of the way so he can get into the cupboard.* Baby had locked up her life savings in a stainless steel cupboard in her room. At last count, there was gold jewellery and piles of currency—Rs 20, Rs 50 and Rs 500 notes totalling Rs 3 crore.[47] She loved stacking notes in order.

On Kalokhe's insistence, she had rigged up CCTV cameras outside her room.

'The next time the police come to search you, the cameras will record everything they do,' he had told her.

Baby's gut told her that it was only a matter of time before Kalokhe made his next move. She would have to beat him to it.

There was no one at Worli ANC Baby could trust anymore. She tried her older contacts instead. Inspector Sanjay Nikam of the crime branch would surely help. After all, he had helped get Deputy SP Dhawale off her back. Nikam's colleagues and rivals called him 'builder', as in bodybuilder, for the muscles straining to rip through his shirt-sleeves. He fit the image of an all-action head-cracking cop. Now though, he was rotting in a desk job in the computer wing of the crime branch. Field policing was out of bounds. There was nothing he could do for Baby.

Other contacts were strangely evasive. One, who she met at Worli Sea Face, promised to speak to Commissioner Maria about Baby's tip-off. When Baby rang to follow up, the cop wouldn't answer.

Another contact, who she met at the domestic airport in Santacruz, simply said, 'Let's see.'

She even turned to Inspector Gautam Gaikwad, who had investigated the suspected murder of her sister-in-law Bharti Mazgaonkar more than twenty years ago. Since that first encounter, Gaikwad had turned his life over to practicing vipassana and worked in the quiet hill town of Igatpuri near Nashik. He had been close to S.N. Goenka, the founder of Dhamma Giri International Vipassana Centre, and retained by the police in Igatpuri on Goenka's request even after his tenure there ended.

At the time when Baby turned to him for help, he was serving a suspension after being accused of bribery. He couldn't help either.

Jyotiram Mane, her contact at Worli ANC in the late 1990s, only made things worse. She had sought him out the previous summer, when she had been looking for a place to stash Samuel's product. She did not want it lying unattended in her bungalow. Mane had refused. He didn't want to know anything about it. But curiosity had led him back to Baby's home a few days later.

'Don't waste your time,' Baby had told him, 'there's nothing illegal about it.'

Mane asked for a small packet anyway and Baby gave it to him. Mane's inquiries didn't lead anywhere. Other cops told him to not bother with Meow Meow. It wasn't worth the trouble. Mane had thrown away the packet and forgotten about it.

But now, in February, Baby needed his help. Mane went over to Marine Drive police station and tried reasoning with Kalokhe. But Kalokhe simply denied having the stash on him.

Baby had never been in a situation like this. She couldn't understand where the Mumbai Police's risk-taking appetite had disappeared! Did mephedrone not matter to them anymore? In all her time as a *khabri* or informer, this was the single-most explosive bit of information she had shopped around: *My man has stashed a huge amount of mephedrone in his home, go get him!*

The central tenet of Maria's legendary detective work was his network of *khabris*.

Was this still his police force?

Time was running out. At any moment, Kalokhe could strike.

The last contact Baby went to didn't show any promise either. 'Go to the press,' said Constable Yashwant Parte, another one of her former contacts from Worli ANC. 'Meet with reporters and tell them that the police have framed you in false cases. Humiliate the police,' he advised. Baby didn't agree.

Parte could have chosen to step away at that point. He didn't need to get involved with his old informant. Yes, she'd helped him catch a few brown sugar peddlers, but that was fifteen years ago. How many times had he told her to go clean?

Like Mane, Parte too had once dropped by at Baby's home to see her packing white crystals into plastic pouches. They looked a lot like cocaine. Baby did not sell cocaine.

'What is it?' he had asked her.

'Sugar,' she said, 'taste it.'

Parte didn't want any sugar.

Baby laughed.

'It's called MD,' she said.

Parte had a different job now. He was an immigration supervisor at the international airport. As far as comfortable assignments in the Mumbai Police went, there were none cushier. Technically, he wasn't even a regular policeman. He was deputed temporarily to the Bureau of Immigration and a minor cog within the Intelligence Bureau.

He didn't need to help Baby. He risked suspension if caught. On the other hand, there would be a substantial reward from the department if things went right, an opportunity to add some shine to an uneventful career. Parte decided to help.

But shopping around for information on Baby would not be easy. She had insisted on staying in the shadows and did not want anything traced back to her. But, then again, no serious police officer would agree to act without verifying who Parte's *khabri* was. Narcotics policing was a no-win situation with no prize for winning. Lose, and you lose everything.

Parte rang up Sudhakar Sarang, a former colleague at Worli ANC. Sarang was now a sub-inspector deputed to the ANC unit in Azad Maidan. Sarang advised his friend to meet his unit chief, Senior Inspector Suhas Gokhale, who was running a personal crusade against Meow Meow. Gokhale spent his mornings lecturing young people about its dangers, afternoons meeting with parents of users, and evenings planning operations on peddlers and suppliers. He devoted his spare moments to efforts at getting the drug classified as a controlled substance under the NDPS Act, which mandates the central government to maintain a list of dangerous substances and constantly revise that list every time a new illicit substance surfaces in the market.

On 5 February, the Department of Revenue under the Union Ministry of Finance issued a notification in the *Gazette of India Extraordinary* stating it was satisfied 'on the basis of information and evidence available to it' that mephedrone, its salts and any other preparations ought to be added to the Act. The threat of a ten-year jail term if convicted temporarily took a small quantity of mephedrone off the streets of Mumbai.

For Gokhale, who had a hand in supplying the decision-makers in New Delhi some of the information and evidence, it felt like the end of his life's work. He had four more months left in the force and awaited a final, much-delayed promotion. He intended to stay out of the news and cross out squares on his calendar until he retired and returned home to Nashik. His plans were disturbed one afternoon in late February by the arrival of Gaikwad in his office, who had now decided to help Baby.

Gokhale couldn't take on the case. His jurisdiction was confined to the geographic limits of Mumbai. In the absence of an FIR, he couldn't go charging into another district and search a private property. He wasn't going to sidestep procedure on the word of an informant who had been useful to him more than a decade before. There was also the niggling chance of not catching Kalokhe in conscious possession of the drug. The fallout of accusing a cop of trafficking and hoarding drugs and failing to prop up irrefutable evidence could wreck him. Gokhale had had too adventurous a career to attempt such a risky operation at the end of his term. He didn't want to end up on the wrong side of the law again.

'There is nothing I can do,' he said.

Gaikwad passed on the message to Baby. It seemed to Baby that she had exhausted her final option.

# 10

Parte wasn't ready to give up. It was time to go to the big boys—central government police agencies unencumbered by jurisdiction that paid a premium for high-value, actionable intelligence.

The Narcotics Control Bureau (NCB), the Central Board of Indirect Taxes and Customs (CBIC), the Directorate of Revenue Intelligence (DRI) and the National Investigation Agency (NIA) are all empowered to make drug seizures. It was just a question of identifying an officer who would take the risk, protect the informant and give them a suitable reward.

Parte sought out Rafiq Bam, a *khabri* to central police agencies who spoke with a pronounced lisp. Over chai at Lucky Restaurant in Bandra, Parte asked Bam to find a police officer with the appetite and authority to sanction a delicate operation.

Bam's contact in the NCB showed no interest. His contacts in Mumbai Police passed up the chance too, citing the same restrictions as Gokhale. Bam could only think of one other man to whom good information would matter more than such trivialities.

That man was Sameer Wankhede, an Indian Revenue Service (IRS) officer posted as a superintendent of police at the NIA in Mumbai. Wankhede had an unusually public profile for an officer of the revenue service—almost like a celebrity cop. Wankhede had been a civil servant for only seven years at that point, but his career path was interspersed with stints at the Customs' Air Intelligence Unit at Mumbai's international airport and the CBIC. It would seem like he had developed the curious tendency of being in the right place every time a famous personality got into trouble.

In 2011, he had kept the original gold-plated ICC Men's Cricket World Cup trophy locked away until the importers paid duty and forced India's captain, Mahendra Singh Dhoni, to hoist a replica trophy after helicopter-ing the side to victory at the coincidentally named Wankhede Stadium.[48]

He had fined film stars returning from vacations for evading customs duty on their baubles[49] and raided several more for evading service tax.[50]

In the last week of February, Bam set up a meeting for Parte with Wankhede at the New Customs House canteen in Ballard Estate. Wankhede had questions for Parte: How sure was he that hundreds of kilos of mephedrone were hidden in a home in a remote corner of Satara? Had he personally verified the information?

In any event, this was not a case for the NIA; there was no narco-terror connection. Wankhede would refer Parte to another federal agency, but only after he did his homework. A federal law enforcement agency would not authorize a drug search without due diligence. No agency could afford to mount an unsuccessful operation. The intelligence had to be of unquestionable authenticity.

Parte would have to find some answers.

---

Meanwhile, Baby needed a holiday. She needed to get out of Mumbai for some time. She asked Kalokhe to come with her. It was the only way she could think of keeping an eye on him and also stop him from hurting her. Besides, they always travelled together. Every time she took a holiday or went away for the weekend, he was there. A few days in Goa would set her right. She hoped that Parte would have a plan ready by the time she returned. She was growing impatient with him.

Kalokhe took ten days off from work, telling Senior Inspector Pravin Chinchalkar that he needed to visit his ailing mother in Satara. Police constables didn't get such long leaves easily. Most bosses either rejected their applications outright or made up creative reasons to deny leave or simply bullied them into cutting down their holidays by half. But Kalokhe was too valuable an asset to be treated like everyone else. He was so good at his job that his leave applications were never denied.

Early morning on 2 March 2015, Baby dropped in at Dev Nursing Home in Prabhadevi where Sarika was being treated for malaria. After a short visit, the driver Madan Singh picked up Baby and Kalokhe at the Buddhist temple at 9 a.m. In the two months that Singh had spent in Baby's employ and lived on the hill, he had heard about Baby's troubles with the police. Knowing that Baby might be a drug peddler made Singh queasy about driving her out of the city, no matter how much money Kalokhe's police identity card saved them. He could never wriggle out of those trips. Singh wasn't happy about having to drive her and that cop to Goa.

After clearing Vashi, Singh turned the car south to the potholed Mumbai–Goa Highway. Baby asked Singh to head south-west on National Highway 66. On that route lay the town of Kolhapur and its temples.

Only God could help her now.

They got as far as Karad in Satara district that night. The couple checked into a cheap highway hotel called Koyna Lodge. Kalokhe identified Baby as his wife in the guest register and paid Rs 700 for a room. Singh slept in the car.

The next morning, the couple left the lodge at eight to visit the Mahalakshmi and Jyotiba temples, before proceeding towards Goa.

That same morning back in Mumbai, Gokhale came to a crucial realization. He couldn't keep Gaikwad's information to himself. He *had* to let his superiors know. Let them evaluate its worth.

Namdeo Chavan, the Deputy Commissioner of Police in charge of ANC and the traffic police was out on a routine inspection of traffic arrangements in Ghatkopar when Gokhale rang.

Chavan cut Gokhale short before he could finish.

'This is too important to discuss on the phone. I am proceeding to the Trombay traffic police chowki. Meet me there,' he said.

Gokhale and his deputy, Inspector Rajani Salunkhe, sped off in the office jeep. An hour later, Gokhale outlined the situation to Chavan: half a kilogram of mephedrone was allegedly hidden in Kalokhe's cupboard at Marine Drive police station and another kilogram in his home in Kanheri village.

'Who is your informant?' Chavan asked.

'It is the suspended police inspector Gaikwad.' Gokhale said. 'He has confirmed that Kalokhe has taken leave to go to Kanheri as his father has passed away.'

Chavan was caught in a deeply uncomfortable situation. The summer session of the Maharashtra state assembly was to begin in six days. Arresting a policeman in possession of drugs would put Chief Minister Devendra Fadnavis, who headed the Home Department, in an extremely vulnerable position on the eve of the assembly session. That would not bode well for Chavan's future in the department.

Chavan rang his own superior, K.M.M. Prasanna, Additional Commissioner of Police of the crime branch. Prasanna was second-in-command of the crime branch.

The men discussed the implications of raiding a home plunged in grief. 'Have you corroborated this information?' Prasanna asked.

'At this stage, sir,' Chavan replied, 'it's just a piece of information. It could be either true or false.'

Prasanna lapsed into thought. To charge into the home of a son grieving his father expecting to find a hidden stash of drugs on the basis of an unverified lead would be unspeakably cruel. Then again, a delay could be just as fatal.

'Is there any other way we can corroborate this information?' he asked. A successful recovery of drugs would be a plain tragedy. Failure, too horrible to think about, spelled disaster.

'No, sir,' responded Chavan.

'What do you suggest then?' asked Prasanna.

It was Chavan's turn to take refuge in thoughtful silence. He took a moment to confer with Gokhale and Salunkhe. Then he returned to Prasanna.

'I think we should wait two to three days before doing anything, sir,' he said. The situation called for caution.

Prasanna concurred. 'Report to me when you conduct the raid,' he said, ringing off.

Chavan didn't repeat the conversation to the waiting inspectors. They had heard. Before he left, Gokhale gave Baby's and Parte's phone numbers to his boss. Chavan, in turn, sent the phone numbers to Prasanna and to Dhananjay Kulkarni, DCP of the crime branch. For now, the operation was on hold.

Baby and Kalokhe stopped that night in Savantwadi town in Sindhudurg, the southern-most coastal district in Maharashtra, and checked into Hotel Shreyas after spending the evening visiting more temples. Hotel manager Mangesh Niwjekar was delighted to host a policeman. At this hotel, police personnel were given a discount of Rs 100 on room rent and exempted from entering their names in the guest register. Niwjekar didn't ask for copies of his guests' photo identity cards either. It was, he thought, the least he could do. Kalokhe showed the night manager his police identity card and identified Baby as his wife. The night manager charged Kalokhe a subsidized tariff of Rs 900 and showed the couple into Room 203. Singh had to make do in the car again.

An entire day of devotion must have paid off. While Baby tucked herself in for the night, Bam called Parte with good news: Wankhede wanted them to go to Pune and brief the Customs field officer there.

The next morning, Baby and Kalokhe checked out of their hotel at eight. It was 4 March when they finally entered Goa. They found a tour guide and spent the day visiting beaches. They returned to Hotel Shreyas at nearly one in the morning and checked back into Room 203.

The morning after, they headed north and stopped at some more temples en route before checking into Hotel Shraddha in neighbouring Ratnagiri district that night. In the visitors' register of the hotel, the occupants of Room 108 were identified as Mr Dharmaraj B. Kalokhe, aged 52, and Mrs Shashikala B. Kalokhe of Prabhat Welfare Society in Century Bazaar, Worli. That night, Baby received some much-needed cheer.

She and Kalokhe had been on their phones constantly throughout the trip. They had travelled together like preoccupied strangers. Baby was making dozens of phone calls to Parte every day. Her furtive conversations made Kalokhe uneasy. He asked her who she was speaking to and instantly regretted it.

'It is Customs officer Suryavanshi,' she said.

Baby had made up that name to conceal her conversations with Parte. It also scared Kalokhe into believing that she might rat him out to Customs. Suryavanshi was code for *don't mess with me*.

Parte had been busy. That day, he had driven down to Pune with Bam to meet the Customs officer. In his briefing, Parte left out the part that Kalokhe was a cop. He didn't want to give everything away until he was sure of the agency's co-operation.

The officer was convinced and began planning the operation. He wanted Parte to visit Kanheri and scope out Kalokhe's house, study its entrances and exits, identify how best to approach it unseen and prevent the target from fleeing or destroying his stash. He promised to reward Parte and Bam if the operation was successful.

'Report to me once you've been there,' he said. Parte returned to Mumbai that evening in good spirits.

Singh got a break from driving the next day. Baby and Kalokhe stayed back at the hotel and stepped out only to visit some temples. She prayed that God would help her screw over her companion.

The following day, on 7 March, Baby and Kalokhe travelled further north to spend a quiet day in Chiplun, Ratnagiri. In Mumbai, Parte set off for Satara. He had brought along Bam and his cook. Two strange men driving into a small village in a white Maruti Eeco would look far too suspicious. A woman gave observers the impression of them being a family. Parte's car was a smaller version of the classic onscreen 'kidnap car' and not exactly an innocuous vehicle. The Mumbai number plate was, in any case, bound to stand out. He was eager to avoid attracting any more attention.

He drove past fields of sugarcane, jowar and onion before arriving at the village bus stop deep in the countryside. Kanheri was another kilometre off the main road.

Parte didn't stop for directions. For a few minutes, he manoeuvred his car through Kanheri's narrow lanes, reading names on front doors as he drove along. It was useless. He would have to ask someone. He drove back to the bus stop and stopped at a shop to buy biscuits.

He told the shopkeeper that he was a friend of the policeman Dharmaraj Kalokhe and needed directions to his home. Following the shopkeeper's directions, Parte drove back and turned inside the first lane to his left to reach a locked house bearing the nameplate 'Kalokhe BB'. He drove past it twice to make sure. A neighbour watched as Parte finally drove away around 6 p.m.

Once outside Kanheri, Parte called the Customs officer. But the officer wouldn't proceed with the operation until he had personally verified Parte's observations. The officer wanted to see the house for himself.

The next morning, while Baby and Kalokhe roamed about the seventeenth-century Pratapgad fort in Satara, Parte drove back to Pune with Bam and his cook. He picked up the Customs officer and headed south-west to Kanheri. In the evening, the white 'kidnap car' made another slow pass of Kalokhe's home.

The neighbour did not dismiss this as a coincidence. She dialled Kalokhe's sister, Baidabai Veer, who lived 12 km away in the village of Sangvi and reported what she had seen. Baidabai immediately called her brother.

'Some men who look like the police have been asking about you in the village, Dharma. They even drove past your house,' she said.

Kalokhe was furious. Baby and he had just checked into an upscale guesthouse owned by the textiles firm Century Rayon in Mahabaleshwar. Ganesh Sherigar, an assistant manager at the firm's factory in Thane district, was indebted to Kalokhe after he had managed to prevent a disgruntled former employee from protesting outside its headquarters in Churchgate in 2011. Four years later, Kalokhe called in a favour and requested Sherigar for a place for him and wife to spend the night.

He spoke to Baidabai briefly, giving nothing away that would prick Baby's ears. He hung up the call and turned to Baby. 'If you betray me, I will make sure that you and your family go to jail,' he warned her, eyes blazing with anger.

Later, when she found a moment to herself, Baby dialled Customs officer Suryavanshi.

'What was the big rush in going to the village? He knows you were there, and now he's going to move the drugs elsewhere and destroy them,' she erupted.

The next morning, Kalokhe announced a change of plans. They were supposed to return to Mumbai but he wanted to drop by Kanheri first.

'I have to take care of urgent business,' he said.

He needed to move the contraband before the police showed up again. This time they wouldn't just drive by. He rang Baidabai and asked if he could store some chemicals at her home. She didn't understand what her brother was saying and asked him to speak to her husband.

Popat Veer was in a gram panchayat meeting when Kalokhe called him at 10.30 a.m. to make the same request.

'I can't talk now Dharma. Can you call me later?' he said. Kalokhe did not.

Baby watched Kalokhe's sudden burst of activity with a growing sense of dread. *He's going to get away.*

At eleven, Singh and his jittery passengers arrived Pargaon Khandala, a town close to Kanheri. Kalokhe asked Singh to park on the shoulder of the highway.

'I'm going to visit my mother. Wait for me here. I'll be in back in fifteen minutes,' he said.

The previous night, Parte had instructed Baby to alert him once she and Kalokhe were close to Kanheri. So, as soon as Kalokhe had stepped out, Baby rang Parte. The operation was a go.

# 11

Anusuya Kalokhe did not know what to make of her son's sudden appearance. He made straight for the large plastic barrel sitting in a corner of the living room. From it, he extracted three plastic gunny sacks containing Samuel's five travel bags.

'There are chemicals in them, *aai*,' he had said when he brought home the bags last year on similarly unexpected visits.

Anusuya hadn't known what to make of her son's luggage then, and she didn't know what to make of it now. Just like before, he was in a great rush.

Kalokhe did not have any time to lose. With no other family member to turn to, he could no longer shift his cargo out of the village. But he could still get it out of his home. The police could not charge him with possession if the drugs weren't found in his home. He went out to check if his neighbour, Jagannath Pawar, was home. He wasn't.

Pawar and his wife Shaila were feeding their cattle in a pasture about a kilometre away from the village when his phone rang.

'*Kuthe aahes, Jaggu? Lavkar ghari ye!* [Where are you Jaggu? Come back home quickly!],' Kalokhe said.

Pawar was surprised, both by Kalokhe's sudden visit and his command. But whatever his neighbour wanted, Pawar couldn't help him. As soon as their cattle had grazed to their fill, he and his wife would have to rush home, wash, change and set out for a wedding celebration. Pawar told Kalokhe as much.

Kalokhe was desperate.

'I just need your help for ten minutes. Can you please come home?'

Shaila Pawar wasn't pleased to hear her husband agree, reluctantly.

'You know we have a wedding to go to,' she reminded him.

'It's just ten minutes,' he told her, already walking away.

### Busted!

Back in the operation's command centre—the white Maruti Swift Dzire parked off the highway—Baby was on the phone, hectoring Parte for an update. Had Customs reached Kalokhe's home or hadn't they? She couldn't drive away unless she knew for sure.

Parte had been in the middle of an average working day at the airport when Baby, as agreed, had called. In turn, Parte rang the Customs officer.

Parte had decided against driving to Kanheri that day, choosing instead to monitor the operation from the safety of his office desk. He couldn't understand what was taking so long and didn't have any answers to give Baby.

The Customs officer had assembled a search party and was ready to proceed. But he would need clearance from Wankhede before he did so. Wankhede ordered him to go to Kanheri but not get involved. 'We can't trust Baby,' Wankhede told him.

'Why does she want to get her own partner arrested? It doesn't make sense,' he said.

In the end, Wankhede simply said, '*Local police la sanga. Tyana karu dya* [Inform the local police. Let them handle this case.]'

---

The average resident of Satara in need of a fix is usually too poor to buy anything more than a few grams of *ganja*. Also, there are no pharmaceutical factories producing illicit drugs in the district. Meow Meow had not travelled this far. In fact, drug abuse was never a cause for concern in Satara.

So, Abhinav Deshmukh, then the District Superintendent of Police, was more than a little surprised to hear from the Customs officer that someone in his district was possibly sitting on a few dozen kilograms of Meow Meow. Deshmukh did not probe where the information had come from—he never did that. The message was precise. It mentioned the exact address where a police search party could expect to find the contraband, and the name of the homeowner. Yet one thing nagged at Deshmukh: why hadn't he heard of this from any of his own men?

He passed the name and address to Inspector Padmakar Ghanvat of the local crime branch and Inspector Ashok Shelke of Khandala police station and asked them to prepare for a drug seizure.

One police constable was dispatched to the Tehsildar's office in Pargaon Khandala to secure the cooperation of three state government employees to participate in the search as independent witnesses.

Another constable went to Kailas Sweet Home shop and requested its owner Ajay Yadav to lend the police his electronic weighing scale for the search. Yadav was also asked to come along.

Others piled a laptop, portable printer, the police station's seal, stamp pad, pens, sheets of blank paper, chemical analysis forms addressed to the state forensic science laboratory, envelopes and ziplock plastic pouches into a police vehicle.

What the police did not have was a field drug-testing kit. Without the kit they would have to rely on their senses of sight and smell and above all, hope that the information they were acting on was correct. Not a single member of the search party had ever seen or touched mephedrone before. They did not even have rudimentary forensic equipment, such as a set of chemicals known as reagents that change to specific colours when a drug is dissolved in them.

Sixteen policemen, the independent witness, DRI officer, informant Bam and a private photographer departed Khandala police station at 11.55 a.m.

Pawar reached Kalokhe's house by 1 p.m. to find the policeman fiddling around with three gunny sacks. Kalokhe wanted Pawar to store the bags for him.

'You know that neither *aai* nor I are home much. Can you please keep the bags safe for me?' Kalokhe said.

'What's in them?' Pawar asked.

'Chemicals,' Kalokhe said. He did not offer further explanations. 'Come on, I'll help you carry them,' he pressed.

The men picked up the gunny sacks printed with the logo of a urea manufacturer. The plant fertilizer urea, like mephedrone, is a white crystalline substance. It is usually odourless but can at times smell faintly of ammonia. Kalokhe hoped that no one who looked in the sacks would recognize the crystals as mephedrone.

Pawar made three trips to and from Kalokhe's home, holding the gunny sacks over his shoulders. To the shopkeeper and two neighbours Pawar passed on the way, he looked like just another farmer carrying sacks of urea home.

Kalokhe walked with Pawar on the final trip. Inside Pawar's home, they stacked the gunny sacks with another identical gunny sack piled around a grain drum. But Kalokhe didn't want his luggage left out in the open. From his wallet he extracted a thick bunch of currency notes and peeled off Rs 10,000.

'I want you to buy a cupboard and a lock. Store my bags inside it and keep the keys safe,' he said.

Pawar protested. He didn't want money to help his neighbour. But Kalokhe was insistent. 'Buy a cupboard soon and don't tell anyone about this,' he said and left.

Around the time that Kalokhe had returned home, confident that for now at least his possessions were safe, a convoy of police vehicles entered Kanheri. The Customs officer and Bam guided them to the lane leading to Kalokhe's home. The vehicles stopped at the mouth of the lane and policemen slowly filed out and surrounded Kalokhe's home. Ghanvat took his position outside the front door and called out 'Dharma!'

Kalokhe did not panic at the sound of the official tone. He had been expecting this. The cops could search his home but they would find nothing.

The search party entered Kalokhe's home. They knew what to look for but within a few minutes, it became clear that the house did not contain any bags filled with white powder. Kalokhe did not utter a word while the police rummaged through every room, not even to explain the sight to his bewildered mother.

Frustrated, the Customs man rang Parte.

'There's nothing here!' he said.

At his desk, Parte grew pale. He was at work, he reminded himself. He had to stay calm.

'How can you say that? You were there when we surveyed the house. Look again!' he said.

'I told you we've looked already. Ask Baby to wait where she is. Tell her not to leave until the search is over,' commanded the Customs man.

Parte refused. The Customs officer's instruction was out of order. You *never* go after the informant.

'Okay look … I can arrange for you to speak with her. Why do you need her to wait? She is not going to run away. I know where she lives. If you need to speak to her later I can arrange that,' he said.

But neither man would relent. Finally, Parte said that he would have a word with Baby and call back the Customs officer.

Baby wasn't expecting this.

'Have they checked the barrel? The MD is in there!' Baby snapped.

The search party had looked inside the barrel, Parte told her, but it had yielded nothing.

'Arre, search his neighbours' homes then. He must have given the MD to someone else!' Baby said.

Parte relayed Baby's instructions to the Customs man. Kalokhe watched as the Customs man pulled Ghanvat and Shelke to a side and whispered to them. The police team did not appear dispirited. It didn't look to Kalokhe that they were about to give up the search.

The officers broke their huddle. Ghanvat addressed Kalokhe.

'We know you've given the MD to a neighbour. Show us where he lives,' he said.

Kalokhe was stunned. Had Baby followed him? Had Jaggu talked? He'd only been back ten minutes ago. How could the police have known what he had done with the bags?

Lost in a fog of questions, it did not occur to Kalokhe to flee. He would not be able to outrun more than a dozen policemen. He would have to give up Jaggu.

'I'll show you,' Kalokhe said and started walking.

At Pawar's front door, Kalokhe called out his name. Pawar, still fretting over the money, went to the door. The search party filled into Pawar's home before he could make sense of what was happening.

'Bring out the sacks I gave you,' Kalokhe said.

Word spread quickly in the village. A crowd of neighbours had gathered outside Pawar's home. One of them rushed to the forest to inform Shaila that the police were in her home.

Pawar dragged the three gunny sacks into the living room and Kalokhe removed five bags from within. One by one, the police opened each bag and found transparent plastic packets stacked inside.

Ghanvat slit open one packet and laid a pile of tiny white crystals on the palm of his hand.

'Somebody Google what MD looks like!' he ordered.

A constable handed him a phone with a page of image search results open. Ghanvat scrolled through endless images of a white powder. They looked remarkably like the crystals on his palm. He then looked at the heap of white powder lying at his feet. He looked at Kalokhe, who had lapsed into a stunned silence.

'Is this MD?' Ghanvat asked.

Kalokhe nodded.

Using Ajay Yadav's weighing scale, the police weighed each packet. The final figure was 112 packets and 112.029 kg of mephedrone. The internet informed them that current value of their seizure in the international market was Rs 22.40 crore.

From the five bags, the police drew samples of 20 grams each and stamped and sealed them in envelopes. Ghanvat, Kalokhe and the three witnesses signed each envelope. These samples would be sent for testing to the Regional Forensic Science Laboratory in Pune the next day.

While the search party worked, the Customs officer told Parte that the police had found the contraband. 'You can tell Baby to leave,' he said.

After all those hours of waiting by the highway for the news, Baby and Madan Singh drove back to Mumbai.

Darkness fell over Kanheri by now. The search party had been working since afternoon without food or water. Deshmukh had also driven to Kanheri to personally supervise the search.

The search party frisked Kalokhe and Pawar next. A familiar-looking laminated plastic identity card in

Kalokhe's wallet identified him as a head constable in Mumbai Police. It was now the search party's turn to be stunned into silence.

'How do we proceed, sir?' Ghanvat asked Deshmukh.

The case hinged on Deshmukh's decision. Unfazed, he said, 'File an FIR.'

But even as the men proceeded with their paperwork, Deshmukh contemplated the unpleasant task ahead of him. Protocol dictated that he convey the news of Kalokhe's arrest to the IPS officer of whose jurisdiction Marine Drive police station was a part—in this case, Ravindra Shisve, DCP, Zone I, in Mumbai.

The phone call was brief and devastating, like a doctor ringing in with news of a terminal illness.

Once the search party was ready to leave, the police informed Anusuya Kalokhe that her son was under arrest for purchasing and trafficking drugs. Kalokhe was allowed to inform his wife.

Save for the pinpricks of light peeking out from homes, Kanheri was in near darkness as the police cars wound their way out, taking one of its sons away. Anusuya was left alone in the empty house.

At Khandala police station, Kalokhe was booked for possessing and transporting a psychotropic substance under the NDPS Act. The sum of Rs 10,000 Kalokhe had paid Pawar was cited as an indicator of his guilt. The police did not book Pawar.

A phone call was also made to Gokhale, who had lectured some members of the search team at the Maharashtra Police Academy on investigating drug seizures. Gokhale passed on his phone number at the end of the lecture, but he had not expected any representative of Khandala to ever have to use it. Now they needed him to walk them through every procedure, step by step.

Gokhale kept his questions in check. This wasn't the time. There would be a furious inquest in Crawford Market the next morning. But he didn't fear being caught up in it. He had done his job six days ago.

News of the search and Kalokhe's arrest first reached local journalists working in Marathi language newspapers. Late that night, the news also reached Mumbai.

In her room in Siddharth Nagar, an exhausted but ecstatic Baby congratulated herself on a job well done.

The holiday was over.

## 12

In Mumbai, Shisve informed his immediate superior, Krishna Prakash, the Additional Commissioner of Police, South region. Then he rang Pravin Chinchalkar, the good-natured Senior Inspector of Marine Drive police station, hoping to receive some enlightenment. Chinchalkar could not provide any.

Chinchalkar had, at least mentally, already begun packing his bags. Commissioner Maria was ruthless in punishing the slightest oversight, packing off senior inspectors to the backwaters of the armoury division in Parel if their subordinates were found to have committed any misdemeanour.

Protocol dictated that the police look through Kalokhe's belongings, if any, at the police station. Constables and officers at the police station were assigned lockers to store their bags and case papers. Kalokhe had his own cupboard.

The cupboard was lying unused in the basement parking lot at the National Centre for Performing Arts in Nariman

Point when Kalokhe and his fellow mill special, Constable Krushnat Mane, called on the manager, Prabhu Tiwari, one day early in 2014. The policemen wanted to know if Tiwari could spare an extra cupboard. The pair needed one to store their files, diaries and registers. In the past, they had been able to persuade the management to donate to the police station ageing chairs that would otherwise have been replaced.

Tiwari didn't have the sturdy Godrej model that the policemen were after but did have a plywood cupboard that no one was using. It was large enough to accommodate both their belongings. At the cops' request, Tiwari hired and paid for a carpenter to partition the cupboard into two horizontal levels and install separate locks for both men. Once the cupboard was ready, Kalokhe got it picked up and placed in a corner of the common room at the police station.

The new piece of furniture did, however, arouse some surprise among Kalokhe's colleagues and superiors. Only the four inspectors and Chinchalkar had their own cupboards.

Shisve and Prakash decided to wait until morning before acting. Rifling through Kalokhe's possessions in the dark would only arouse further suspicion. They wanted to be seen following proper procedure.

Chinchalkar came in to work at 8 a.m. to find the usual stack of newspapers waiting on his table. Only the English tabloid *Mumbai Mirror* and the Marathi daily *Pudhari* had the story of Kalokhe's arrest.

The headline in Pudhari read: '100 kg drugs found in Marine Drive police constable's home'. The article began below a one-word subhead: 'Shocking'. Looking at the printed copy in his hand, Chinchalkar felt the full force of his subordinate's alleged crime. The next paper to land on his desk would surely be his transfer order.

Till date, there had been no complaints about Kalokhe. He kept to himself and went about his work with a quiet, almost robotic efficiency. Even his fellow mill specials, Constables Mane and Suresh Jadhav barely knew him.

Prakash called almost as soon as Chinchalkar had finished reading the article. It was almost as though Prakash had allowed Chinchalkar time to digest the facts before commencing the morning's grim business.

Once Chinchalkar had summoned Mane and Assistant Police Inspector Janardhan Patil in the common room, it became clear that the top half of the cupboard—Kalokhe's half—would have to be forced open. Only Kalokhe had the keys.

Chinchalkar dispatched one constable to locate a carpenter and another to the New India Assurance Company—the office was located in the art deco Moti Mahal building a short walk away—to find two employees willing to participate in the search as independent witnesses.

Prakash rang DCP Chavan for assistance. Chavan, who was engaged in a meeting to finalize traffic arrangements for the state assembly session, had been expecting that call. Only minutes earlier, Gokhale had called to brief him about the previous evening's events in Kanheri.

'Is this the same case you had told me about?' he asked.

'Yes it is, sir.'

Only those in the room witnessed Chavan's reaction to letting the headline-making case slip away from his grasp. On the other line, Gokhale was unaware that his boss had nearly suffered a meltdown.

'Kalokhe's cupboard is being opened. Go and help,' Chavan said.

The men gathered in the small common room towards the end of the barracks that housed the police station. It was one of eight built by the British to house soldiers during World War II. After Independence, the police department took over four barracks while the Government of Maharashtra housed some of its obscure departments in the others.

In 1999–2000, when the then Bombay Police Commissioner M.N. Singh felt the need to establish another police station to secure Mantralaya and Vidhan Sabha, he chose the first barracks. Today, the ageing building is surrounded by some of the most exclusive apartment buildings in the city. Its roof is propped up by bamboo poles and appears to be in imminent danger of collapse.

Kalokhe was not the first constable posted at Marine Drive police station to disgrace himself. Almost exactly a decade back, Constable Sunil More had raped a seventeen-year-old college student inside a sea-facing police chowki.[51]

By the time the carpenter and independent witnesses arrived, Chinchalkar had his men put together equipment for the search—an electric weighing machine, the police station's stamp and seal, chemical analysis forms, labels for seized samples, a laptop and printer. The carpenter brought along sample keys and his tools. Just like in Kanheri the previous evening, the missing item here was a field drug-testing kit.

The carpenter unscrewed the latch to Kalokhe's half. Inside, the policemen found his personal effects stored on three shelves. Carefully, the policemen stripped the shelves of their contents. The largest item was a black backpack with the words 'Express Tower' and its familiar blue-and-green skyscraper logo printed on the front. In 1970, Ramnath Goenka, founder of *The Indian Express*, had commissioned the construction of the tower, which overlooked Marine Drive. The empty backpack was put aside as the policemen turned their disbelieving eyes to the rest of Kalokhe's belongings.

There were two 750 ml bottles of rum—Blender's Pride and Lord Nelson XXX; a thick wad of Indian, Indonesian and Filipino currency notes; police health insurance cards for Kalokhe, his wife, kids and mother; a pair of spectacles; a bottle of cleaning liquid; four umbrellas; three vests; two caps; a visiting card holder; two paper folders; two bottles of perfume; a knife; an elephant figurine; a 2011-year diary; three other diaries; a notebook; Titan and Citizen sunglasses; a Blackberry phone and a smartphone; and one nail cutter. A small plastic packet contained a dark brown substance that Gokhale recognized as charas.

That left twelve plastic packets. Each packet bulged with white crystals like a pack of unbranded salt. It was ten minutes to noon now, nearly four hours since Chinchalkar had begun what was surely his final day in charge of this police station.

Complete silence descended on the search party as one packet was slit open for Gokhale to examine the white crystals. In his five years on the narcotics beat, Gokhale had discovered drugs concealed in photocopy shops, warehouses and in too many pockets to count. This would be a first.

He took a pinch out of the packet and held the crystals to his nose. The search party waited for his verdict. Gokhale inhaled deeply and turned to Chinchalkar.

'It seems to be mephedrone,' he said, 'but could easily be Ajinomoto.'

The second half of his sentence was left out of the FIR filed against Kalokhe at five minutes past five that evening.

# 13

But for an act of violence, Suhas Gokhale would never have become a policeman. As a young man, the image he had of the police was that of a group of corrupt men. He seemed predestined for a life in the mountains.

Growing up by the banks of the Godavari river in the town of Nashik in Maharashtra, his parents, both teachers in a private school, could never keep young Gokhale away from climbing up trees and hills or jumping off bridges long enough to attend school.

In the family of two boys, Gokhale was the outdoorsy, rebellious one while his elder brother, Nandakumar, was the serious, studious one. Nandakumar could have walked right out of one of the government Adarsh Balak posters, designed with the purpose of cultivating the right habits in young boys and girls. Naturally, he was the more responsible sibling, prayed devoutly, read war stories and wore his shirt tucked in. As a teenager, he joined the National Cadet Corps

(NCC) and yearned for a life in the military. He consciously avoided trouble and could never be convinced to go trekking. He feared heights.

The family lived in relative comfort in a home that Gokhale's paternal grandfather had built in Panchavati, a locality by the river that got its name from five ancient banyan trees and its holiness from a cave in which Lord Rama, Sita and Laxmana are believed to have stayed during their exile.

While Gokhale's preoccupations lay chiefly in getting into trouble, scouting tougher hills to scale and taller bridges to dive off, Nandakumar had formed strong patriotic feelings at a young age. When both children were quite young, the parents had taken them to a playground to hear a retired Army Major speak about the history of officers from Maharashtra in the military. At the end of the speech, their father had vowed to the Major that at least one of his sons would join the military. In school, those passions were further stoked when Nandakumar won a national-level essay competition and was rewarded with trips to Mumbai, Calcutta and the Andaman and Nicobar Islands. Paying a visit to Vinayak Damodar Savarkar's jail cell in Kala Paani made Nandakumar even more of a patriot.

Despite having to wear glasses to remedy frequent and painful headaches, Nandakumar excelled at shooting and handling a bayonet. But his dreams were scuppered when his eyesight was adjudged to be too poor to graduate to the NCC's advanced course. Nandakumar didn't sulk indefinitely. Before long, he joined the gym and karate classes and enrolled in college.

In the meantime, Gokhale had moved to Chinai College in Mumbai to study microbiology. While his studies confined him to airless laboratories in Andheri East, his head was stuck in the mountains. He led treks to the upper reaches of the Himalayas once a year and went away to climb peaks in the state every chance he got. The boy from Nashik with bad Hindi and non-existent English language skills had struggled in the big city college until he joined the college's hiking club and basketball team. Much to his surprise, Gokhale graduated college voted the best student in his year.

While his younger sibling remained in Mumbai, having secured a job at a private company, Nandakumar struggled to find employment in Nashik. He had had an ill-fated spell at a relative's garage in Mumbai and nothing to show for his two years' work experience when it shut down without notice. He returned to Nashik utterly dejected, but he didn't stay down for too long.

Though a career in the military was out of the question, his skills easily earned him a spot in the Maharashtra Police. After training at the Maharashtra Police Academy in Nashik, Nandakumar was posted to Nagpada police station in south Mumbai as a probationary police sub-inspector.

Nagpada in the early 1980s was home to gangster Dawood Ibrahim and, as a result, the epicentre of the city's criminal activity. While full-scale gangland killings were still a decade away, tense relations between communities living in close quarters meant a constant fear of communal riots in Muslim-majority Nagpada. It was a tough first assignment for a rookie cop.

Gokhale resisted Nandakumar's efforts to draft him into the police department. He would not change his opinion of the police.

The new sub-inspector soon made himself indispensable to the police station and was rewarded with the responsibility of heading its Anti-Goonda Squad—police parlance for keeping small-time criminals in check. Nandakumar also married a teacher at his mother's school in Nashik and they had a son. Nandakumar's wife feared for his life every time he left home to capture a fugitive criminal. He assured her that nothing would happen to him.

'And even if something does happen, Suhas will rush to your aid like Laxmana,' he'd tell her.[52]

She was right to have been afraid. Bombay was on the edge all through 1984. Shiv Sena founder Bal Thackeray had floated the idea of a Hindu Mahasangh in an incendiary speech on 22 January. He followed that up with more invective directed towards Muslims at a Mahasangh meeting on 21 April.

*India Today* journalist Coomi Kapoor reported on the speech in these words:

> By his own admission he used the derogatory Marathi term 'landiya' to describe Muslims, and declared that they were spreading like cancer and should be operated upon like a cancer. The country, he said, should be saved from the Muslims and the police should support them [the Mahasangh] in their struggle just like the police in Punjab were sympathetic to the Khalistanis.[53]

Thackeray's comments, including those allegedly insulting Prophet Muhammad, were largely ignored by the press in Bombay but picked up and printed prominently by an Urdu publication in Bangalore on 9 May.[54]

As a result, the situation was particularly restive in Bhiwandi, a Muslim-majority town on the outskirts of Bombay and a large textile power loom centre. Fierce protests broke out over Thackeray's comments. The atmosphere was further vitiated in Bhiwandi when the police granted the Shiv Sena permission to carry out a procession to commemorate Shiv Jayanti.

The Shiv Sena countered those protests by enforcing a bandh in Bombay on 16 May. The same day, a politician in Bhiwandi announced the formation of the 'Muslim Sena'.

'Nobody took the announcement seriously till green flags started appearing mysteriously in parts of the city as if to counter the saffron flags, symbols of the Shiv Sena,' *India Today* reported.[55]

Two days later, riots erupted in Bhiwandi and spread swiftly to Bombay. On 18 May, Nandakumar had changed into his street clothes and deposited his pistol in the police station's armoury at the end of his shift. All day, rumours had been rife of a flag belonging to a particular community being desecrated and dumped in a garbage bin. By 8 p.m., trouble broke out in Nagpada. A colleague rushing to quell the rioting requested Nandakumar to back him up. It would be just the two of them against a mob of unknown numbers. Nandakumar went in unarmed.

The policemen reached the locality to find a full-scale riot underway. Nandakumar was armed with only a lathi and asked his colleague to provide cover fire. The rioters overpowered him when he started to swing the lathi around. He turned back to see why his colleague wasn't helping him but could not spot him. They were separated by the crowd. That was the last time Nandakumar was seen alive.

At 3 a.m., Nandakumar's body was found beneath a metal sheet in a drain in the neighbouring brothel district of Kamathipura. Coroners counted thirty-eight small and large injuries on his body. They were the clues to his final hours. He had probably slipped while surrounded by rioters, who then pounced upon him. His left arm was fractured in multiple places, most probably from trying to protect his head. The rioters then beat Nandakumar senseless and dragged him up the terrace of a three-storey building on Kamathipura's 3rd Road. There, they threw a bucketful of water on Nandakumar's face before hurling him off the roof. The fall broke his head. The mob then dragged his body to the gutter and covered it with a metal sheet to hide it from the view of passers-by.

The young acrophobic patriot met his end after being thrown off from a height.[56]

Nandakumar's was the first death of a Mumbai Police personnel in a communal riot. Strangely, a list of martyrs on the Maharashtra Police website does not provide any details of Nandakumar's death beyond saying that 'PSI/Nandakumar Gokhale laid down his life in the line of duty.' His first name is misspelt in the entry.

Among the visitors to Nandakumar's home in the days after his death were Nagpada's poor and destitute who spoke of how he had helped them. Their words came back to Gokhale at the funeral, where the younger brother made the decision to join the police department.

His parents were aghast at his announcement. They could not countenance losing another son. It felt to them like a rash decision, but Gokhale's resolve would not be shaken.

'I could have lost my life on a trek had I made a mistake or had luck deserted me,' he told them, 'but nothing of that sort happened.'

In the end, with much reluctance, his parents yielded. The family now truly fulfilled the promise made to the Army Major all those years ago.

Gokhale breezed through the physical and written tests for the Maharashtra Police's sub-inspector exams. He faced his actual test when he was shortlisted for the final round, an interview with three stern-faced police officers who knew exactly who he was.

'We have heard that you have joined the police force to avenge your brother's killing,' the panel said.

Gokhale was taken aback but kept his composure. 'I am not influenced by Hindi films in which people carry out their revenge on every bad guy individually after fifteen to twenty years. I am neither Amitabh [Bachchan] nor Dharmendra.'

He asked a question of his own. 'I know I am not allowed to ask questions during the interview but can you tell me why people think so about me?'

The panel responded. 'That is because despite a good academic record and despite losing your brother, you still want to join the police force.'

Gokhale retorted forcefully, 'Just like Nandakumar was a brother to me, he was also a brother to each of his colleagues. As along as everyone remembers that, I won't have to do anything differently. Some people say that my brother was Hindu and his murderers were Muslim. I do not believe that. My brother was a police officer and policing was his religion. The murderers were criminals and committing crime is their religion. Whenever I catch a criminal I will feel like I have avenged my brother's death. If that's what you call an act of vengeance, then I will carry out my revenge until the day I retire.'

The interview hall was silent after he had finished speaking. He quietly took his leave. Soon after, he was selected to join the Police Academy.

Gokhale spent the first two years after graduating from the academy as a sub-inspector in Jalgaon. Young police officers begin their careers in the countryside before the inevitable call to serve in the big city. It was no different for Gokhale. The first police station to which he was posted had under its jurisdiction villages with historical communal tensions.

Soon, Gokhale was part of a large police deployment meant to ensure peace at a Navratri festival procession. The police apprehended that members of the procession would stop at a mosque en route and chant aggressive and provocative slogans. To head off trouble, the police surrounded the mosque and forced the procession to move on. But violence broke out nonetheless and a colleague, sub-inspector Mandaleshwar Kale, dove in alone with his lathi. He was quickly overwhelmed.

Visions of Nandakumar outnumbered by the mob less than three years ago rose before Gokhale's eyes, and he prepared to charge in to help. But Deputy Superintendent of Police Ramrao Pawar ordered him to stay where he was.

Ignoring the direct order, Gokhale said, 'My brother lost his life because his colleague did not help him. I will not let that happen to Kale.' Gokhale managed to save his colleague that day, but Pawar ordered him to stay calm the next time.

Occupied with quelling riots and solving thefts, Gokhale had little time left to give to his family. He almost missed the birth of his first-born, Saket, because he was chasing a lead one night when his wife unexpectedly went into labour. With no other way to reach her husband, she had contacted the police station and demanded that Gokhale be sent to the hospital right away. After his wife had delivered the baby safely and fallen asleep, Gokhale slipped back to the police station to finish his shift. He returned the next morning to find her awake and furious. She gave him hell for leaving. He promised to stay for the birth of their grandchildren. She was not impressed.

## Encounter

A transfer to Mumbai came in 1988. The officer Gokhale reported to on arrival was tempted to post him in Nagpada but he was talked out of it. Gokhale thus began his tenure in Mumbai at Mata Ramabai Ambedkar Road police station, down the road from CSMT, overseeing the security of Crawford Market and all of the historic Bombay Fort area. His duties in the big city gave him very little time for his family or leisure. Work always got in the way of every opportunity to relax and to be a father to his two young children. He could take them on only two vacations—one to the beach town of Ganpatipule in Ratnagiri District and a day trip to the hills of Matheran. When his wife was pregnant with their daughter Shruti, he was also forced to leave her at the gynaecologist's office after receiving the news of a shootout in south Mumbai. When Shruti was older, he had spent her dance recital preoccupied with thoughts of a violent revenge killing reported in his jurisdiction. There were also the first stirrings of disciplinary issues.

In a routine shake-up of its personnel before the 1996 General Elections, Gokhale was transferred to the ANC. Gokhale wasn't happy with the move.

In the mid-1990s, the ANC had acquired the reputation of being poorly managed and staffed by inefficient personnel of questionable integrity. It was an image that the new DCP in-charge of the ANC, a promising IPS officer named Hemant Karkare, planned to change.

On Gokhale's first day there, Karkare ordered him to begin studying the NDPS Act, a short but exacting piece of legislation the ANC had been formed to enforce. It was a part of the reason cops rarely volunteered to work there. It only intensified Gokhale's dislike for his new job.

It was the words of his superior officer in the ANC, the encounter specialist and 26/11 martyr Vijay Salaskar, that proved to be a guiding light. One evening, Salaskar passed by Gokhale's wife at the police quarters in Kurla while she was on her way to the market and asked her to pass on a message to her husband.

'Please tell Suhas to put his heart into his work. I know he will do well in the ANC,' Salaskar said. That piece of advice would change Gokhale's outlook of the ANC.

Karkare's first commandment was to raise the ANC's abysmal record of securing convictions in court. So, even as his new charge immersed himself into studying the Act, Karkare also wanted him to observe trials in the special NDPS Act courtrooms at the Sessions Court in Kala Ghoda.

Gokhale's first day in court as an ANC officer was an eventful one. That day, the special NDPS Act court would pronounce its verdict in the seizure of 485 kg of heroin from the possession of the notorious Afghan drug smuggler Noor Mohammed Khan alias Nari Khan.

Gokhale noticed that the courtroom was extremely tense. The judge appeared petrified. From his raised seat on the bench, he had a clear view of Khan, who was seated in the accused box and praying under his breath.

The judge acquitted Khan on minor technical grounds. He pronounced his judgment so softly that even the lawyers seated in the front row could not hear him clearly. Gokhale discovered later that the judge had received a threat to his life on the eve of delivering the verdict. At the back, Khan lowered his head to the wooden railing of the box and prayed in relief. More out of curiosity than disgust, Gokhale went up to Khan and asked him what he was doing. Khan was ecstatic.

'It is by God's grace that I have been acquitted. I had trouble falling asleep last night. When I did get some asleep, I dreamed that Allah recited some verses of the Holy Quran and ordered me to stop selling heroin. I will never sell heroin again,' he said.

Gokhale was amused by the story. 'What is a Pathan like you going to do if not sell heroin? Will you sell Mandrax now?' he asked.

'*Nahi, sahab* [No, sir],' Khan said. 'There is too much competition in Mandrax. *Ab se main hashish bechunga* [I will sell hashish from now on].'

Gokhale was left speechless.

A week later, Gokhale and two other colleagues were hiding behind bushes in pitch darkness on the Eastern Express Highway in Vikhroli. They had been called in by the local police to assist with preventing a sale that was expected to take place on the service road.

They watched as a car slipped off the highway and into the service road and came to a stop close to a cluster of slums. A gigantic man dressed in a Pathani suit and holding a plastic bag emerged from it. Gokhale had a funny feeling that he had seen the man quite recently but needed to be sure. Then the figure passed under a streetlight and Gokhale recognized Nari Khan.

Gokhale stepped out of the bushes and ordered Khan to stop. Khan whipped out a pistol and shot at Gokhale. But the target was standing in darkness and Khan wasn't a good shot. The bullets missed. Gokhale fired back, shooting Khan in the knee and bringing him down. Before Gokhale could even think of subduing Khan, his colleagues fired and killed him. It was yet another encounter in Mumbai in the 1990s.

The erasure of Khan from Mumbai's drug market made Gokhale the ANC's undisputed star. Even as the fame brought informants to his door and added significant busts to a burgeoning record, Gokhale wrestled with the fact that he had actually killed a man.

The good times however tended to be tempered with bouts of trouble. Gokhale's job was on the line soon after, when a subordinate arrested a wealthy young man for evading Customs Duty on the import of four hundred mobile phones and allegedly demanded a bribe to let him go.

Already reeling from the possibility of an arrest or a suspension, Gokhale received news that evening of his father's sudden passing from a heart attack. He left for Nashik, knowing fully well that skipping town without notice would make him a suspect.

Some days after the funeral, Gokhale's partner, Arvind Wadhankar, pleaded with him to return to Mumbai. Wadhankar had received information about plans for a massive drug sale in the suburbs and needed Gokhale's help. Gokhale did not want to leave his mother on her own but she told him to stop moping.

So Gokhale joined Wadhankar on a late-night stakeout in Goregaon. When they spotted the suspects, they identified themselves and ordered them to stop. But just as Khan had done, the suspects shot at the policemen. One bullet struck Gokhale on the ear. The cops had no choice but to fire back. The men killed in Goregaon were later identified as an operative of Pakistan's Inter-Services Intelligence (ISI) spy agency and his local contact. They had been attempting to smuggle six tonnes of heroin from India to a drug cartel in Cambodia.

Gokhale now had three kills to his name but thankfully hadn't earned the tag of an encounter specialist.

# 14

Tense faces greeted Dipti Patankar when she returned home at half past two in the afternoon on 11 March. She had been out for just an hour to pick up her son Saurabh from school in Dadar. The mood at home had been relaxed when she had left. Now her husband Girish and brother-in-law Satish were huddled around the television. Baby was throwing clothes into a bag.

The news of Kalokhe's arrest and the contents of his cupboard at the police station the previous morning had not caused any worry. Today's top story, attributed to the Mumbai Police, was the name of his alleged supplier, a 'Drug Mafia' named Baby.[57] The reports were sketchy on the details. They speculated that the police discovered hundreds of kilograms of Meow Meow in Kalokhe's home.

Kalokhe had not spilled her name instantly. On his first full day in custody at Khandala police station, he had stayed quiet during questioning. Kalokhe's interrogators thought that he looked scared. But Kalokhe was seething inside. From the moment the police search party had arrived at his front door, it had become clear to him that Baby had ratted on him. He wasn't going to let her get away with it.

It had taken investigators several hours to come to terms with what exactly sat in the police station's storage room aka *maalkhana*—112.029 kg of a drug never seen before in Satara. SP Deshmukh didn't take any chances. He deputed one of his most experienced officers to head the investigation: Deepak Humbre, the Deputy Superintendent of Police of Wai taluka, who had served in the department for over thirty years and been awarded the President's Police Medal for his services.

Deshmukh passed on what little his investigators had learned from Kalokhe to DCP Shisve in Mumbai. They would have to locate this Baby before the story got away from them. After obtaining her address from Kalokhe, Humbre and his detectives set off for Mumbai.

Their first stop was at Marine Drive police station where it immediately became evident that the contraband found in Kalokhe's cupboard and in Kanheri had common origins. The contraband in the cupboard was part of the stash Baby had purchased from Samuel and stored in her bungalow.

The police declared Baby as a wanted accused.

This was not part of the deal Baby had negotiated for herself while delivering Kalokhe. Baby had failed to factor in just how deeply Kalokhe's capture had rattled his bosses in Mumbai. They had now decided to break a cardinal rule of crime detection: leave the informant alone. She rang Parte for an explanation. But he did not have one. She needed to disappear. Quickly.

Dipti watched as Baby finished packing, grabbed Nishigandha and left without a word. Girish's actions were just as urgent.

'We're going to your parents' place. There's no time to pack,' he told her.

Girish phoned his schoolmate and fellow Siddharth Nagar resident Sachin Dhayalakar, whom he fondly called 'Chooha', the Hindi word for mouse. Within an hour, Girish, Dipti, Saurabh and daughter Sayali were driving to Vasai with Sachin at the wheel of the family's Toyota Innova. He was to drop them at the home of Naresh Pardeshi, Girish's business partner in Vasai.

Just before they turned into the Bandra-Worli Sea Link, Girish got out of the car and promised to join them in Vasai later that evening. He asked Sachin to return to Worli once he had dropped Dipti and the children.

With his wife and children safe for the moment, it was time for Girish to think about his mother. The only hiding place he could think of would not be a pleasant one.

## *Flight*

Satish, Sarika and their children, Soham and Sonali, didn't leave Worli until much later. Their first priority was to lock up their home and put some distance between themselves and Siddharth Nagar. It would give them time to think.

The sight of the locked homes had puzzled Madan Singh when he had arrived at 4 p.m. to collect his salary. Someone was always home. With no choice but to return later, Singh walked out of the lane when two policemen in plainclothes stopped him and asked him why he was lurking outside Baby's home. More importantly, the cops wanted to know where everyone was.

'I'm just the driver,' Singh explained. 'I came to get my salary. I don't know where everyone has gone.'

Once the policemen allowed him to go, Singh rang Satish, Girish and Baby but could not reach any of them. Then he returned home.

The previous night, Satish wanted to drive to Sangvi to look for Kalokhe at his sister's home. But after a full day of driving the kids to and from school on the back of a week-long jaunt across Maharashtra and Goa, Singh had begged for some rest and talked Satish into leaving early the next morning.

They set out at five in the morning and stopped outside a temple near Baidabai's home three hours later. Satish walked the rest of the way. He was back minutes later after ascertaining that Kalokhe was most definitely in police custody.

By the time the men returned to Siddharth Nagar, the children were waiting for Singh to drive them to school. Before leaving though, Singh told Satish that he wanted the rest of the day off after the school run.

Back home after that uneasy chat with the police, Singh nodded off. At 6 p.m., his phone rang. It was Satish, asking to be picked up outside the Buddhist temple.

'That's not a good idea,' Singh told him, 'the police are watching your house.'

Singh surmised that the police would have surely placed spotters all along the main entrance. There was no chance of getting away.

'Meet us at the back entrance then,' Satish said.

A few minutes later, Singh drove into a lane that snakes away from Worli Naka and leads to Prem Nagar, on the other side of the hill. Satish and Sarika were waiting with their children.

The police searched through Baby's home after Singh had disappeared. They made three discoveries—Baby's ration card, her driving licence and a picture. It showed an unsmiling Baby and Kalokhe standing in front of a coconut tree and posing for the camera. Kalokhe had an arm across Baby's shoulders. They looked like an average middle-aged couple on holiday, not an alleged drug supplier and a serving policeman.

There were no signs of any more contraband or clues to where she might be.

It took the police another forty-eight hours to obtain five mobile phone numbers used by Baby and her sons and request telecom companies to provide Call Detail Records (CDRs). The companies sent a sheaf of pages detailing every call and message made to and originating from those numbers since the beginning of the previous year. The records also showed the cell tower closest to those phone numbers, placing their locations within a radius of a couple of kilometres.

A CDR sheet is easy enough to read but needs a skilled analyst to decipher. Cell towers in Mumbai serve tens of thousands of mobile phone users. For the police, relying solely on CDRs for tracking down a suspect is like looking for a needle in a haystack. It needs a skilled analyst to spot patterns in the jumble of phone calls and text messages, to identify phone numbers which account for the most activity and cell towers they originate from. It is laborious, patient, time-consuming work.

The investigators at Marine Drive police station didn't have time.

Cooped up in Mira Road with his employer, Singh wanted answers but on the first evening, found no one willing to give him any. The next morning's newspapers quelled some of his curiosity but left him with the same uneasy sensation he felt every time he had to drive Baby out of the city.

There was a knock on the door on the third day in Mira Road. It had taken the police less than twenty-four hours to track down Satish's location using his CDRs. Satish and Singh were hauled off to Marine Drive police station.

Neither had seen or heard from Baby since their hurried departure from Siddharth Nagar four days ago. Satish let on very little, telling his interrogators in vague terms of one occasion when he'd accompanied Baby to Pune to pick up two bags of mephedrone from a man whose name he didn't know and whose car registration number he couldn't recall.

Singh was allowed to leave. Satish was a resident of the police station until his mother was found.

---

Baby spent the first twenty-four hours in her hideout in a state of disbelief and silence. The disbelief of a master schemer who has suffered her first-ever loss, and silence of one who disapproves of her surroundings.

Baby hated the idea of hiding at the house of Reshma, Girish's second wife. But, for the moment, it was unlikely that the police would look for her there. She had never accepted Reshma—not even visited her in the hospital last month when she gave birth to a baby boy.

So, when Girish called Reshma at 7 p.m. and asked if his mother and cousin could stay with her for two days, Reshma was inclined to say no. Girish preempted and stonewalled all her questions. Reshma gave in.

Baby and Nishigandha arrived two hours later and went straight up to the first floor of her *jhopdi*. Reshma noticed that something was bothering her mother-in-law but neither of them attempted to make conversation. Reshma served her guests dinner and then withdrew downstairs. There was nothing to talk about and no sense probing the cause of her distress. Baby slept fitfully that night.

The next morning, Nishigandha descended the stairs for breakfast. Baby stayed where she was.

It was now two days since the police had begun looking for Baby. Her picture and news of her continued disappearance had moved from brief news bulletins to prime-time slots on Marathi and Hindi news channels. Reshma's neighbours in Prem Nagar were also watching. No one was very surprised that *gard-powder-waali* Baby *tai* was in trouble again. They asked Reshma where she thought her mother-in-law might have gone. Reshma hadn't watched the news until then. She dreaded what the police would do to her son, mother, brother and sister-in-law when they discovered she was sheltering Baby. It was only a matter of time before they would. Baby and Nishigandha couldn't stay.

Reshma rang Girish and ordered him to take his mother away; she was not going to a harbour a fugitive from the law a minute longer. Girish kept her waiting the entire day and finally arrived at nine after a few more angry phone calls.

Reshma was relieved to see Baby leave but couldn't resist asking Girish where he was taking them next.

He said nothing.

From Prem Nagar, Girish took Baby to Kamothe, Navi Mumbai, where his third wife, twenty-three-year-old Rachna Singh lived. There, they laid low for a few days until Baby fell ill. It was too risky to come out in the open and walk into the neighbourhood clinic. On the spur of the moment, Girish bundled everyone in the car and ordered Sachin to drive to Surat. The police would never think to look that far. A Surat doctor patched up Baby. She was in better spirits on the drive back to Mumbai.

The party split up on the Western Express Highway in Borivali. Rachna returned home. Baby, Girish, Nishigandha and Sachin boarded a bus heading south to Kudal in Sindhudurg district. Baby had an acquaintance named Prakash Jadhav in Kervade village. They could lie low at his home.

---

While Baby crisscrossed Mumbai in plain sight, Kalokhe was about to feel the wrath of a humiliated police department. Shisve and Prakash conducted a swift inquiry and sent a report of their findings to Commissioner Maria. Using powers vested in him under Article 311 (2) of the Constitution of India, Maria signed an order dismissing Kalokhe from the force. The actual investigation was anything but this straightforward.

The man running the investigation was Inspector Vijay Darekar, whose bloodshot eyes, growl and hair-trigger temper made him a fearsome presence. His permanent mask of irritation discouraged small talk, back chat or conversation.

Sarika spent most of the next fortnight at the police station. After dropping the kids off the school in the afternoon, she would answer the police's questions until late evening. The police took her to Siddharth Nagar dressed in a burqa and made her unlock all of Baby's rooms. There was no sign of drugs.

The police also tracked down Dipti in Vasai on 15 March. Girish rang her twice the next morning. Dipti urged him to surrender. When she reported the calls to the police, they asked her to come down to the station. The police put Dipti in a burqa too and in Prem Nagar, asked her to identify Reshma's house.

Much to Dipti's chagrin, the police also brought Reshma and Rachna's mother Babli and her brother Pankaj Singh to the police station. Darekar was certain that tracking down Girish was the key to locating Baby. The fact that this might inflict irreparable damage to Girish and Dipti's marriage in the process did not bother Darekar.

He conceded that the possibility of Baby still hiding in Mumbai was remote. It was time he expanded the search beyond city and state borders. Babli and Pankaj Singh provided him with vital clues. They were natives of Agra's Bodla neighbourhood and had migrated to Mumbai to live in the Congress House in Grant Road, once the city's commercial sex activity hub.

Girish had visited Rachna in Bodla twice the previous year, first in March when she was pregnant and then in June, when her grandfather passed away. He had brought along his cousin Upendra for the first trip and Sachin for the second.

Babli hadn't spoken to Rachna in weeks. Was it possible that she had snuck Girish and Baby away to Agra? Darekar needed to find out and Pankaj wanted to help. Darekar sat the teenager on a flight to Delhi with two officers and two constables.

Next, Darekar sent details of Baby's passport to the crime branch. He wanted a Look Out Circular (LOC) issued against her at every airport. It wasn't an excessive precaution.

Darekar's bosses had put every cop in south Mumbai at his disposal. His informants reported that Baby had fled southwards and could either be holed up in Panvel or Alibaug in Raigad District or Savantwadi in Sindhudurg. Even as he awaited news from Agra, Darekar assembled another team to seek out Baby's brothers, beginning with Arjun in Panvel. She wasn't there. Nor was she in Alibaug.

That left only Shatrughna. But he had vanished. It finally emerged that Shatrughna was being held at Unit IV of the crime branch in Antop Hill. They had hoped to beat Darekar to Baby's capture but were getting nowhere, not with Shatrughna, nor with any of Baby's peddlers. Darekar was a lot more confident in his ability to get something out of Shatrughna. All he needed from Shatrughna at this point was some sign, any sign, that Baby might have fled to Savantwadi. His team in Raigad was awaiting orders: should we return or proceed to Savantwadi?

But Unit IV wouldn't release Shatrughna just yet. As a favour it advised Darekar against looking in Savantwadi. She couldn't have run that far.

'You'll be wasting your time,' the unit chief had said.

Darekar asked the team to return.

Baby was sheltering in a village less than fifty minutes away.

# 15

Darekar expanded the scope of the search in Mumbai. He sent two subordinates to Gorai, where Baby owned two apartments. She had leased them out to two families. He didn't learn much from either tenant. Baby had last visited them in 2011, the year she last renewed their lease agreements.

Baby's daughters-in-law received no respite from their daily summons. The strategy produced marginal gains. On the third day of questioning, Reshma produced a mobile phone Baby had left behind in her home. Dipti told him about the CCTV cameras Baby had placed outside her home. Darekar disabled the cameras and took away the recorder. Now he'd know who visited her.

The other team returned to Mumbai after an unsuccessful two-day-long search in Agra. Baby had definitely not fled north. That did not help improve Darekar's mood.

Neither the daughters-in-law nor Satish gave him a lead on day four. But Naresh Pardeshi admitted to the police that Girish had called him twice. The CDRs showed that the phone calls had originated from cell towers in Santacruz and Dadar. But by the time Darekar sent his men to both locations, Girish was long gone.

Kalokhe had now spent eight days in Khandala police custody. Under Indian law, the police can keep a person in its custody for only fourteen days at a time. Six more days and Kalokhe would be sent to prison and Darekar would be free to seek his custody. He submitted before the Esplanade Court in CSMT a transfer warrant addressed to the Judicial Magistrate First Class in Khandala.

Pardeshi, a friend of Girish, arrived in the afternoon. Girish, Pardeshi and their friend, Satish Hasbe, had tried unsuccessfully in 2013 to open a bar in Mira Road. They had identified the perfect premises, leased it but fallen short of money. Girish and Pardeshi had stayed friends. Now that Girish's wife and children had nowhere to go, Pardeshi took them in.

Pardeshi did not deny receiving phone calls from Girish ever since he'd gone on the run. Darekar suspected that he knew more than he was letting on. But since Pardeshi wasn't a suspect, Darekar could not detain him.

As the sun set on 20 March, Darekar was interrupted by a commotion outside his cabin. A loud voice hurled accusations of illegal detention. Darekar stepped outside to have a look. A man who claimed to be Pardeshi's lawyer demanded that he was set free.

'Why have you brought him here? Release him now!' the lawyer said.

Not a patient man at the best of times, Darekar controlled his urge to snap back. He didn't want Pardeshi zipping his mouth any tighter than he already had done. With considerable difficulty, Darekar contorted his features into what he hoped was a pleasant smile. It fooled no one.

'Your client seems to know where Baby is hiding. Once he tells us, we will let him go,' he said.

With utmost politeness, Darekar requested the lawyer, who was cursing under his breath, to leave.

The next day, a Sunday, began disastrously for Darekar. The team he'd sent to Kolhapur with Kalokhe's transfer warrant had returned embarrassed. The prison superintendent had spotted an error in the warrant. Darekar was supposed to have addressed it to the Satara City Civil and Sessions Court, not the magistrate in Khandala. The superintendent had refused to hand over Kalokhe's custody to the police until they returned with the correct warrant. Darekar submitted yet another transfer warrant at the Esplanade Court.

Pardeshi returned that afternoon with Satish Hasbe—and fortunately for Darekar—sans his lawyer. He couldn't pretend to be nice to him twice in the space of twenty-four hours.

The businessmen gave away nothing, and yet again Darekar was left with the feeling that vital information was being concealed from him. By evening, he was compelled to let them go. Once they were out of earshot, Darekar ordered his detectives to tail them. 'Follow them and learn what you can. Do not let them see you!'

Darekar entered the following week cautiously optimistic. He still didn't know where Baby was and had no arrest to show for the first eleven days of his investigation. But, provided he hadn't cocked up the transfer warrant once again, this could be the week the tide turned in his favour. He sent his team to Kolhapur with the warrant, praying that they returned bearing the captive.

The man produced in Darekar's cabin a day later bore none of the aloof formality that had marked Kalokhe's years in service. No matter how distasteful Darekar found having to poke into Kalokhe's personal life, he had no choice now. Kalokhe did not deny owning the packets of mephedrone found inside his cupboard.

Kalokhe was produced in Esplanade Court the next afternoon. The court sent Kalokhe to police custody for a week. His lawyers, Naveen Chomal and Jayesh Wani reached the courtroom seconds after the hearing had ended. They had just enough time to get Kalokhe's signature on the *vakalatnama*—a document that empowers a lawyer to represent a person in court—before the police led him away.

DCP Chavan questioned Kalokhe that afternoon. Darekar retreated to his cabin to take stock. Tailing Girish's business partners had produced no results. So he summoned the Singhs and reminded them to get in touch if Girish contacted them.

Darekar then turned his attention to Girish's friend Sachin Dhayalkar. Someone in his family was bound to talk. But neither Sachin's father Dattaram nor his wife Manisha knew where he had gone. He had fled without saying goodbye. He had switched off his phone but called Manisha from an unknown number the day before.

The police traced the calls to a PCO near Siddhivinayak Temple in Prabhadevi. CCTV footage showed Girish and Sachin using two landline phones at 2.41 p.m. on 27 March. While Sachin had only spoken to Manisha, the police were puzzled by the number Girish had dialled. The address in Agripada in central Mumbai to which it was registered simply did not exist!

Dhayalkar's calls to Manisha on three consecutive days held a glimmer of hope. Dhayalkar wouldn't tell her where he was but did mention that Baby was sick. It meant that they still might be in Mumbai. The police staked out the PCO until dawn on 31 March but neither men showed up.

The detectives also searched a nursing home close by but it had not admitted or treated any patient matching Baby's description. It was clear to Darekar now that both Girish and Sachin were responsible for shielding Baby. He would have to consider booking them too.

Meanwhile, as the budget session of the Maharashtra State Assembly wound up, Jayant Patil of the Nationalist Congress Party questioned the need for the Mumbai Police to file an FIR.

'I have serious doubts about the intentions of senior police officers in the Mumbai police. There could be deliberate attempt to weaken the case, to safeguard the interests of the officers involved. By registering a parallel case, officers with vested interests are likely to create loopholes in the case,' Patil said.[58]

Fadnavis promised to look into the case personally. If needed, he would even direct a senior police official to conduct an investigation.

However, he did not intervene.

While his detectives chased shadows in Prabhadevi, Darekar experienced contrasting fortunes questioning the Kalokhe family. The wife and children claimed to be ignorant of his work life. Kalokhe was more obliging. He gave Darekar a detailed list of Baby's real estate investments with precise addresses.

The two witnesses Darekar spoke to next were both taxi drivers. Yunus Makrani was a taxi driver in Siddharth Nagar. He was mates with Kisan back in the 1980s when he drove a taxi to earn an honest living. After Kisan fled Worli in 1993, Makrani spent the next two decades driving Baby around on her errands. In 2014, he had loaded two large bags into the trunk and driven her to the state transport bus depot in Parel. A man was waiting for Baby there. Makrani watched the man load the bags into a bus and bid Baby goodbye. That was the last time Baby had contacted him for a ride.

The other driver was Mayur Kadam, the son of a policeman and resident of Worli Police Camp. He recalled the time he had driven Baby and her family to their bungalow in mid-2014. The trunk of her car had been empty on the drive there. On the way back though, he found the empty space filled with some bags. Baby's grandson Saurabh had to hold his toys in his lap.

This was information to be filed away for the future. For now, the detectives had found sixteen phone numbers used by Baby and Kalokhe.

It had been a good week.

This was Baby's Bridge of Khazad-dum moment. Surely she would give herself up and stay behind to fight the Balrog so that the rest of her family could go free? She had half a mind to emerge from hiding. She was tired of running. She offered to surrender before Gokhale but he didn't want to get mixed up in the case any further. She asked lawyers in Mumbai what she should do. All of them advised her to stay hidden.

# 16

*Breakthrough*

Gokhale informed DCP Chavan about Baby's phone call. It was from an unknown phone number and the first solid lead the police had received after weeks of groping in the dark. Chavan and Gokhale hastened to Crawford Market to apprise Additional Commissioner Prasanna of the development.

Phone numbers that Baby and her companions were using were under 24/7 interception. A single phone call would pin down her location to the nearest cell tower. But their phones remained stubbornly switched off. The crime branch also wrote to the phone carrier for their CDRs.

Now that Baby's phone number had landed in the crime branch's lap, Inspector Shelke of Worli ANC, whose men had failed to locate a woman living less than 2 km from the office, saw it as a way to redeem himself. Parsing through thousands of pages of CDRs for hidden patterns and connections was a skill he had picked up and perfected over his decade-long stint in the crime branch and Anti-Terrorism Squad.

The surveillance wing did not immediately acquiesce his request to sit in to listen to intercepted phone calls and for copies of Baby's CDRs. In the crime branch's informal hierarchy, the ANC figured somewhere at the bottom. When the CDRs did arrive on Shelke's desk after some delay, they were raw. The surveillance wing had not even bothered to mark out the phone numbers they had identified. Studying raw CDRs would take hours.

Meanwhile, unfettered by intra-departmental rivalries, Darekar had made headway with Baby's older CDRs. He had closely examined the number she had used the longest and found four of her most frequent contacts.

The first number belonged to Inspector Gaikwad, who in 2014 had made at least 115 phone calls to Baby. In a written statement, Gaikwad explained that Baby had inquired about a meditation course. Later, she had sought his help to trap Kalokhe. Through a batchmate posted in Mumbai, he had passed Baby's information on to Gokhale.

The second number belonged to Inspector Jayendra Sawant of Worli police station. In 2014, Sawant had called Baby thirty-eight times. Sawant had an explanation ready. Late in 2014, Baby's teenage niece had gone missing from Siddharth Nagar. Baby suspected that she had run away with her boyfriend. After a frantic search, Sawant's detectives found the girl unharmed at Worli Sea Face. The police arrested the boyfriend.

Sawant had not contacted Baby since then.

The third number belonged to Parte. Darekar asked him to come down to the station at 7 p.m. one evening but Parte skipped the summons.

So did the owner of the fourth number, Parte's cousin, Advocate Anil Parte. Despite making 570 phone calls to Baby in the preceding seven months, Advocate Parte managed to wriggle out of his summons. Darekar did not pursue him, but he would not allow constable Parte to get away.

The Partes weren't the only ghosts Darekar chased as the investigation entered its third week. The possibility that an officer of the Customs department might be involved had spooked him. Kalokhe could not shed much light on the elusive Customs officer Suryavanshi. He had never seen him. He only had Baby's word that Suryavanshi was one of her suppliers. It was a dead end.

Shatrughna was also proving impossible to locate. Even though the crime branch had not been asked to assist, it seemed to be placing minor impediments in Darekar's path. He couldn't put off speaking with Shatrughna any longer.

Once again, Shatrughna had been detained by Unit IV. Darekar's detectives reached Antop Hill only to find that Shatrughna had been released and immediately picked up for questioning by Unit II in Agripada.

At Unit II, the detectives were informed that they'd just missed Shatrughna by a few minutes. Two days later, word came through that Shatrughna was still in Agripada.

Shatrughna's account blew away the cobwebs of doubt surrounding Customs officer Suryavanshi. Baby's supplier was in fact Shatrughna's former Arthur Road Jail cellmate Gyan Samuel. That didn't mean Shatrughna knew where Baby had run off to. He had fallen out with her in 2014 because he couldn't bear to see Satish working with her. He drew a line at involving children in the trade. Baby didn't agree. So Shatrughna stopped visiting her.

Like so many skeletons tumbling out of a closet, the next phone number of interest in Baby's CDR was of constable Jyotiba Mane of the crime branch's Anti-Extortion Cell. From the off, Darekar could tell that Mane was attempting to conceal the extent of his involvement with Baby.

Mane admitted being in touch with Baby since 2001. Darekar wasn't convinced that all of Mane's contact with her had been in the capacity of a policeman tapping an informant. Kalokhe helped fill some of the gaps.

It emerged that before Baby handed over her stash of mephedrone to Kalokhe, she had promised to give it to Mane. She was to pay Mane to keep the contraband safe. When Baby reneged on her word, Mane rounded on her. He marched to Marine Drive police station to confront Kalokhe. Not wanting to make a scene in front of his colleagues, Kalokhe denied having the contraband. Mane did not buy the lies. He continued looking for *his* contraband.

Darekar needed to speak to Parte to verify these claims. But Parte had switched off his phone and locked his apartment at the Kalina Police Quarters. His neighbours had last seen him painfully limping away on a swollen foot.

The other phone number on the frequent callers list belonged to the driver Madan Singh. He had safeguarded his employer's secrets during his first round of questioning. Now he saw no reason to do so. He told Darekar about the trips Satish had made with Baby to pick up bags of mephedrone in Pune and the early morning visit to Kalokhe's sister's home. Satish had warned him against mentioning the last of these to the police.

Darekar wanted to rip out his moustache.

'Call Satish here!' he barked at his detectives.

But Satish was locked inside Khandala police station. The score was 2-0 to Satara Police.

Over at Crawford Market, Prasanna found himself involved in the case once more. On the one hand, he had to frame the police's response to a query raised by the Opposition in the state assembly. On the other, he wasn't happy with Gokhale. A CDR analysis of the phone numbers Gokhale had provided showed numerous phone calls between him and Baby.

Prasanna summoned Gokhale to his office for an explanation. The meeting did not go well. Gokhale repeated what he'd told Baby on the phone. Prasanna wasn't satisfied.

On 10 April, Darekar filed an application in the Esplanade Court seeking the transfer of Satish's custody from Kolhapur central prison. That was his last act as investigating officer for the next two days. Policing several thousand fans attending the Indian Premier League clash between the Kings XI Punjab and Mumbai Indians at Wankhede Stadium demanded his complete attention. It was dull work. Shisve had his men on their feet from dawn until well past midnight on both days rehearsing and perfecting anti-hijack, anti-terror and crowd management drills. He would not tolerate a single error on match day.

The home team seemed to sleepwalk through the run chase. Darekar forged a momentary kinship with Rohit Sharma. He never been further behind in his pursuit of Baby.

Chastened by his failure to obtain Kalokhe's custody on the first attempt, Darekar was much more careful with Satish's transfer warrant. With her husband in trouble now, Sarika tried limiting the damage.

She had warned him against working with Baby, she told Darekar.

'I tried keeping him away from it. Baby and I used to fight. I told her never to take Satish along with her to Pune again,' she said, adding, 'it's Ballu and Samuel you should be speaking to, not Satish.'

Darekar wrote to the court to have Ballu and Samuel released from Arthur Road Jail and into his custody.

Satish was brought to Mumbai on 14 April and placed under arrest. On his last visit, he had outwitted his interrogators with lies and half-truths. Now Darekar wanted some real answers. Satish wouldn't breathe a word.

Two days later, Ballu and Samuel were temporarily released from jail. Darekar hoped to fit the pieces of his puzzle together.

Samuel remembered his dealings with Shatrughna and Baby differently. Soon after the two men were released from jail in 2009, Shatrughna had asked Samuel to source a plant fertilizer for his fields. Samuel obtained a white crystalline substance at Rs 2,000/kg from an acquaintance named Pawan. He sold it to Shatrughna at Rs 22,000/kg. Within no time, Shatrughna was placing orders for large sacks of the stuff. Finally, he took Samuel to Siddharth Nagar.

'From now on, I want you to supply directly to Baby,' Shatrughna informed Samuel.

Ballu recounted Baby's early years in the drug trade and her alliance with Kalokhe. He knew they were working together to source and sell mephedrone.

But Darekar couldn't get a peep out of Satish. It was Samuel who pointed out the rendezvous point on the Pune–Satara highway where Satish had accompanied Baby for the pickup on two occasions.

Satish said, 'I don't know where she's gone.'

Satish wasn't lying. To contact the outside world, Girish and Sachin used the only PCO in Kervade. They had made at least three trips to Mumbai in March and April to consult with their lawyer, N.N. Gavankar, at his office in Dadar. At the third meeting, Gavankar had convinced Girish that the only recourse left was to turn themselves in to the police. Baby agreed.

On 15 April, Girish rang Dipti and Sarika to tell them that Baby would return to Mumbai to surrender. She would need a week to prepare.

On 22 April, Baby walked into the police headquarters with Gavankar's *vakalatnama*, Rs 23,130 in cash, a mobile phone and a change of clothes.

The next day, the police scheduled a press conference at the press room on the ground floor of the crime branch building and triumphantly announced that they had captured Baby in a carefully planned operation.

The new Joint Commissioner of Police (Crime), Atulchandra Kulkarni, briefed the press that afternoon. An IPS officer of the 1990 batch, Kulkarni was posted as the crime branch chief a week after Kalokhe's arrest. He had returned to the state police after close to a decade in India's domestic spy agency, the Intelligence Bureau (IB), in Mumbai and Arunachal Pradesh. He was on the verge of being posted to the Indian Embassy in Dubai. But that was not to be. India's foreign spy agency, the Research and Analysis Wing (R&AW) already had an officer posted there. There was no need, the central government decided, for two spies in the same city. When the move collapsed, Kulkarni was asked by the Maharashtra government to fill the vacant post in the crime branch instead.

Kulkarni told journalists that the police had found Baby, Girish, Sachin and Nishigandha returning to Mumbai in a tourist bus. A team from the crime branch's Social Service Branch (SSB) had been tipped off and they intercepted the bus at a toll plaza in Panvel. They were brought to Crawford Market where Baby was placed under arrest. Despite allegedly assisting a fugitive evade arrest, Girish and Sachin were allowed to leave after they narrated their accounts of the past six weeks. Nishigandha, a minor, was also allowed to go.

The official line in the crime branch was that a month-and-a-half of ceaseless searching had finally yielded a lucky break to the most unlikely wing of the crime branch.

After leaving Kervade, the four travellers reached the Kudal bus stand on the Mumbai–Goa highway in Kudal at 8.30 p.m. on 21 April. They had asked travel agent Ashok Kande when the next bus was expected. Since they hadn't booked tickets, Kande asked the travellers to wait at the bus stop. Once a bus arrived, he would find them seats.

One person at the bus stop had recognized Baby as she crossed the road from Kande's office to a hotel restroom. The gawker was cashew trader Bhiba Dhuri. He sent regular parcels of cashew from his factory to Mumbai by bus and knew Kande well. Dhuri thought the woman looked a lot like the 'drugs mafia' featured in a Marathi news bulletin a few days ago.

He needed to be sure. Dhuri called Police Constable Chandraprakash Ghag of the Mumbai Police. He had met Ghag the previous year while protesting at Mumbai's Azad Maidan to demand tax exemption from the state government for a jamun wine factory he hoped to set up. Ghag had since joined the SSB.

When Dhuri rang, Ghag was out conducting an inquiry with his senior officers. SSB chief, Senior Inspector Shirish Sawant, asked Ghag to text his informant a picture of Baby. He wanted to be absolutely certain that the woman was her. Dhuri only had a few seconds to walk towards the bus Baby was about to board and confirm the image which Ghag had sent him.

'I'm sure it's her,' he wrote back. He also sent Ghag the registration number of the bus.

A squad from the SSB was waiting at Kharpada toll plaza in Panvel when the bus arrived at six thirty the next morning. A woman matching Baby's description was seated on seat number one. The chase was over.

Baby's arrest was, as the saying goes, a story made for television. A ZEE 24 Taas report[59] on 23 April 2015, had branded her 'India's biggest woman drug supplier' and likened her to 'Maya Memsaab', the 1993 Hindi film adaptation of French writer Gustave Flaubert's *Madame Bovary*.

Other news reports had also speculated on property worth 'crores of rupees'[60] that Baby had acquired through the drug trade. Television news channels, especially Hindi and Marathi ones, extracted as much sleaze as they could out of the story. The reportage centred on a few predictable points: that a *woman* had been selling drugs, that she was sleeping with a policeman, that she was rich and had been smart enough to avoid trouble until now.

Baby was news TV's warm-up act for its coverage of another self-made woman being accused of a much more serious crime five months later. Unlike media executive Indrani Mukerjea, Baby was spared the indignity of TV news speculating on the contents of her breakfast on her first morning in police custody.[61]

It was a minor consolation. The circus was in town.

# 17

Darekar hared over to Crawford Market the minute the crime branch rang with news of Baby's surrender. He placed her under arrest and produced her in court the same afternoon. Baby was remanded to police custody until 28 April. That was Darekar's final act as investigating officer.

While his subordinates announced their triumph to journalists in the press room, Maria signed an order transferring the investigation to the crime branch with immediate effect. Among the crime branch's twelve field units spread across Mumbai, Unit I, situated in a crumbling stone building within the headquarters was chosen to lead the investigation. The Unit I chief, Senior Inspector Avdhut Chavan relieved Marine Drive police station of all its case papers. Now he had to pick an investigation officer from among his subordinates.

Chavan didn't want the case. It didn't make sense in his opinion for Maria to pull the case away from Marine Drive police station at that stage. But now that he had, Chavan wanted the ANC or an external agency like the Maharashtra Criminal Investigation Department (CID) to handle the investigation.

When news of the new assignment reached Unit I, Chavan turned to the five inspectors who reported to him, silently praying that none of them would volunteer. Everything that had happened since Kalokhe's arrest told Chavan that the crime branch was the wrong agency to investigate this case. There was no glory to be found in investigating another cop, and certainly not *this* one. Any investigator would only find dirt the deeper he dug. He didn't want any of his men to be in those shoes.

One by one, three inspectors feigned sickness and proceeded on sick leave. The fourth refused outright. That left Inspector Rajesh Kasare, a long-distance runner who commuted 60 km to work from Kalyan to Crawford Market and had a wife with chronic diabetes whom he cared for.

Chavan hoped that Kasare too would invent some excuse. Maybe, just maybe, he could then ask for Unit I to be excused from the case. Unfortunately, Kasare said yes.

## Distractions

Kasare had inherited from Darekar an investigation beset with distracting sideshows. That was one reason Darekar had precious little progress to show for two-and-a-half-months of investigating Kalokhe and Baby. To be fair to Darekar, he was not at fault for the development that nearly derailed his investigation.

When Kalokhe was first produced in Esplanade Court on 25 March, his lawyers, advocates Chomal and Wani, moved a bail application. Chomal read out the grounds for seeking bail. Paragraph eight of the application caused consternation in the courtroom:

> The applicant submits that there is a situation where the original investigating police from the Khandala police station Satara are going to root of the matter and even trying to ascertain the roles of the concerned customs officials who the senior police officials involved in the entire crime. The present accused/applicant was thoroughly questioned as regards his knowledge about the involvement of the said custom official, which the present applicant does not know and so also was interrogated regarding the role of senior IPS officer in Mumbai Additional Commissioner of Police Shri K.M.M. Prasanna.

'An inquiry,' Chomal told the court, 'should be conducted to find what his links are.' Kalokhe was stunned. There had been no forewarning from his lawyers.

The previous evening, Chomal and Wani had disagreed over including such a serious allegation against a senior IPS officer in the bail application. Wani warned his boss that there was no way to prove such a claim. Chomal overruled him.

After the hearing had ended, Chomal was swarmed by reporters who wanted further details of his allegations. Chomal had claimed, wrongly, that immediately before being posted as Additional Commissioner of the crime branch, Prasanna had been Superintendent of Police of

Satara. Prasanna, in fact, had served DCP of the Special Task force in Mumbai in between his stints in Satara and the crime branch. That afternoon, for the first time since the story had broken, the headlines on TV were not about Baby's whereabouts.

The Mumbai Police immediately issued a statement defending Prasanna. 'There is no truth to Kalokhe's allegations,' the police spokesperson said.

Prasanna's response was equally swift. Before the week was out, he sent Chomal and Wani a legal notice.

Allegations of his involvement in the drug seizure are 'absolutely false, concocted and were obviously made as part of a motivated and malicious campaign against him at the instance of Kalokhe,' Prasanna's lawyers wrote in the notice.

The notice further stated that:

'I was also convinced that since the said application was brought to the Court by both the accused duly prepared when the said Kalokhe had no occasion to give any instructions to the accused, it was done with a prearranged plan of certain vested interests working behind the scene who wanted to settle score with me on account of their anger and frustration against me for a certain action I might have taken while discharging my duty as a public servant.'

Prasanna had suffered 'irreparable damage to his clean image' and demanded that Chomal and Wani tender a written apology. He would sue them for defamation if they didn't.

Prasanna also took the matter up with the Maharashtra Director General of Police, who in turn inquired with the the Satara Police. SP Deshmukh 'confirmed' that there was no basis to Chomal's allegations. His men had neither interrogated Kalokhe about Prasanna's alleged involvement in the case nor had they had an occasion to.

The lawyers did not back down. Chomal was insistent that an inquiry would absolve Prasanna if he was linked to the case in any way.

'Whatever I have done is in the capacity of an advocate and upon instructions from my client. Certain aspects have been assumed in his [Prasanna's] notice. We will reply to it and clarify any misunderstandings and also bring this to the notice of our Bar Association,' he told reporters afterwards. Prasanna went to court.[62]

On 27 March, the next hearing, Darekar also rubbished Chomal's and Wani's claims. Their allegations, Darekar told the court, were made with the dual intentions of hampering his investigation and demoralizing the investigators.

The drama temporarily deflected attention from the police's hunt for Baby but left the crime branch with some uncomfortable questions to answer. It was the reason Avdhut Chavan preferred that an external agency investigate the case.

Kasare had willingly walked into a shitstorm of an investigation.

## *New boss*

There was little time to think, even less to map a coherent strategy for the investigation. His immediate priorities were to question Baby, Kalokhe, Samuel and Satish, visit the crime scenes, unearth any conspirators among his own colleagues and hope for good news from the FSL. Only then would the complete picture emerge.

It looked good on paper but in essence, Kasare was like a captain airdropped onto a troubled ship and expected to steer it to safety while a storm gathers quietly on the horizon.

The first question Kasare wanted answered was where and how Baby had managed to stay hidden for five weeks. He sent a team of detectives to Kudal to find out. Next, he took custody of Satish and sought CDRs of his and Baby's mobile phones.

A clear division of labour was enforced. His two DCPs and an officer brought in specially by Kulkarni from the IB questioned Baby and Kalokhe. But for Maria, this would have been Darekar's denouement.

Beginning 24 April, Baby talked for three straight days.

She spoke of how as a fledgling peddler in the 1990s she'd pay off cops and how being with a cop protected her business from other policemen. She accused Parte of buying packets of brown sugar from her twice a week.[63]

She had three constables at Worli ANC on her payroll. The constables had developed a profitable business on the side. They'd keep aside a quantity of drugs seized in each case, and like Dhawale, sell it to Baby the next day.

She hadn't shared Samuel's optimism about mephedrone at first. No one had heard of it and there didn't seem to be a market for it. She had passed on samples to Constable Shingate, formerly of Worli ANC on at least ten occasions but he didn't take the bait.

The more she fed it, the larger the market for mephedrone grew. Baby was amazed to see just how quickly it had become popular among young people. She began to place ever larger and more frequent orders from Samuel. For the first four months, Samuel supplied her free of charge.

'Pay me when you make some money,' he said.

The policemen in her life would not be left behind. Both Parte and Kalokhe began to source mephedrone from her. Kalokhe supplied it to guests at hotels in south Mumbai. Soon he established a direct line with Samuel.

Girish did not approve of her work. In 2013, he gave her an ultimatum. But Kalokhe wouldn't allow her to quit. He pressured her into meeting Samuel. When she refused, he hit her.

She had made three trips to Pune in 2014 and bought a total of 150 kg of mephedrone in six bags from Samuel. She stored the bags in her bungalow. Since Baby's visits were irregular, a watchman at the bungalow ran away with 20 kg of her contraband. She discovered the theft when she found the bungalow untended on her next visit. She did not report it to the police.

The bungalow was no longer safe. Baby and Kalokhe shifted the contraband to Siddharth Nagar. Every time Kalokhe visited Kanheri, he took along some of the contraband with him. By June, he had moved all of the remaining 130 kg to Kanheri. On the way back home, Kalokhe would bring small quantities of mephedrone back to sell in Mumbai.

With this money she purchased a Toyota Innova car and Rs 80 lakh worth of gold jewellery. But Baby was uneasy having so much gold at home, so she sold it to two jewellers in Zaveri Bazaar. She asked to be paid in four different cheques—two to her bank account and one each to Dipti and Sarika's accounts. Later, she transferred the money from their accounts into hers. She used Rs 25 lakh to purchase a commercial space in Worli and gifted Girish Rs 3 lakh to set up his bar in Mira Road.

She spoke of her desperate attempts to rid herself of Kalokhe's unceasing pressure and abuse. She corroborated what inspectors Gaikwad and Gokhale had said in their defence.

Helplessly, she flitted from one contact to the other but no one would commit. Mane screamed betrayal. He turned up at her home and left with two packets of mephedrone and Rs 10,000 in cash.

On 27 April, the interrogators took a break to reflect on what they'd heard and formulate their next questions.

There was no respite for Baby though. Satara Police's DSP Humbre used the day's break to interrogate her.

The next day, Kasare produced Baby in the sessions court to seek another week's time to question her. Before hearing Kasare's plea, Judge U.B. Hejib of the special NDSPS Act court asked Baby if the police had treated her well in custody.

'Yesterday, DSP [Humbre] had come. He told me he would throw me off a cliff. He made a lot of dirty hand gestures and yelled at me. He told me I would be beaten up badly,'[64] she said.

Judge Hejib was outraged. 'Any lady having decency would not like or tolerate vulgar gestures ... hand gestures are worse than any third-degree torture to a woman,' he observed.

Henceforth, the court ruled, only a female police officer would interrogate Baby. Kasare could not allow anyone else to enter the interrogation room.

Once she had returned to Crawford Market, the team asked her its final set of questions—for now. They wanted to know more about Kalokhe.

'He has no interest in his job,' she said, 'he's been buying from Samuel because he's going to retire soon and needs the money. Why do you think he hid so much mephedrone at home?'

Kalokhe was cautious, she said, almost paranoid, about his phone use. When off-duty he never used a phone or SIM card for more than a few days at a time. Baby also claimed that a journalist working at a leading tabloid, who had broken some sensational stories thanks to Kalokhe, was also working with him. Unit I found no substance in this allegation.

At Unit I, Kasare dug into Baby's disappearing act in January 2015. He found that Baby hadn't just enjoyed the hospitality of Garware Club House between the nineteenth and the twenty-first, she had spent the preceding twelve days at Marina Guest House—the cream-coloured Art Deco building on the junction of Veer Nariman Road and Marine Drive. The guest register confirmed that she had checked in on the seventh.

Kasare then produced before Baby two constables from Worli ANC. She didn't recognize either man. He also absolved Shingte of any wrongdoing. He had not spoken with Baby after the police had declared her a suspect.

Kasare also recorded the statements of Parte, Mane and constable Chandrkant Gurav of the Azad Maidan ANC. On 1 May, Kasare and Avdhut Chavan briefed DCP Kulkarni and Joint Commissioner Kulkarni of their progress.

Things were not looking good for Baby's friends in the department.

Worli ANC chief Shelke was not among them. He had sulked for a while after the surveillance wing had sent him raw CDRs but soon found another way to prove valuable to the investigation.

Close to three decades of police work told him that the best way to put the squeeze on an absconder was to hit them where it hurt the most. Baby, who had homes all over Mumbai and Pune and several crore rupees in her bank accounts, presented him with sufficient targets.

Shelke cracked open his copy of the NDPS Act to Section 68F, which allows the police to seize or attach any property it suspects has been acquired through proceeds of the drug trade. He listed down all of Baby's moveable and immovable assets and sent the dossier to Darekar.

Shelke would not get to bask in his achievement. Joint Commissioner Kulkarni suspected that moles within Shelke's unit were deliberately scuttling the search for Baby.

Still new to the crime branch, Kulkarni may have wanted to give his charges a clean slate to begin with, but the fact that Baby's CDRs were riddled with phone calls to and from police personnel did not help. The men under his command were wary of the new boss. They knew that officers who came from the IB saw corruption and incompetence in even the slightest misstep.

In the press conference announcing Baby's arrest, Kulkarni had told journalists that a major impediment to the search was that her phone was switched off. Once the journalists had been dispatched, Kulkarni summoned the heads of every crime branch department for an explanation. How could a drug dealer from a slum in Worli have eluded so many of them for a month-and-a-half?

He wanted answers from senior inspectors of the ANC's five field units. Shelke was the last of them to speak.

'Worli! What is happening? How many of your people are under inquiry?' Kulkarni asked.

'Three, sir,' Shelke replied.

'Your unit is corrupt!' Kulkarni shot back.

Shelke tried to hold his fury in check. It was useless to mention his dossier of Baby's assets or to point out that within a month of taking charge he had filed the first FIR against her in fifteen years.

'Sir, I have been in charge of the unit for only six months. I cannot speak of what might have happened before I came but I can guarantee that since I have arrived, none of my people have done anything wrong.'

It was true. When Shelke heard that the crime branch was digging into Baby's contacts in the police, he had taken Shingte and two other constables to Maria's office and personally vouched for them. *Baby is their informant. They are only doing their jobs by communicating with her*, Shelke insisted. Maria agreed, the constables had done nothing wrong.

Kulkarni wasn't in such a forgiving mood. There was no absolving Shelke for failing to locate a criminal with roots in his jurisdiction. The ANC's DCP Namdeo Chavan spoke up in Shelke's defence but Kulkarni shushed him.

'If we are at fault, sir,' Shelke said, cutting in, 'you may take action against us.' It was bold of Shelke to stick his neck out but his conscience was clear.

After the meeting ended, Kulkarni apologized to Shelke. It was not meant to be personal, he told Shelke.

'I am angry with everyone.'

# 18

For the present, Kasare had learnt what he could from Baby. He still didn't know from where the mephedrone had originated. Baby had nothing to add on that subject. Samuel had changed the name of his supplier from Pawan to Paulraj Duraisami Padaiyatchi. Kasare did not know where to begin looking for this new man.

Even as the answers to the larger questions eluded him, Kasare had to gather seemingly irrelevant information, such as the fact that Baby had previously travelled to Mauritius using a hitherto unknown passport.

These bits of information were useless to Kasare but invaluable to DCP Kulkarni and Joint Commissioner Kulkarni, who briefed journalists every evening. They were usually morsels that were slipped in at the end of briefings—always prefaced with a 'by the way …'

The foretold storm crept up and bore down on the crime branch now. The investigators were oblivious to it. Like a pre-monsoon sound-and-light show heralding the end of the earth, a blinding peal of lightning and the deafening boom of thunder struck on Day 10 of Kasare's investigation.

On 2 May, both the Mumbai and Pune FSL coincidentally completed their analysis of their samples of the substance taken from Kalokhe's cupboard and bags, respectively. Their findings to the Mumbai Police and the Satara Police were identically worded:

The exhibits do not show presence of mephedrone.
The exhibits examined do not show presence of narcotic drugs like mephedrone, alprazolam, diazepam, lorazepam, nitrazepam, morphine, heroin, cocaine, methaqualone, methylenedioxymethamphetamine (MDMA), ketamine and methamphetamine.
Sodium Glutamate is detected in the exhibits.

In simple words, Ajinomoto. The *salt* in Chinese bhel!

The Pune FSL dispatched its report to the Satara Police by Registered AD post. Kasare waited until 13 May to personally collect the report and remaining samples from Mumbai FSL.

The case was over before Kasare could even take a proper crack at it.

He chose to plod on.

The breakthrough on Padaiyatchi came with the discovery of his criminal record. The NCB had arrested him in 2007 for allegedly smuggling 90 kg of Mandrax valued at Rs 2.25 crore. He was eventually acquitted.

In the meantime, he turned informer for the agency, conveniently taking up work as a cargo-clearing agent at the Mumbai international airport. He was last believed to be living in Sanpada, a suburb of Navi Mumbai.

New information on Baby also came in from Bhandup, Manickpur, Shahu Nagar and Worli police stations—places where she was suspected of supplying mephedrone. The way forward, Kasare realized, would be to give wider publicity within official channels, to Baby's arrest.

He had details of the charges against Baby published in the Mumbai Police's daily bulletin, available to all of its 40,000 personnel and also widely read in neighbouring police jurisdictions. It was bound to jog some investigator's memory.

Mumbra police station in Thane city got in touch about a peddler arrested in November 2014. Kasare explored Baby's links to him but found nothing conclusive.

On 4 May, the team of detectives Kasare had sent to Kudal returned to Mumbai with their findings. They had pieced together a broad picture of Baby and Kalokhe's holiday until the day of his arrest.

Unit I, meanwhile, played host to a nervous stream of Baby's cop contacts. Gaikwad was a frequent visitor. Summons were also sent to Sub-Inspector Sarang of Azad Maidan ANC and Assistant Police Inspector Sanjay Nikam of the crime branch's computer cell.

Mane had woken too late to the possibility that he might be in trouble. He had not been bothered by news of Kalokhe's arrest or by the phone call from Satara's SP Deshmukh a week after to ask if Baby had contacted him the previous summer.

Once summons went out to every cop in Baby's contact book, Mane panicked. He told his boss, Inspector Vinayak Vast in the AEC, about Baby, Kalokhe, mephedrone and the phone calls. There was nothing Vast could do now.

'You should have told me this earlier,' he told Mane.

Two days later, Baby was sent to Byculla women's jail after her police custody ended. Samuel was sent back to Arthur Road Jail a day later. As his fortnight-long stay at Unit I came to a close, he told Kasare that Padaiyatchi was most likely hiding in his native Tamil Nadu.

The steady stream of cops threatened to widen when the informant Rafiq Ahmad Sayyad alias Rafiq Bam showed up two days later to answer Kasare's questions. Bam provided Kasare with a list of police officers whom he had approached with Baby's information.

Before he got to work on the list, Kasare needed to gather his thoughts. He was to brief DCP Kulkarni and Joint Commissioner Kulkarni the day after.

A breakthrough arrived when the earliest record of Baby's criminal activity was obtained in a file wrapped in cloth on a dusty shelf in the Cuffe Parade headquarters of the ANC. The Worli unit had arrested her on 21 March 2001, allegedly in possession of 30 grams of heroin valued at Rs 6,000. Baby was out of jail before the turn of the year. The Special NDPS Act Court acquitted her on 7 November.

Kasare would have to be much more thorough than those detectives had been.

---

As summer drew to a close, Baby was back in a world where the names in her phonebook meant nothing. She had no friends and little money with which to buy influence or comfort. She could only hope that those of her family not already in jail were doing their damnedest to get her out.

The jailors found it hard to bully Baby. As per the unwritten code that governs life in jail, undertrials give head and body massages to the jailor and wash and iron their uniforms after the lights go out. On days when they fast for religious reasons, undertrials fetch them snacks from the canteen. Undertrials also wash the bathrooms and toilets.

At meal times, jailors skimmed all the fat out of the milk and left a whitish watery swill for the inmates. The jailors delegated part of the authority to a select few trusted convicts who were designated as warders of each barrack. It was the warders' job to distribute two boiled eggs, two bananas and four pieces of *paav* to each inmate every day. But the jailors made sure that no inmate received more than a single boiled egg, two pieces of *paav* and one overripe banana.

The first time, the warder in her barracks ordered Baby to wash the jailors' uniforms, Baby refused.

'You are here to look after us, not to order us around. Only the court can tell me what to do,' she spat at the jailors.

As punishment, Baby was made to sleep that night by the toilet.

Baby made no friends and did not complain about either the eggs, the bananas or the milk. She chanted her prayers whenever she found moments of peace. Those were in short supply. Every day, her refusal to fall in line was weakened by seeing her fellow inmates, both female and male, being thrashed mercilessly for the most trivial reasons.

She needed to get out. And soon.

## The end?

Padaiyatchi was holed up in Trichy, a town in the state of Tamil Nadu. The crime branch found him on 12 May. At last, Kasare could feel the knots untangling themselves.

He put Samuel and Padaiyatchi in the same room. Samuel claimed that he'd met Padaiyatchi back in 2009 when he was working as a cargo-clearing agent, helping smuggle drugs abroad. Padaiyatchi denied being in contact with Samuel.

In the meantime, Unit I had readied a report on the extent of Baby's contacts in the police. Gokhale, Gaikwad, Sarang, Parte and Mane were among those named in the report.

Kasare had spoken frankly with each of them but found no evidence that they had committed a crime. Featuring prominently in Baby's CDRs was not sufficient evidence.

Kasare followed up three days later with another report, which he marked to the DCPs and the additional and joint commissioners. He wasn't convinced that any of those cops had broken the law. There was insufficient evidence to charge them with a crime. He recommended that the department deal with them internally. Prasanna agreed.

The next day, Kasare, Chavan and DCP Kulkarni met Joint Commissioner Kulkarni. The agenda was the fate of the cops under suspicion. Kasare listed the charges and repeated his recommendation.

It was the joint commissioner's decision now.

While he awaited the verdict, Kasare had a more pressing lead to follow. Samuel had changed his story. He had lied about Padaiyatchi. He had a score to settle for getting him mixed up in the botched attempt at smuggling methamphetamine back in 2009. Samuel retracted his statement incriminating Padaiyatchi and told Kasare what he hoped was the truth.

He had taken Shatrughna's request for ketamine to his friends, drivers Varun Kumar Tiwari and Nityanand Thevar, whom he had met in April 2013. Both men transported illegally produced ketamine from Rukhma Industries, a pharmaceuticals firm in Jalgaon to Tiwari's boss Vikas Puri, a pharmaceuticals executive in Mumbai. When Samuel met them at a bar one night, they offered to bring him mephedrone a few days later. They didn't have any ketamine.

Once Shatrughna and Baby approved of the new product, Samuel devised his own routine with the drivers. Tiwari and Thevar would bring a sack of mephedrone from Jalgaon and pick up Samuel from Mumbai's eastern suburbs. They'd then drive Samuel home to Wadala and help him unload the sack. They would also drive him to the drop-offs in Pune. Samuel would pay them with the money that Baby passed on to his wife in Mumbai.

The arrangement had worked smoothly until 13 December 2013, when Tiwari and Thevar drove to Jalgaon for another assignment. They were to deliver 1,175 kg of ketamine to Puri. The DRI had been surveilling Rukhma Industries and its management for some time. The drivers were arrested before they could leave Jalgaon.

When Samuel heard of the arrests the next day, he packed up his sacks of mephedrone and fled to his uncle's home in Tamil Nadu. For the next few months, he travelled alone to Pune every time he had to meet Baby.

Once Tiwari and Thevar were released on bail in 2014, they began driving him to Joshi Vadewale again.

Now that Kasare needed to speak to the two drivers urgently, they were back in Jalgaon prison.

For the rest of the week, Kasare's colleagues questioned two real estate agents with whom Baby had done business, a man who had painted her homes in Siddharth Nagar and Malavali and exchanged notes with counterparts at Bhandup police station.

Kasare was preparing to leave for Kolhapur. The court had approved his request to question Kalokhe in jail on everything he had learnt from Baby and Samuel in the past month.

The next day, a week after he had recommended disciplinary action against Baby's police contacts, Kasare received an order to arrest five of them.

The four inspectors who had passed up the assignment a month ago unanimously decided to call in sick the next day.

# 19

29 May 2015, Friday. It was an ordinary day at work for Gokhale. It was also his final day of meaningful work as a policeman after thirty years in the department. Gokhale looked forward the most to spending the first half of Saturday as an assistant commissioner of police.

As a parting gift, his employers had awarded him the promotion he would have earned years ago along with his batchmates had his life and career been uneventful. For one entire day he would hold the rank of assistant commissioner of police. The real reward would be the higher pension.

In the evening, he would join 425 others in a retirement ceremony at the Mumbai Police Gymkhana on Marine Drive. At various points in his career he had been kicked out of the police department and come within a whisker of dying. To now retire quietly felt like a welcome return to normalcy.

His colleagues in the ANC had pooled money to buy Gokhale's favourite articles of clothing—a pair of denims and a polo neck shirt. This would be their farewell present.

Gokhale departed his office near CSMT at 7 p.m. after a final check of the locations where his subordinates would conduct anti-drug awareness campaigns the next day.

At home, his son Saket had kept his uniform neatly pressed. He had taken off two strips of red and navy blue cloth from each shoulder pad, leaving behind only the three silver stars. Saket insisted that his father put on his uniform and pose for a picture. Gokhale didn't smile at the camera then but surely, Saket thought, he would tomorrow.

A phone call disturbed what should have been a quiet evening at home. It was from Kasare. After spending much of the summer answering questions from Prasanna and Kasare, Gokhale had hoped, finally, to be left alone.

Kasare wanted him to come to Crawford Market urgently. There were a few questions left to ask. The timing of Kasare's summons made Gokhale and Saket uneasy. Nevertheless, he would have to go.

The Unit I office is located at the very rear of the headquarters and accessed by a vertigo-inducing wooden staircase. The climb was steep enough to tire out a fairly fit person. For a fifty-seven-year-old man with a paralysed left half, a visible depression on his skull and one who needed the assistance of a walking stick, the ascent was unimaginably arduous. Gokhale could not help thinking that this was a walk to certain doom. Every slow, painful step only served to increase his dread.

Upstairs, he found four other policemen, some of whom he already knew: Sarang, Mane, Parte and Gaikwad, who was also due to retire the next day but would not receive a ceremonial farewell.

Neither policeman was surprised when Kasare informed them that they were being placed under arrest. They were shocked, however, at the charges brought against them: operating a drug syndicate with Baby, advising her to flee Mumbai and helping her to stay hidden,[65] making no attempt to arrest her and drug consumption.

Kasare needed to probe the extent to which each cop was involved in Baby's drug trade and what kind of assistance he had rendered. The inquiry had revealed that Parte and Mane had an active role in the crime and that Gaikwad frequently visited Baby's home. This meant Kasare needed to take a fresh look at all other cases registered against Baby in the past six months for any sign that the policemen might be involved.

Kasare would also explore the possibility that the cops might have operated their own syndicate with Baby as a front. This also opened up the possibility of the involvement of other members in the department.

Before confiscating their cell phones, Kasare allowed them to inform their families. Gokhale contacted Saket and filled him in. Saket knew what to do next. Then, Gokhale used a different phone to make another phone call.

It was past 11 p.m. I was walking home from work and had stopped at a shop in Four Bungalows to buy ice cream. It was a muggy night at the end of a routine day at work: the murder of a child at a shelter home and the arrest of two policemen for allegedly accepting a bribe.

I hadn't even unwrapped my ice cream cone when the phone rang. It was an unknown number but the voice at the other end was unmistakable.

'Hello,' Gokhale said, more out of habit than greeting.

'*Gokhale sir? Sab theek hai?* [Is everything okay?] *Yeh koi doosra number hai kya aap ka?* [Is this your alternate phone number?]' I enquired.

'*Haan, suno* [Yes, listen up]. I am at the Unit I office. They have placed me under arrest in the Baby Patankar case. There are five of us. They have seized our phones. *Kal Qilla Court* [Esplanade Court] *mein produce karengey* [They will produce us at Qilla Court tomorrow].'

Click.

That was all. No context. No explanation. No time for questions.

At that time, I hadn't imagined that Gokhale was a suspect. I was aware that Unit I had summoned and questioned Baby's contacts in the police but there had been no talk of any arrests. The possibility of Gokhale even being considered a suspect had never crossed my mind. We hadn't spoken about the case much since Baby's arrest. Her capture had seemed to me the end of the story.

It took a few phone calls and text messages to eke out what little the police would admit about the involvement of five of their own at that point. I finished my ice cream, sent off a hurriedly typed report just before midnight and considered where this left me.

For any police organization, it's bad PR when a man widely considered one of the state's foremost narcotics offences investigator is arrested on suspicion of aiding an alleged drug peddler and accused of being on her payroll. For the Mumbai Police, it was a disaster.

For a reporter, it's a sickening feeling when a source is accused of committing a crime. It makes you question your ability to identify and befriend reliable, trustworthy and clean contacts in the police department. It makes you a lousy judge of character.

I hadn't moved an inch while making phone calls and attempting to type a coherent copy. To borrow my mother's favourite cricketing phrase, I was '(Joe) rooted to the spot', and that too outside a shop in a respectable upper-middle-class Four Bungalows neighbourhood outraging customers with panicked phone calls—full of disturbing words—to policemen! This was now more than an ordinary crime story.

## The charges

There was too much activity in the courtroom the next afternoon to notice, let alone digest the irony of the situation. Gokhale was, after all, the Mumbai Police's spearhead in its battle against mephedrone. There was no denying his contribution in bringing it under the law's purview. The office he had headed until a day ago was also located in the same compound as the Esplanade Court.

He was produced before a magistrate in a courtroom he had entered on countless occasions over the past two decades as a member of the prosecution. His place was either in the front row of seats facing the magistrate or in the witness box, not on a bench in the accused box at the far end of the courtroom.

I reached the gates of the complex with just enough time to spare before the hearing was scheduled to begin. Now to run up two flights of stairs and hunt for an empty seat in the courtroom. But before I could take flight, I was stopped by the sound of my name. A senior reporter at a tabloid newspaper was calling out to me. He had the unnerving habit of cracking a joke and unleashing a subtle personal jibe in the same casual tone. I could never tell when he was making fun of you or when he had something on you.

'*Aye Srinath! Rukh na. Hearing ko time hai re* [Hey Srinath! Wait up. The hearing hasn't begun yet],' he said, beckoning me towards him.

This reporter had been extremely close to Kalokhe, right until he was caught. After spending most of March and April fretting over the consequences of his source's arrest, he looked at peace that afternoon, serene even.

'*Maine suna tera bhi naam hai Gokhale ke CDR mein* [I have heard that your name is also part of Gokhale's CDR],' he said.

What I wanted to ask was: *How the fuck do you know about last night?* But what I said was, '*Nahi toh. Tumko kisne bataya?* [Of course not. Who told you that?]' It was a poor attempt at sounding unperturbed.

'*Abhi tereko bhi bulanyengey yeh log. Sambhal ke reh* [They'll call you too for questioning. Be careful],' he said. I mumbled something in reply and walked away from him, trying not to run.

Inside courtroom No. 8 on the first floor, Gokhale was grim-faced and dressed in his other uniform—a polo shirt and denims. His left arm hung limp and useless at his side. He met my eye for a split-second before turning his attention to the magistrate. I couldn't read anything in that exchange.

With five arrested men, as many lawyers, numerous family members, a dozen policemen and journalists packed inside, there was barely enough space to stand. Shocked colleagues and subordinates in the ANC, who returned Gokhale's farewell present, had also come. The flip side was that every word spoken inside was perfectly audible.

In his application seeking custody to question them, Kasare told Magistrate R.K. Deshpande that the arrested policemen were aware of Baby's hidden stash of mephedrone. Despite knowing that she was a wanted fugitive, they had refrained from arresting her.

The allegations against Gokhale were damning. 'Gokhale told Patankar to switch off her cell phone and run away and also helped her to escape from the police. The crime branch wants to investigate his links with Patankar,' Public Prosecutor Kiran Bendbhar told the court. The crime branch also cited Gokhale's alleged delay in providing his superior officers with Baby's phone number as the reason she was able to evade arrest for a month and a half.[66]

Furthermore, the crime branch accused Gaikwad of paying a visit to Baby's home and of failing to inform investigators of her whereabouts.

Lawyers for the policemen argued that the crime branch had not produced any evidence to support their allegations.[67]

However, Magistrate Deshpande noted that on the face of it, the policemen seemed to be directly involved in the crime. He remanded them to the custody of Unit I.

'Considering the serious nature of the crime and the involvement of the accused policemen, custodial interrogation is required. Sufficient ground has been shown by the investigating officer for believing that the accusation is well-founded. Police remand is justified,' he observed.[68]

Gokhale had remained calm throughout the hearing. After it had ended, the crime branch gave him a few minutes to confer with Saket and his lawyer before leading him away. For the second time in his life and an hour before he was supposed to have walked away from it all with only a bouquet of flowers, a coconut and wristwatch as a gesture of gratitude for three decades of service, Gokhale was once again accused of a serious crime.

# 20

Gokhale can't resist telling stories. He has lived that kind of life. He barely scratched the surface during the many late afternoons I'd spent in his office between 2014 and 2015. I had hoped to come away with a story fit to publish in the next day's paper but left well after sunset with another episode of his life story. Even so, he never fully explained how he had become partially paralysed. I wanted to know but could think of no tactful way of asking. From the action-hero stories he had told me about his time as a detective, I assumed that he had been in an accident. But like so much else about Gokhale, it wasn't so straightforward.

In 1999, while working on one of his final cases in his first stint at the ANC, Gokhale and his team of detectives had travelled to Savantwadi to track down a suspected heroin supplier. They'd caught a drug peddler in Worli with 1 kg of pure heroin and were desperate to trace its source.

Night had fallen on the coast by the time the team found the supplier. An exhausted Gokhale wanted to stay the night in a hotel and start for Mumbai at dawn after a few hours' rest. But the driver of the police jeep vetoed the idea. He did not want to take any chances while transporting an arrested man across the state and was confident that he wouldn't fall asleep at the wheel.

He stuck to his word and navigated the jeep expertly in complete darkness through most of the night. But once he was clear of the hills in Satara and half-way home, he was overcome by a spell of drowsiness.

Within seconds, the jeep veered sharply off the road and crashed into a tree. Badly hurt but alive, the occupants of the jeep managed to extricate themselves from the wreckage and waved to oncoming traffic for help. But car after car rushed past the bloodied men without slowing down to check on the crash site.

Realizing that he needed to get his colleagues to the hospital immediately, Gokhale took out his pistol and stood in the middle of the road in the path of an oncoming tourist bus. A colleague had tried to push Gokhale away but he wouldn't budge. The bus showed no signs of slowing down. Finally, with Gokhale less than ten feet away and clearly determined to stand his ground, the driver of the bus jammed the brakes. At gunpoint, Gokhale persuaded the driver to take him and his men to the nearest hospital. Fortunately, none of them had suffered life-threatening injuries. Gokhale walked away with a fractured arm and stitches on his head. Doctors could do nothing about the dent in his cranium.

After three years in the ANC, Gokhale was drafted to Dharavi police station. 'Asia's Biggest Slum' is a pretty sterile descriptor for Dharavi. It fails to account for the occasional bursts of toxic blue and green dyes coursing through its drains, the wail of scrap metal being picked apart by calloused fingers on open roads, the odour of fresh leather from a million purses on shopfront displays, the sound of a thousand quarrels ringing through paper-thin walls, and the smoke from burning plastic melding with the fragrance of clay pots drying in the sun to form a solid, stinging sensation that settles on the tongue and never quite leaves. But that's only a romantic outsider's view of Dharavi.

For a cop, policing Dharavi is *the* nightmare.

It took just one patrol of his new workplace for Gokhale to realize just how little he knew about this part of the city. Spotting a long queue of men lined up on the pavement early one morning, Gokhale asked a constable if they were waiting to buy sugar or kerosene at the ration shop. The constable laughed at his superior officer's naivety.

'That is a country liquor store, sir. And those men are most likely sanitation workers who need a drink before they start cleaning drains,' he said.

The chaos on the streets spilled over into the police station and into Gokhale's life. Just months into his new post, the entire crime detection squad of the police station was shunted out over allegations that they had raped a bar dancer brought to their cabin for questioning.

Gokhale was chosen as the new detection officer and had to build a new team of constables with little experience of detective work. The new squad would have no time to bed in.

Twenty-two murders were reported in the jurisdiction in Gokhale's first year in Dharavi. Three took place on a single terrifying day.

In the first of those, two men murdered a drunk man for bumping into their father on the road. The detection squad had barely arrived at the scene of the crime when word came in of another killing not far away.

A young man had sexually harassed a girl in a public place. Her neighbour had intervened and slapped the attacker away. But the humiliated assailant returned minutes later with a knife and stabbed the neighbour. Gokhale dispatched another team to track down the killer.

But even as the police attempted to make sense of the two unrelated murders, a chilling scene of violence unfolded in Naik Nagar. Neighbours heard a woman screaming in her first floor home and rushed out of their homes to see pieces of torn paper floating to the ground. They watched in horror as the woman's husband tore her clothes and pushed her down. No one dared to intervene as the husband grabbed two 20-kg stone weights and pummelled her head with it, stopping only when she stopped twitching. A neighbour quietly contacted the police.

Gokhale arrived to find the woman lying on the ground with her head cracked open, her husband holding two large and bloodied stones over her and pages from a religious text scattered all around. Gokhale's first act, since the woman was beyond help and her husband subdued, was to gather up and account for all the loose pages. He could not risk witnesses believing rumours that the text had been desecrated. Gokhale would later learn that the husband nursed an inferiority complex since his wife was better educated and could recite verses from the text faster than him. His resentment had simmered until that afternoon, when he finally snapped. After their children had gone to school, he dragged his wife upstairs and unleashed a frenzied attack. Doctors who performed the post-mortem examination of the woman's body found some more pages torn from the text lodged inside her throat. The husband's explanation horrified Gokhale.

'Why wouldn't I hit her? How can a woman read the text better and faster than me?' he told his interrogators. It seemed that people in Dharavi killed each other at the slightest provocation.

Shootouts continued to remain a disturbingly regular feature of Gokhale's work. An attempt to capture a murder suspect in Aarey Colony resulted in an exchange of gunfire. Once again, Gokhale escaped with his life while his colleagues gunned down the suspect. The policemen involved in that incident did not face disciplinary action since they had acted in self-defence.

But the next time Gokhale drew his weapon, in a sugarcane field on the outskirts of Ahmednagar district, the consequences were grave. It had gone spectacularly wrong right from the off. A stranger entered the detection room one day and offered to lead Gokhale to a man in Daund, Pune district, who traded in stolen gold and silver jewellery. It was a vague, unverified lead from a man Gokhale had never met and knew nothing about. He was not inclined to take the lead seriously but procedure demanded that he run it by his senior inspector. The senior inspector sanctioned a trip to Daund before the detection squad could even begin a preliminary verification of the informant's claims. Daund was miles away from their jurisdiction and any trip to another district in order to pursue a lead required the permission of the assistant, deputy and additional commissioners of police. The senior inspector had not bothered to inform them.

Trouble began mere hours into the trip. The team, which was travelling in two cars, split up when one of the vehicles broke down. Gokhale, who was travelling with the mysterious informant, was reunited with his colleagues only in Daund once they repaired their car. In Daund, the informant picked up two friends who offered to show the police the way to the rendezvous. The plan was for the officer leading the team to pose as a trader, a constable as his servant and Gokhale and two others as their friends.

The locals directed Gokhale to drive towards Ahmednagar while his colleagues followed in the other car. Suddenly, the locals asked Gokhale to make a U-turn and directed him to a muddy road off the main road and into a sugarcane field. His colleagues in the other car had not spotted Gokhale's car abruptly changing direction. They drove on ahead.

Inside a clearing in the field, the policemen were completely hemmed in by sugarcane plants towering above their heads. An old man holding a bagful of silver coins was waiting for them. As per plan, Gokhale stayed close to the car while his colleagues negotiated the purchase. The 'buyer' inspected a few of the coins and asked where the rest of the silver was. But the old man wanted to see the money first. The undercover policemen had rehearsed this part. The 'servant' produced a briefcase filled with a stack of currency notes. Each stack was piled with a few genuine currency notes on top and pieces of blank paper underneath. As soon as the briefcase was opened, the man yelled out a command and at least fifty men and women armed with wooden sticks, axes and sickles emerged from their hiding places behind the sugarcane plants.

Joined by the informant and his friends, they formed a ring around the policemen, cut off all exit points and circled in for the kill. The policemen flashed their ID cards and warned the mob not to attack. The mob ignored the command and drew closer. Gokhale and his colleagues fired warning shots in the air. At such close quarters, the sound of each shot cannoned through the clearing but not a single member of the mob flinched in fear. They fell upon the policemen.

Gokhale ducked just as a sickle flew past his head. He was thrown off balance and fell on a mound of earth where something stung his hand. It was chilli powder. The mob were members of the Pardhi tribal community, some of whom were notorious for waylaying unsuspecting travellers with chilli powder, chopping them down and looting whatever they could find. Had the attackers reached the chilli powder, Gokhale and his colleagues would probably not have survived.

A sudden gunshot, fired below waist height, sent the mob scattering. The policemen made it out alive, unaware that in the melee, a man lay dead in the field, struck by a bullet.

In Daund, the local police refused to register a complaint. The other police station in the vicinity told the weary cops that they had no jurisdiction to investigate the incident.

Upon returning to Mumbai, Gokhale and his colleagues faced a departmental inquiry for conducting an investigation outside city limits without the permission of superior officers. Once the body was discovered in the sugarcane field, the Maharashtra Police's CID registered a case of murder against Gokhale and his colleagues. Pending the outcome of the probe, Gokhale was transferred out of Dharavi to an office where he had no contact with citizens.

Gokhale was already facing a departmental inquiry into allegations of bribery from his time in the ANC. A second one stretched his capacity to endure suffering. He started experiencing severe stress headaches.

On the way to the doctor with Saket one afternoon, Gokhale collapsed. At the hospital, a neurosurgeon discovered internal bleeding and performed an emergency surgery. Gokhale remained unconscious for eight days. When he came to consciousness, he could not move his left arm or leg.

## Redemption

After three bed-ridden months, Gokhale commenced physiotherapy and step by agonising step, regained enough strength to walk again. Though disabled, he was still a murder accused. The department assigned him to a desk job.

Meanwhile, the CID continued to question Gokhale's colleagues, forcing them to sit on an uncomfortable wooden bench with no backrest for hours at a stretch. The last of these interrogations took place in the sugarcane field, where the CID wanted to recreate the events of that day. Gokhale couldn't travel to Ahmednagar that day. One of his old cases had gone to trial at the Sessions Court in Mumbai, and he was summoned to depose as a witness. Two days later, he learnt that the CID had arrested his colleagues. He immediately applied for and secured anticipatory bail. He was safe, for now.

In the midst of all this chaos, Gokhale was also learning to come to terms with the new limitations of his body. At his next posting, as an inspector at Pant Nagar police station in eastern Mumbai suburb of Ghatkopar, he needed help to climb up and down a short flight of stairs to his office. Saket would seat him in an autorickshaw and send him off to work. Gokhale would return home in another autorickshaw at the end of his shift and meet Saket at the gate of the police quarters. Every step hurt, and his body could take no more than fifty of them without tiring. It was a cruel twist of fate for a man who had scaled 22,000-foot-high mountains in his youth.

For the murder trial at the Sessions Court in Ahmednagar, Gokhale chose not to engage a lawyer. He knew the law well enough to argue his own case. On the eve of the first day, he was deep into his notes at home when veteran NDPS Act lawyer Ayaz Khan, a man he had sparred with and consistently lost cases to, dropped by to check on his preparedness. Khan looked through Gokhale's homework and was convinced that he was ready. Then Khan called up senior lawyer Shyam Keswani, another regular opponent in court, and informed him that Gokhale was prepared for the trial. Their support gave Gokhale much confidence.

Gokhale could not afford to miss work to attend the trial. A day before each hearing, he would work the day shift, take an overnight bus, check into a hotel for some rest, attend the hearing and head back the other way once court was adjourned, just in time to start the night shift.

By the time the trial had ended, Gokhale was reasonably confident of an acquittal. He had managed to get a crime scene forensic analyst to admit that the deceased had suffered fatal injuries most likely from a lead bullet found in a country-made revolver and not a brass-coated one used in a police weapon.

But the judge was unmoved and sentenced Gokhale and his colleagues to life imprisonment. The convicts were transported to Ahmednagar District Prison the same day. The jail superintendent refused to admit them as 95 per cent of his inmates belonged to the Pardhi community. He could not guarantee the safety of the convicts. So they were transported to Yerwada Central Prison in Pune on the same night and lodged in a cell in the yard where freedom fighter Lokmanya Bal Gangadhar Tilak had been incarcerated between January 1898 and February 1899. All through the drive, Gokhale thought about his mother, who was now lonelier than ever before.

He had only just begun to adjust to life in prison when he was summoned to the superintendent's office one day. A guilty-looking constable from Mumbai had brought him a letter. He had expected to receive news of his removal from the police force at some point but when it arrived, it still hit him hard. The policeman in him died that day.

Saket had filed an appeal against the conviction in the Bombay High Court. The appeal allowed Gokhale's colleagues to seek and secure their release on bail until he and another constable were the only ones left behind bars. Gokhale had delayed filing his own application for bail until the constable was granted bail. He did not want a subordinate to be the last one left inside. Gokhale finally walked free after eight months at Yerwada.

Gokhale emerged from the prison's main gate early one morning. Just like Ellis Boyd 'Red' Redding in *Shawshank Redemption*, the outside world felt alien to him. The thought of crossing the road terrified him. With no stomach to move, Gokhale sank into a bench outside the gate and waited for his family to arrive. His mother and a friend from Nashik came moments later.

But the moment he reached his flat at the police quarters in Kurla, all of Gokhale's joy evaporated. An eviction notice was stuck to the door. He could keep the flat if he paid the department rent equivalent to the market rate. Gokhale explained to his old bosses, who were now in leadership positions, that he could neither afford to make rent nor imagine having to vacate the house. They permitted him to retain his home provided he paid a discounted rent.

But while he was able to secure a roof over his family's head, he would not stay with them for long. Gokhale's relationship with his wife had strained over the years. His conviction and imprisonment pushed the couple past any possibility of reconciliation. The old cliché about some people being committed to their jobs to the point of complete devotion held true to Gokhale. He was married first to his job and then to his wife. He had just not been enough of a husband or a father. When his wife eventually asked him to move out, Gokhale did not protest or put up a fight. Quietly, he returned to Nashik to stay with his mother, who was then battling cancer. In her final years, he could at last be a son to her.

Gokhale found work as an assistant to the editor of an English-language daily newspaper and briefly as its editor when the boss moved abroad. But this upswing in fortune was temporary. His mother's health continued to slip. She did not respond either to chemotherapy or blood transfusions. The Bombay High Court had also not ruled on his appeal. Gokhale could no longer tolerate the judicial delay.

'If something happens to my mother,' he wrote in an application to the bench hearing his appeal, 'it will not matter whether you acquit me, award me life imprisonment or the death penalty. It will all be the same to me.'

That rare outburst of emotion seemed to have an effect on the court. In the next fortnight, the court heard final arguments from counsels for Gokhale and his colleagues and the state government pleader, and in the end, overturned the trial court's conviction. The verdict meant that they got their jobs back.

Gokhale returned to Mumbai; this time with his mother. She lived long enough to see him back at the job he loved and worked hard at. Gokhale wanted her to see that he had truly turned around his life. He would return home every evening wearing his uniform even though the norm was to change into civil clothes before heading home. That sight brought a smile to her face. She passed away in 2010 after less than a year in Mumbai.

### Back from the wild

By 2013, Sadanand Date—Gokhale's DCP in Dharavi in the early 2000s—was the new joint commissioner of the crime branch. Date brought Gokhale back into active policing and posted him as senior inspector of the ANC's south Mumbai field unit.

In his second stint in the ANC, Gokhale fashioned himself as more of a mentor and counsellor in the police's war on drugs than a detective. There was good reason to do so. Unlike in the 1990s, drug cartels no longer smuggled hundreds of kilograms of heroin or Mandrax into Mumbai. That version of Gokhale's ANC had ceased to exist. The era of spending entire nights inside warehouses counting several thousand tablets of the banned anxiety medication Diazepam and discovering sacks of hashish hidden in the roofs of photocopy shops was also over. Mumbai was still a major harbour in cocaine's dash across the globe but on the street, only its poor imitation ruled.

With the emergence of an unknown chemical powder at every street corner, Gokhale foresaw usage, dependence and addiction on the scale of an epidemic. He was not wrong. Cocaine was the Lindt chocolate bar of drugs. Meow Meow was Melody toffee, cheap and easy to find.

The death of a suspected Meow Meow user in September 2013 forced Gokhale to step out into the field again and campaign against the drug publicly.[69] As part of the ANC's Drug Free Campus programme, he lectured at colleges in south Mumbai. He pleaded with students not to experiment with drugs, especially not with Meow Meow. At the end of each lecture, he gave out his phone number and promised to attend each phone call or message seeking help. Once the calls started to come in, Gokhale spent most afternoons meeting worried parents in his cabin.

With the law yet to take note of Meow Meow, Gokhale was forced to turn to unconventional solutions. A 'music therapist' from Oshiwara had offered his services to Gokhale. Music therapist didn't quite do justice to DJ Roshan Mansukhani. With his beret, hipster beard, tattooed shoulder, sleeveless shirts and cargo pants, he was more of a fun dad to whom kids experimenting with alcohol or drugs could speak to more openly than with their own parents.

Mansukhani had offered his services to the police after noting an increase in mephedrone usage among his daughter's friends in the glittery western enclave of Oshiwara. Through a combination of counselling and DJ-ing classes, Mansukhani had managed to persuade three teenagers to quit.[70] Gokhale had forwarded Mansukhani's proposal to his superiors and they promised to consider it. They did, but weren't interested in it.

Malishka Mendonca, the popular radio jockey at Red FM, took note of Gokhale's activism. She hosted a three-part anti-drug week special on Meow Meow on her morning show on 15, 16 and 18 December 2014.

Her first guest was Dr Yusuf Merchant, a psychologist who had filed a public interest litigation in the Bombay High Court seeking an immediate ban on the drug. To the tune of suspenseful music and goofy sound effects, Dr Merchant repeated several unverified Meow Meow horror stories from Europe. He also speculated that Mumbai had at least one hundred thousand Meow Moew users.

'*Yeh zombie drug hai* [This is a zombie drug],' he warned listeners.

Malishka, though, was not as sensationalist. 'Meow Meow makes it sound like a pussy cat drug but it's not. It's a dangerous drug. It is very lethal and it is very easily available,' she said at the end of her first show.

Gokhale appeared on the show the next morning. He spoke in plain terms. There was no need to lecture or scare his listeners.

'School and college exams begin in a few months,' he said. 'If Meow Meow is not banned by then, a large number of students will use it as an aid to last minute revision.'

He also warned users that the product available on the street was often adulterated with dangerous chemicals. 'Meow Meow crystals look quite similar to Ajinomoto. *Toh uska bhi thoda usme mixing ho raha hai* [So Ajinomoto is also being mixed into it].'

Before signing off, Gokhale read out both his phone numbers on air. He was doing all he could.

In the meantime, the Government of Maharashtra stepped in. Maria's lobbying had paid off. The government commissioned a state-wide report on drug consumption and trade for the urgent notice of the NCB. The rise of mephedrone had also raised concerns in the NCB, which separately wrote to the central government to regulate its production and sale.[71] Date entrusted the job of reporting the mephedrone situation in Mumbai to Gokhale.

The political push came from CM Fadnavis, who in December 2014, wrote to the central government seeking a ban on mephedrone.[72] The central government responded two months later, notifying mephedrone as a controlled substance under the NDPS Act. The Maharashtra government and the Mumbai Police claimed victory but Gokhale was its public face.

It looked like he had finally caught a break.

# 21

Friday, 29 May began differently for Kasare. In the morning, he informed the Sessions Court of the FSL's findings and submitted a request to have the samples resampled and retested by one of the central government's Central Forensic Science Laboratories (CFSL). He ended the day with the arrest of the five policemen.

The case could have ended that morning had the crime branch accepted the findings of the Kalina FSL.

Instead, Kasare told the court that he had only received the FSL's report on 14 May, twelve days after Assistant Chemical Analyser R.K. Oberoi had completed the analysis.

The NDPS Act does not contain any clause that allows for the retesting of seized drugs. When Parliament passed the Act in 1985, it expected the police to trust the results of forensic analysis and withdraw its prosecution in the event that a sample was not found to contain a prohibited substance.

But the law also provided a way out. State and central police agencies began adding to their FIRs sections of the Drugs and Cosmetics Act 1940, Prevention of Food Adulteration Act 1954, and the Central Excise Rules 1994, which permit retesting as long as a request is made within thirty, ten and twenty days, respectively. The persons under arrest for allegedly dealing drugs could only watch helplessly from prison as courts across the country allowed the police to have the samples retested—a procedure that ordinarily takes at least three months.

This state of lawlessness was somewhat curtailed in 2013 when the Supreme Court issued guidelines to judges in trial courts and state high courts that they could no longer entertain requests for retesting 'as a matter of course' under the NDPS Act. The police was given a fifteen-day deadline to submit requests. Judges could only permit such requests under 'extremely exceptional circumstances'.[73] If the police missed the deadline by a single day or failed to persuade the judge, the case was over.

By Kasare's calculations, his fifteen-day window began on 14 May, the day he became aware of the report. He made no attempt to explain to Sessions Judge U.B. Hejib what he had been doing in the preceding twelve days and why he had suppressed knowledge of the report from the court for nearly a month.

In Satara, Deputy SP Humbre did not accept the findings of the Pune FSL either. But unlike Kasare, he moved an application for retesting in the Satara Sessions Court within the prescribed time. It was up to the two sessions judges to rule whether the applications for retesting had been filed on time and if police made a compelling case for another shot at salvaging their cases.

Additional Sessions Judge V.R. Kachre of the Satara Sessions Court instantly granted permission for a retest. There were no defence lawyers present in court to oppose retesting. On 4 June, two officers travelled from Satara to CFSL Hyderabad with a sealed packet of white crystals and a poorly worded letter from SP Deshmukh.

FSL Pune has submitted report to investigating officer and according to it, sample doesn't have 'Mafedron'. However the investigating machinery is not agree with said report and wants to challenge the said analysis report dtd 2/5/2015 before CFSL. CFSL Hyderabad being the expert laboratory, it is opinion will be very important for investigation of this case. Hence it is requested that the enclosed second sample of Mafedron along with report and to be examined by CFSL.

In Mumbai, Sessions Judge Hejib was not as hasty. His interpretation of the law would also affect bail pleas filed by Baby, the five policemen and Padaiyatchi.

A negative forensic report wasn't a knockout punch. Kasare could see another way of establishing Baby's wrongdoings. To do that he would need to account for every last rupee in the Mazgaonkar–Patankar family bank accounts and every inch of property they owned.

A bank in Worli where Baby held an account reported that she had fixed deposits totalling Rs 1.3 crore. The bank had approved a loan of Rs 1.7 crore against the deposits.

Meanwhile, Kasare wanted to personally search Kalokhe's cupboard. He had not had the opportunity to look through it since he had volunteered to lead the investigation. The cupboard had stayed locked since it was first forced open on 10 March. A fresh search by a new pair of eyes might just rescue the sinking investigation.

Judge Hejib allowed him to proceed. A carpenter was not needed this time. The key to Kalokhe's half of the cupboard was found in the luggage box of his motorcycle. Kasare had also taken the precaution of requesting a scientist from the FSL to be present for the search.

The twelve plastic packets of white crystals were where they had been left three months ago, on the topmost of the three shelves. Kasare also found some articles that had been overlooked in March: a bottle of Kingfisher Premium beer, Baby's PAN card, Satish's Aadhar card and three voter ID cards—the first belonging to Sarika Patankar, the second with the name Ramesh Kamlakar Patankar but with a photo of Kalokhe, and the third with the name Ramesh Kamlakar Patankar but with a photo of Ballu. There were no records of the last two voter ID cards in the electoral rolls of the Worli Assembly constituency, clear grounds for Kasare to suspect forgery.

The forensic scientist took samples from the shelves, the Express Tower backpack and three other articles in the cupboard. Kasare prayed for a different outcome this time. The only positive outcome he had achieved at the FSL so far was confirmation that a bar of blackish substance discovered in the cupboard in March was *charas*.

But if he thought that he had bought some time, Judge Hejib reminded him the next day that there was no escaping the inevitable. He had decided the bail pleas of the five policemen and with it extinguished all of Kasare's lingering hopes.

In Judge Hejib's mind, the police had not produced any evidence to support its claims that the policemen had entered into a conspiracy with Baby to supply mephedrone. The CDRs did not persuade Judge Hejib that the policemen had advised and assisted Baby to evade arrest since Kasare had not produced transcripts of their conversations.

Also, unlike Kasare, Judge Hejib had no reason to mistrust the analysis of the Mumbai FSL. He had not yet decided whether to grant Kasare permission for resampling and a retest but he was not going to deny the arrested men their liberty while he made up his mind.

The men were free to go.

Despite the unfolding of events, Kasare refused to accept that the ship was sinking. Back from court that evening, he discussed with DCP Kulkarni and Joint Commissioner Kulkarni the possibility of asking the court to draw fresh samples of the contraband and having them tested at any of the six CFSLs in the country.

Both officers agreed.

The only judicial victory Kasare was able to savour came from the sessions court in Jalgaon, which permitted him to question the two drivers, Thevar and Tiwari, who were then inmates at Jalgaon Central Prison.

In Mumbai, Judge Hejib had so far refrained from conducting a 'mini trial'. But while granting bail to Baby in July, he delved into the merits of the case. During the bail hearings, Baby's lawyer, advocate Gavankar pointed out a major flaw in the police's case—Baby had not been found in possession of mephedrone. The only evidence tying her to the substance discovered in Kalokhe's home and cupboard was his word.

In his order, Judge Hejib settled the chicken-and-egg question. How could Baby have broken the law by allegedly being in possession of mephedrone in 2014 when the drug was only notified as a controlled substance by the central government on 2 February 2015? That made every other allegation against her hypothetical. Kalokhe's 'confession', which the police recorded without the presence of an independent witness, held no value in court.

Judge Hejib did not entertain hypothetical situations.

Taking into account the hypothetical case that the application of the prosecution for resending the sample is allowed and going a step forward even assuming that the CFSL report supports the case of the prosecution case that what was found with the accused was Mephedrone, then in that case, the prosecution would be at liberty to move with an application to cancel the bail. But in any case, pending the determination of the application other for retesting or thereafter pending the analysis and report, the grant or rejection of the bail cannot be postponed for indefinite period as it is common knowledge that reports of either FSL or CFSL except in exceptional cases are not received timely or quickly may be for diverse reasons.

Judge Hejib did not share the police's apprehension that Baby would skip town if granted bail. He further wrote:

To say about her probable abscondence in India, the prosecution story itself indicates that the accused has many properties and it goes without saying that the value thereof must be about crores having regard to the location at Mumbai (Worli), Ratnagiri, Lonavala and so on. Having regard to the nature of the offence, to my mind, the accused would prefer to face the trial instead of losing right to enjoy aforesaid properties.

The month did not get any better for Kasare. Less than a fortnight later, the FSL concluded its analysis of samples taken from the second search of Kalokhe's cupboard: the white crystals in the twelve packets had not magically metamorphosed into mephedrone.

They were still stubbornly Ajinomoto.

## 22

Consumed by his standoff with the court, Kasare could not spare time to question Kalokhe. He had submitted an application to have the samples redrawn and retested.

Unit I Chief Avdhut Chavan made the trip to Kolhapur Central Prison instead. On 29 June, after a month's delay, the crime branch finally heard Kalokhe's side of the story.

He contested, denied and refuted every allegation Baby had made against him. It wasn't so much as presenting a differing point of view as narrating a completely different story.

'Who was Baby's supplier?'

'She told me it was Customs officer Suryavanshi. She never once mentioned Samuel. But believe me, I hated that she sold drugs.'

'What do you mean?'

'For the past one year, I had been trying to get her to stop. Parte and Mane could not let that happen. If Baby stopped selling, they stood to lose a lot of money. That is the reason Parte worked with Gaikwad to trap me.'

'How is Gaikwad involved?'

'He used to visit Baby's home regularly. He used to hit her too. He forcefully enrolled her into a *vipassana* course. Baby and I have been together for eighteen years but because of Gaikwad, we grew apart. We stopped speaking to each other.'

'Then why did you go to Pune with Baby to meet Samuel?'

'I didn't. She's lying!'

'Why did you store mephedrone in your mother's home?'

'Baby told me it was a chemical not covered under the NDPS Act. Whenever I asked her if I could get rid of it, she wouldn't give me a straight answer. That caused many arguments.'

'Why did you store mephedrone in your police station cupboard?'

'When I visited my mother in January, Baby asked me to bring back twelve kilos. She promised to take it from me but kept putting it off. Since mephedrone wasn't banned at that time, I knew I wouldn't get into trouble if anyone found it. In February, she also gave me a small packet of charas for safekeeping.'

'Why didn't you dispose of the mephedrone after it was banned?'

'I wanted to but couldn't. I love Baby.'

Kalokhe's acts of love helped explain some of the more startling revelations of the investigation. He denied having the power of attorney over Baby's bungalow.

He admitted to using his contacts to house Baby at Garware Club House in January. Staying at Marina Guest

House had become too risky. At some point, the police was bound to start searching hotels and guesthouses.

'What is your photo doing on Ramesh Patankar's voter ID card?'

'There was a room in Siddharth Nagar registered in his name. Baby wanted to transfer it in her name. So she forged his identity cards using mine and Ballu's photos.'

'And you agreed to store the cards in your cupboard?'

'Yes.'

He made no allegations against Gokhale and Sarang. He had seen Gokhale speak at an anti-drug seminar at Islam Gymkhana the previous year but hadn't met him. He didn't know who Sarang was.

While Gokhale savoured freedom, his former boss at the ANC, DCP Chavan, threw him under the bus. In his statement to Unit I, he accused Gokhale of concealing the fact that he had been in contact with Baby immediately prior to and after she was named as an accused.

Gokhale, oblivious and uncaring, claimed to journalists that Unit I had arrested him despite a lack of evidence. Kasare complained to the court: Gokhale's comments were affecting his investigation. The court barred Gokhale and the others from giving interviews.

Kasare, meanwhile, followed Baby's money. He found that she had booked and paid an advance for two flats and a commercial space in a project developed in Palghar town by the real estate firm HDIL. In 2012, she cancelled her registration.

Kasare's quest to unmask other possible collaborators of Baby within the department had not concluded. He questioned two inspectors who in 2013 had sought the assistance of the Bengali-speaking informant Rafiq Bam to track down a suspect in a counterfeit currency case in West Bengal. Kasare cleared them. Bam hadn't gone to the inspectors with the dope on Kalokhe.

Kasare was also keen to appeal against Baby's bail order in the Bombay High Court. But the joint commissioner's legal officer advised against it. He had no case for an appeal.

On 23 July, Kasare sent a report to the Maharashtra home department, similar to the one he had sent to his superiors exactly two months ago. This one also named Baby's alleged conspirators in the police department. Only the tone differed. He alleged that the ten officers and constables named in the report had misused their positions to assist Baby's drug business and had profited handsomely.

Kasare also learnt how Baby conducted her real estate business. Five of her tenants in Siddharth Nagar told him that she had not registered formal rent agreements. They paid her rent in cash every month.

Meanwhile, in courtroom 44, Judge Hejib was ready to rule on the crime branch's application for resampling and retesting. For the past two and half months, Additional Public Prosecutor Usha Jadhav had argued that the discovery of a purported contraband in the cupboard of a police constable was a compelling enough reason to have it resampled and retested. As per the Supreme Court's guidelines, these were 'extremely exceptional circumstances'. It was essential, she argued, that the substance should be identified 'beyond reasonable doubt'.

She accused Gokhale, who was not a suspect when Kalokhe's cupboard was searched on 10 March, of intentionally taking samples from the topmost layer of the twelve plastic packets stored in Kalokhe's cupboard. It sounded like the crime branch had made liberal use of Professor McGonagall's Time-Turner!

APP Jadhav also claimed in court that the crime branch had received the FSL report dated 2 May on 14 May. Judge Hejib had directed Unit I to submit photocopies of its office inward register. An entry for 13 May clearly mentioned receipt of the FSL's report.

When Judge Hejib asked Kasare to explain this twelve-day gap, Kasare admitted that he had personally visited the FSL on 13 May to collect the report. He had falsified an entry in the office's inward register suggesting that the FSL report had arrived on 14 May. He had conveniently played around with dates to file his application for resampling and retesting on the final day of the fifteen-day deadline.

Judge Hejib reserved his order for 17 August.

Something in Baby snapped when she saw Kasare in court at noon on 12 August. It wasn't a lengthy hearing. Judge Hejib sent Baby back to jail for fourteen more days. She would have to stay there until her family could arrange a surety. Before dismissing her, Judge Hejib inquired about her health.

Baby attacked the policewoman in charge of escorting her to and from prison.

'She treats me very badly!' she claimed.

She wasn't done.

'The staff in jail also treats me very badly. They don't allow my family to visit me. I know they are following Kasare's orders!'

Judge Hejib was stunned. He asked Baby's lawyer to detail her grievances in an application. He would meditate on it after lunch.

Once the court broke for lunch, Kasare pulled Baby's escort officer aside for a chat. They retreated some distance away from the courtroom. Suddenly, Baby walked up to them.

'When I go back to jail, I'm going to hang myself. I will blame both of you!' Baby spat in anger.

The escort officer whisked Baby away and asked the jail superintendent to keep a close watch on her. The next day, the police informed Judge Hejib about Baby's threat.

The drama didn't sidetrack Kasare. In the absence of a drug, he had no case. But he didn't need a drug to prove that all of Baby's earnings were a result of historical illegal activity. Section 68 (F) of the NDPS Act allowed the government to freeze any assets it suspected were acquired through the proceeds of criminal activity. He would need to make a convincing case before the Competent Authority under the Smugglers and Foreign Exchange Manipulators (Forfeiture of Property) Act.

The file he had put together included the list of Baby's properties which Kalokhe had very kindly provided, Shelke's dossier of Baby's assets and updated bank account statements of Baby, her sons, daughters-in-law, brothers and nephew. He had also already impounded her cars and scooters.

It was time to turn the screws.

On 17 August, Kasare began posting notices to the Patankar-Mazgaonkar clan, informing them of a freeze on their assets. Baby was served the notice in jail. She refused to accept it. Kasare also sent a copy of the report to the Office of the Competent Authority in Nariman Point. Unless the Competent Authority confirmed the notice within thirty days, it would have no effect.

In the afternoon, Judge Hejib ruled on Kasare's plea for resampling and retesting. He wasn't convinced that Kasare had met the fifteen-day deadline to apply for retesting.

Judge Hejib wrote, 'The application filed on 29.05.2015 is hopelessly barred by the limitation.'

He was also not impressed by the prosecution's attempt to go back in time and attribute an otherworldly level of prescience to Gokhale.

Application rejected.

Kasare had expected the rejection. Like every other reversal in court that summer, he brushed it aside. He sent Kalokhe a notice under Section 68 (F) and dispatched a copy to the Competent Authority. He also sent copies of the notice to the superintendent of Byculla women's prison with a request to serve it to Baby and receive her signature.

One window had opened just as soon as the other had shut.

# 23

*The men from Sangrampur*

Satara Sessions Judge Kachre did not share Judge Hejib's wisdom. It was not his place to weigh the evidence the police had gathered against Baby or to decide if a case against her even existed. Those issues would be addressed in the trial.

On 2 September, the Satara Police submitted a nearly 300-page-long chargesheet against Kalokhe, Baby, Satish and Samuel.[74] Buried among the statements of fifty-eight witnesses was the report of the Pune FSL conclusively proving that the white powder found in Kalokhe's home was *not* mephedrone.

The law allows undertrials to be set at liberty once the police files its chargesheet because it recognizes the fact that a trial, where the person accused of committing a crime receives an opportunity to prove herself innocent, takes years to commence. Judicial delay impinges on an undertrial's fundamental right to life and personal liberty under Article 21 of the Constitution of India. But neither the Constitution nor the forensic report could sway Judge Kachre. He decided that it was too early to completely discard the police's case. Moreover, the magnitude of Baby's alleged offence was too serious to grant her bail. Baby's lawyer appealed the decision in the Bombay High Court.

Judge Kachre's baffling decision capped a disappointing two months for Baby. The temporary euphoria she had experienced after Judge Hejib granted her bail dissipated as soon as she was explained the fine print. The court had set her bail at Rs 5,00,000, but it wouldn't be as simple as depositing the money in the court's coffers and walking free. Baby would have to find at least one surety—a respectable person who knew her well and was willing to take responsibility for her regular attendance in court and to place personal assets valued at least Rs 5,00,000 as collateral. Baby wasn't allowed to leave Mumbai city limits without seeking the court's permission, she would have to report to Kasare every two weeks for the next six months, surrender her passport to the court, provide proof to the court of her residence in Mumbai after release, and refrain from contacting witnesses or tamper with evidence. If Baby violated any of these conditions or jumped bail, the surety risked going to jail and losing their assets. Very few people would consent to undertake such a risk.

Meanwhile at the Mumbai sessions court, Arjun produced a surety. It was a painter who had worked at Baby's bungalow the previous summer. He was a native of Sangrampur taluka in Maharashtra's Buldhana district, located 550 km northeast of Mumbai.

The court ordered the police in Buldhana to ascertain the painter's relationship with Baby and ascertain if he owned assets worth at least Rs 5,00,000. Judge Hejib, not new to dealing with a curious class of men who dedicate their lives to acting as sureties for complete strangers for a considerable fee, was amazed at what the police discovered.

The only ties between Baby and the painter were of a *maanleli bahin* (assumed sister). When he was produced in court in the first week of August, the painter denied being acquainted with Baby. He also lived on daily subsistence. His wages for short-term painting jobs ranged between Rs 300 and Rs 400. And while he did own farmland whose speculative value might have fulfilled the financial stipulation for a surety, the fact that he was still paying off a property loan completely disqualified him as a surety.

Judge Hejib was at his wits' end. His ruling stated the following:

> It is extremely improbable that a labourer working with a lady just for the sake of Rs 300 to Rs 400 would stand for her as surety of Rs 5,00,000 by jeopardizing his immovable property. Therefore, there is reason to believe that the surety must have appeared for some consideration. Acceptance of such a surety will hardly secure the presence of the accused at the proposed trial wherein there may be severe punishment.

Application rejected.

Things began to move in the office of the Competent Authority. It asked to examine all the evidence that Unit I had gathered so far. It also summoned all the respondents to the notice sans Baby on 10 September. They would have an opportunity to present a defence. The world, just briefly, took on the sweetness of freshly watered soil.

Kasare dared to hope.

He was keen to appeal the sessions court's rejection of his resampling and retesting application in the Bombay High Court. He had not been present either in Kanheri or Marine Drive police station when the substance was seized. He had a right to try and conduct the procedure himself.

There was no time to think. His 180-day deadline to file a chargesheet under the NDPS Act ended on 19 September. A failure to file the chargesheet by then would mean freedom for Kalokhe and Samuel. Kasare would go down fighting. He would not hand his opponents a walkover.

He was confident that his chargesheet was strong enough to take Baby and Kalokhe to trial.

The crime branch had to pick an option—either file the chargesheet and end the investigation or file an appeal in the high court and dig in for the long haul.

Kasare and Chavan briefed DCP Kulkarni, Additional Commissioner Prasanna and Joint Commissioner Kulkarni. The final decision rested with them.

Prasanna was sufficiently literate in chemistry to know that drug dealers used substances like Ajinomoto as fillers. He was certain that this was a case where the filler had been packed into the top layers of Kalokhe's packets. Resampling would allow the police to scoop out the lower layers which he hoped contained traces of mephedrone.

Repeating the procedure would be fair not only to the accused but more importantly, also to his investigators. Yes, the months lost to the process were regrettable. But it was the only way to put all doubts about the substance to rest.

On 16 September, Joint Commissioner Kulkarni and Prasanna asked Kasare to appeal the decision. The crime branch had expended too much time, money and effort over the summer to throw in the towel.

Later that day, Kasare informed Judge Hejib that he was unable to file the chargesheet within the stipulated deadline. He sought an extension of six months.

Arjun's second attempt to convince Judge Hejib in the first week of September was, improbably, even worse. The candidate was a wholesale fruit merchant. Arjun—in his job as a driver—had been transporting consignments of fruit for the merchant all over Maharashtra and Goa for the last sixteen years. In its verification report, the police wrote that the merchant had agreed to stand as Baby's surety after Arjun narrated her 'woeful story'.

Despite such a lengthy business association, the merchant failed to tell Judge Hejib what Arjun and Baby's last names were. This indicated to Judge Hejib that the merchant was not a genuine surety. He also found it extremely hard to believe that a fruit merchant who had a non-existent relationship with his driver would risk holding a residential plot worth Rs 19 lakh as collateral. Arjun would have to do better.

Application rejected.

Four days later, the unthinkable happened. The Bombay High Court ruled on Baby's appeal against the rejection of her bail by Judge Kachre in Satara. It took only a cursory perusal of the evidence for Justice Abhay Thipsay to be convinced that over-the-top media coverage of the case had influenced the decision of the Satara sessions judge. Justice Thipsay wrote a scathing six-page order, excoriating Humbre and Judge Kachre. The police's allegations, he ruled, were 'without support'.

He reminded the Satara Police of the moment on 9 March when they weren't sure what the white crystals in Kalokhe's bags were and had Google-searched the answer. Lacking a field drug-testing kit they had assumed that those crystals were a 'mephedrone-like substance'.

Moreover, the only flimsy thread tying Baby to the substance was Kalokhe's word. It would have no evidentiary value if the case went to trial. The police would have to provide tangible proof that the substance had first been in Baby's possession.

The most glaring weakness in the police's case was that in July 2014, when Baby was alleged to have been in possession of the drug, mephedrone was yet to be classified as a psychotropic substance under the NDPS Act. Since that happened only on 25 February 2015, Baby had not committed a crime.

But all of these were hypothetical considerations since forensic testing had proved that the substance seized from Kalokhe's home was not mephedrone at all.

'… there is nothing to show that the substance is indeed mephedrone or any other psychotropic substance. On the contrary, the report from FSL indicated that it is not a psychotropic substance,' Justice Thipsay observed.

It did not matter that the Satara Police had chosen to disbelieve the Pune FSL's report and sought a second opinion from CFSL Hyderabad. 'Even if the best is expected for the investigating agency, and it is assumed that the report from the CFSL would be that the seized substance is "mephedrone", the same would be relevant only with respect to the co-accused Dharmaraj Kalokhe, who was allegedly found to be in possession of the said substance,' he observed.

Judge Kachre had ignored all these contentions simply because the offence Baby was *alleged* to have committed was 'of a serious magnitude'.

Justice Thipsay ended his order with the judicial equivalent of a takedown.

> The learned additional sessions judge forgot that magnitude of the offence is one thing and connection of accused with that offence is quite another. That the offence is of serious magnitude will not excuse the court from examining whether a prima facie case exists against the person alleged to be the offender.

Justice Thipsay ordered that Baby be set at liberty forthwith. He set bail at Rs 30,000 and ordered her to either produce one surety willing to foot the whole amount or two sureties of Rs 15,000 each.

The High Court's order applied only to the case filed against her in Satara. To leave prison, Baby still needed to produce a reliable surety before Judge Hejib in Mumbai. But in setting her bail at the much lower figure of Rs 30,000, Justice Thipsay had provided her a way out. Judge Hejib was forced to follow suit. The law allows persons who are unable to secure sureties to post cash bail on a personal bond of good behaviour instead of undergoing continued incarceration. Arjun's failure to find a surety meant that Baby had spent two whole months in jail even though the case against her had practically collapsed. On 16 September, Judge Hejib set Baby's bail at Rs 30,000, with at least one surety.

Two days later, the office of the Competent Authority issued a confirmation order against Baby and her clan, followed later in the week by a confirmation order against Kalokhe. They were frozen out of their bank accounts. Kasare had got them!

Here at last, Kasare found a friend and ally in the law.

It didn't matter then that on 21 September, Judge Hejib ordered Baby's release. In the four weeks of freedom she had bought herself, she would *have* to find a convincing surety.

But for now, it was time to go home.

Baby asked Judge Hejib to order the police to unlock her rooms in Siddharth Nagar. He obliged.

Baby opened the rooms to find them ransacked. The doors of her cupboard were creaking on their hinges and its contents piled on the floor. She counted Rs 35,000, her bank documents and house property papers missing. The CCTV cameras she had installed on her door at Kalokhe's insistence, and their recorder, were smashed to bits. The Mumbai Police had also seized twenty mobile phones from her family, their passports and two of her three cars. Her lawyer filed an application in the Bombay High Court pleading for the Mumbai Police to return her belongings.

As her four weeks came to a close, Unit I filed the resampling and retesting application in the high court.

# 24

Before spending most of August and September parked outside Khar police station and driving all over Raigad following the twists and turns in the Sheena Bora murder case, I had dedicated the summer to befriending Baby's lawyer, the affable N.N. Gavankar. By September-end, with interest in the murder case seeing a momentary decline, there was time to breathe again.

Justice Thipsay's observation that the police had no prima facie case against Baby[75] was reason enough to ring Gavankar.

Given the vilification that she had endured at the hands of the press, I had expected Baby to turn down a request for an interview. But Gavankar persuaded her to meet me.

So one rainy afternoon in October, Prashant Nadkar, a senior photojournalist at *The Indian Express*, and I, set out for Worli. We knew that she lived somewhere in Siddharth Nagar. On the phone, Baby had instructed us to take the entrance opposite City Bakery and to call her once we reached the top of the hill. Anyone who has ever tried to locate an address inside a slum would know that it compares to no other feelings of confusion and bafflement. I'd been lost in a slum before and not for the first time that year. Only two months previously, I was among a bunch of other reporters circling uselessly inside a slum in Santacruz trying desperately to find the home of Indrani Mukerjea's driver, Shyamwar Rai and speak to his wife. That slum was a maze to begin with and the locals wouldn't help either. We were each working alone, desperate for an exclusive story but ran into each other at every other turn. With the mid-afternoon heat, the flies and the oppressively confined lanes, the search had been so utterly exhausting that an hour later, a rival-reporter-turned-close-friend and I decided to join forces. Working together, we had managed to find Rai's home after unknowingly walking past it at least half a dozen times. That day, we were the first ones to interview Mrs Rai.[76]

In Siddharth Nagar, I experienced the exact same feeling of being completely out of my depth the higher Nadkar and I climbed up the hill. Baby had told to us to make for a Sai Baba Temple with an attached playground at the summit. 'It should not take you more than ten minutes. My home is close to the temple,' she had said.

But as we became increasingly lost, we began to call her for help. Baby didn't answer the phone. Asking locals for directions didn't help either. Most made a face and turned away. The pouring rain made the ascent treacherous. Torrents of water flowing down the cement steps made keeping a firm footing a challenge. We were definitely headed upwards but fifteen minutes into the climb I had lost track of how far we had come. The deeper we progressed, the more maze-like the lanes became. Every few metres we encountered wide, unexplained holes in the paths that exposed heaving drainage lines below. These could only be crossed by walking slowly and carefully on narrow strips of pavement on either side. One slip off the tightrope and our feet would plunge into rat-infested filth.

If we were making any progress, it was only by staying on the central path that inclined upwards and not lanes that veered sideways. After what seemed like a long time but might not have been longer than half an hour, the path opened without warning into a flat concrete playground of sorts with a temple and a sports club at one corner. It was the widest open space we had seen since entering the slum. A few teenagers hung around the club. We asked them for directions but they shrugged their shoulders.

On the phone, Baby gave vague instructions.

'Follow the lane next to the temple, keep walking for a few minutes and you will see my room.'

But which one? There was more than one lane leading away from the temple. We were both soaked in sweat and rain and Nadkar was carrying several kilograms of cameras and lenses on his back. We chose the lane closest to the temple and hoped for the best.

The problem with picking out an individual home in a dense, unfamiliar slum is that house numbers or nameplates which might aid a search are rarely plastered on doors. Some distance into the lane, we passed by a few men wearing bright blue jerseys but still no Baby. I clocked the names on some of the jerseys. We had moved a few paces ahead when the name on one jersey struck me as being familiar. It was of one of Baby's sons.

I asked Nadkar to stop walking and dialled Baby.

'Haan madam, I think we're here,' I said.

'*Accha ruko. Main bahaar aati hoon* [Alright wait. I'll come out],' she said.

And she did. Out of a door closest to the jersey-clad men emerged a woman in her early-fifties with a wide, expressive face. At that moment, her expression was one of deep concern.

'*Tumhich phone kela hota ka? Ya na aatmadhey ya* [Was it you who called? Come in],' she said in Marathi.

The room we were welcomed into held a bed, cupboard, some chairs and a kitchen. Weak monsoon sunlight poured through an open door at the back.

Baby took a seat on the bed. She had agreed to meet but hadn't agreed to talk.

'*Mera koi nuksaan toh nahi hoga na* [Will this hurt me in any way]?' she asked.

She spoke Hindi with a thick Marathi accent but with the unease of someone the language did not come to naturally.

I spent the better part of thirty minutes running through some of the allegations that the police and television news channels had made against her that year, hoping to provoke a response. It didn't work.

'*Tumhala Marathi yet nahi ka? Marathi madhey bola. Mi Hindi madhey neet bolu shakat nahi* [Do you not know Marathi? Please speak in Marathi. My Hindi isn't very good),' she said.

It was my turn to feel uneasy and not in control. This was going to be a huge embarrassment. My conversational Marathi isn't great and it showed as I sputtered through questions. Thankfully, Nadkar jumped right in and took over. Baby was immediately at ease. She would occasionally break into Hindi for my benefit, but she needn't have.

Worli had not been a friendly place to return to from jail. No one would speak to her anymore.

'In my granddaughter's school, other children tell her that her family will be stripped naked and beaten up,' she said.

The police, she said, wanted her to lose all her respect.

'When I was in custody, they kept asking me, "*tu hamesha policewaale ko hi kyun pakdati hai? Tum ne police ko raste pe laaya, tum ko chodengey nahi*" [Why do you always get policeman caught? You have disgraced us; we will not spare you]. If a policeman is selling drugs, why should I not get him caught?' she said.

All Baby had wanted, was for the police to be completely sure of the substance they had recovered before branding her a 'drug queen'.

'Why did the police make such a sensation when they realized they hadn't found drugs? *Dawood ki bhi behan thi, lekin uska matter bhi police ne itna uchala kya?* [Dawood Ibrahim also had a sister, but did the police make such a big deal about her?],' she said.

During the interview, Baby repeatedly stressed that the source of her income was clean. To illustrate, she stepped out of the back door and into what served as her backyard. Nadkar used a temporary break in the downpour as an opportunity to shoot pictures of Baby. The surface we stood on was the littered roof of the house below. The metal sheet groaned every time we moved our feet.

All around Baby stretched aluminium and tarpaulin-covered roofs. Beyond her loomed the incomplete hulks of Palais Royale—interrupted in its quest to become India's tallest building—and the then under-construction hulk of the Konark Empress. One by one, she pointed to each home that she had bought and sold over time, before spreading her arms wide and declaring, 'I have carved homes into this hill!'

Nadkar chose that moment to shoot a picture that shows Baby at her most expressive.[77]

# 25

*The trap*

Baby and Arjun had learnt nothing about finding the right surety despite twice failing to convince Judge Hejib. They tried again in December. This time they produced another daily wage worker with roots in Sangrampur. This man had laid tiles at Baby's bungalow in the summer of 2014. Judge Hejib would have been excused for experiencing a strong sense of déjà vu. The tile layer had no permanent accommodation in Mumbai and stayed at whatever premises his contractor found him.

Judge Hejib could not conceive of a single reason for why the tile layer would offer himself as a surety for a woman whose home he had fixed more than a year ago. After all, how close could he have been to Baby? Judge Hejib had enough reason to doubt that the tile layer must be a 'hired and professional surety'. The fact that the tile layer had the same origins as the painter had also not escaped the judge's notice.

'How many sureties hail from Sangrampur taluka is not free from doubt. I therefore regret that the surety cannot be accepted although apparently everything appears to be all well,' he ruled.

Application, yet again, rejected.

Baby now faced a very real possibility of returning to prison unless she could arrange for a surety who wasn't a daily wage worker or a fruit merchant or an assumed sibling and, at the very least, could tell Judge Hejib her full name! Another man from Sangrampur would not do.

---

Fortunately, the law sympathizes with undertrials unable to arrange for a surety. The law allowed Baby to sign a personal bail bond and deposit Rs 20,000 in court. If she failed to attend court or went on the run, she would forfeit the money. Judge Hejib had little choice but to agree; he couldn't countenance having to quiz one more professional surety from Sangrampur. He forbade Baby from leaving Mumbai except to travel to Satara to attend court and answer summons from the police. Baby was finally free on 14 December.

The next day brought bad news. The high court could not direct the Mumbai Police to return her belongings as it was yet to finish its investigation and file a chargesheet. To get back her impounded Maruti Swift Dzire car, she would have to approach the sessions court in Satara.[78] It meant that she would have to beg at Humbre's feet.

His cooperation came at a price. As the investigating officer and a representative of the prosecution, Humbre was obliged to oppose Baby's attempt to have her car restored to her. But in exchange for a bribe he could make his opposition less vehement. He could inform the court that since he had completed his investigation and filed the chargesheet he had no reason to impound her car any longer. The Satara sessions court sided with Baby and in March 2016, ordered the police to release her car. Kalokhe also found himself having to bribe Humbre to secure the release of his belongings.

Humbre's case had reached a definitive end a month before. The results of forensic analysis at CFSL Hyderabad were the same as those recorded by Pune FSL. The white crystals in Kalokhe's travel bags were Ajinomoto.

There was no higher authority Humbre could approach. He was now duty-bound to file a report in the sessions court discharging Kalokhe, Baby, Satish and Samuel. Unsurprisingly, he would not do it for free. Baby was sick of bribing him. Like Dhawale and Kalokhe, it was time she cut Humbre down to size.

Fixing Humbre would not be easy. He was careful never to accept a bribe in person. He relied on a close friend and local fixer named Yuvraj Dhamal to collect the money. The exchanges were always made in a public place. Humbre waited close by while Dhamal interceded with the victims. Because he kept his hands clean, Humbre had escaped more than one citizen's attempt to record him accepting a bribe. Baby interpreted this to mean that she could not trust the local police.

Baby took her complaint to the headquarters of the Maharashtra Anti-Corruption Bureau (ACB), located on Sir

Pochkhanwalla Road, a ten-minute walk from Siddharth Nagar. The bureau is obliged to look past the antecedents of citizens approaching it with complaints of corrupt public officials. At the very least, Baby would receive a fair hearing.

Since the police is the second-most complained about department of the state government at the bureau, it is not surprising that a majority of the bureau's bribery traps and investigations are directed against its own colleagues. In the bureau's annual reports, the state police department has stubbornly held onto the second spot on its charts of government departments most frequently investigated for bribery.

In 2016, the bureau trapped 277 employees of the state's revenue department in 229 cases of alleged corruption. The police department was one place below: 228 cases filed and 300 employees trapped for accepting bribes.[79]

Baby and Humbre were both known names at the bureau. She was a household name, and he a slippery figure who had frustrated every effort by the bureau to catch him in the act. It would need a dogged, relentless complainant for the bureau to trap Humbre.

Baby walked in at the right time.

The bureau was satisfied by its preliminary investigation into Baby's complaint. It held up on verification. Unless she paid up, Humbre would neither release her vehicle nor submit a discharge application in court. Baby did not want to pay any more bribes. She and Kalokhe had already paid him Rs 40 lakh in the past year.[80] The desperation of her situation also fulfilled a crucial criterion without which the bureau would not take on her case—in this case, she did not have a personal score to settle with Humbre. The police's case against her simply did not hold up in court. She had everything to lose if Humbre got away once more. A squad of officers from the Mumbai office was deputed to execute the operation.

Baby did not give Kalokhe the details. She could not afford any leaks, but he wouldn't stop pestering her.

'Tell me which wing of the ACB you went to and who the investigating officer is,' he asked her. When he refused to back off, Baby gave him some made-up names.

On the bureau's instructions, Baby contacted Humbre, informing him that she was ready to pay. The meet was set up at a restaurant close to the Satara sessions court on the afternoon of 7 May. Baby travelled to Satara with Satish and Kalokhe. The only piece of luggage that she had brought along for the trip was a large travel bag containing the bribe. The bureau's investigators travelled in another car. The previous day, they had run through the operation with Baby. The bureau had devised a simple signal. Once she had handed over the bribe, Baby was to drape the pallu of her saree over her head. In the heat, the action would go unremarked.

It was also her responsibility to procure and assemble the crucial elements of the operation. The bag and Rs 1 lakh in currency notes were relatively simpler to gather. Authentic currency notes would form the topmost layer of the bag. The bureau coated the notes with phenolphthalein—a white powder that on being touched by the suspected bribe-taker and washed with an alkaline solution turns pink—in anticipation that Humbre's intercessor or hopefully Humbre himself, would inspect them. The bureau also noted down serial numbers of the currency notes and took photos of the notes and the bag for its record. The money would be returned to Baby after the operation was over.

Locating mock currency notes worth Rs 4 lakh proved tricky. In the end, Baby had to settle for toy notes meant as children's playthings. They bore a close enough resemblance to the real thing. Most importantly, they were exactly the right size. The bureau gave Baby a voice recorder the size of an internet dongle and showed her how to use it. It was important that she concealed it in a way that it would clearly record all conversation. Baby wrapped it in a handkerchief that she folded in one palm.

Given the scorching summer heat that greeted Baby in Satara, nothing about her handkerchief was suspicious. The trio sat down to lunch. The bureau's officers fanned out and took positions inside the restaurant and formed a discreet ring around the premises.

Baby called Humbre, who waiting inside the public prosecutor's office in court, discharge papers in hand.

'Have you brought the money?' Humbre asked.

'Yes. I want to speak to the public prosecutor,' Baby said.

Humbre handed the phone over. The prosecutor repeated Humbre's question.

'Yes I have. Will Humbre *saheb* give you the papers now?' Baby asked.

'Yes,' he replied.

'Should I pay him the money now?' Baby said.

'Yes, you can go ahead,' the prosecutor said. He returned the phone to Humbre.

'A friend of mine will meet you outside the restaurant,' Humbre told Baby. 'Hand over the money to him.' He rang off.

The visitors finished their meal and walked back out into the sun. Minutes later, Dhamal pulled up in his car. After the introductions were made, he invited Baby, bag in hand, to step into the car with him. Baby had prepared for this possibility. She knew that if she followed Dhamal into the car, she would vanish from the sight of plainclothes bureau sleuths observing the exchange from a safe distance. 'You must remain within our sight at all times,' they'd told her the day before.

'No, thank you,' she told Dhamal.

Dhamal nodded and rolled down a window. She pushed the bag through it and covered her head with her pallu. It really *was* hot. Dhamal barely had time to open the bag before half a dozen men surrounded his car.

The policemen herded Dhamal to court. He had no time to warn Humbre. Inside the public prosecutor's office, the scene outside the restaurant was recreated, with Dhamal playing Baby's role. The bureau's officers took up positions outside the office with Baby, Kalokhe and Satish watching. They waited for Dhamal to place the bag in Humbre's hands before charging into the room. Humbre fell to the floor in shock. His final words, before the police lead him away, were curses for Baby.

'*Majhi kiti haay jhaali* [I have been disgraced]!' he cried.

Baby later learnt that Humbre had evaded seven previous bribery traps. Local residents had given up hope of ever bringing him to justice. The exploits of 7 May made Baby a celebrity in Satara—for the right reasons this time.

'*Sachai ke liye ooparwaala bhi saath deta hai* [God is on the side of the truth],' she told all those who came to shake her hand.

Eighth was a charm.

## 26

Even though the two forensic reports had ended the investigation, Satara SP Deshmukh was not prepared for how spectacularly Humbre would screw up filing a closure report. He had entrusted Humbre with the investigation because he was the most experienced and decorated officer in the district. Despite murmurs of illegal activity, there was no complaint against Humbre. His record was spotless, not even a departmental inquiry.

No one wanted to touch Humbre's files now that he was gone. The discharge reports gathered dust in his office for a year until Baby moved the sessions court. The police could no longer delay the inevitable.

The police argued desperately to prevent Baby walking free. In one breath it accepted that the substance found in Kanheri was sodium glutamate while in another it claimed that on the day it discovered the substance in Kanheri, mephedrone was classified as a controlled substance under the NDPS Act. Baby, the police argued, had allegedly committed an 'anti-social' offence.

The arguments were like water off Special NDPS Act Judge M.J. Mirza's back. Only two facts mattered—first that the substance wasn't mephedrone and second, even if it had been, Kalokhe's word alone wasn't enough to implicate Baby.

Judge Mirza discharged Baby on 28 August 2017.

### Interminable delay

In the Bombay High Court, the crime branch made excuses to defer arguing its case for resampling and retesting the sample taken from Kalokhe's cupboard. It showed no urgency in having the matter decided conclusively. It was almost as though it did not want to.

The police's lethargy affected the five policemen the most. Sarang, Parte and Mane were still some time away from retiring but would have to serve suspension until the case reached a conclusion. Gaikwad retreated deeper into *vipassana*, spending weeks at a stretch meditating in total silence at the centre in Igatpuri. *Vipassana* had helped ease what should have been a very unpleasant three weeks in jail.

Gokhale had begun writing his memoirs once he was granted bail. A Pune-based publisher, Menaka Prakashan, picked it up and published it in Marathi in 2016. The book, *Kaidi Number C – 14861*, ended with his reinstatement to the police department in 2013. He would wait until the case came to an end to write about subsequent events.

Surviving in Mumbai without a pension or retirement benefits was impossible. For a while, Gokhale rented a flat in a depressing part of the city. Eventually, he gave up and returned to Nashik. A builder had acquired Gokhale's ancestral home and turned it into an apartment complex. Gokhale got a flat on the second floor overlooking the Godavari river.

At Crawford Market, the police commissioners who succeeded Maria lacked the will to intervene. It was a pickle best left for the next guy to deal with.

The high court eventually lost patience with the crime branch for chickening out of arguing and requesting an adjournment on every date. Arguments began in the summer of 2018 after counsels for the defendants demanded an end to the crime branch's delaying tactics.

The crime branch reproduced much of the same arguments it made in the sessions court a year ago. It accused Judge Hejib of miscalculating the fifteen-day span within which it was to apply for resampling and retesting but made one small concession. Assuming that it had exceeded the deadline by one day, the delay 'could be condoned, considering the magnitude, seriousness and gravity of the offences,' it told the high court.

It also argued that the discovery of a suspected drug in the cupboard of a police constable made the case 'exceptional … [and] necessary to ascertain the presence of drug in seizure.'

It accused Gokhale of deliberately drawing a faulty sample of the contraband because he would need to shield Baby from arrest a few weeks later, crediting him with remarkable prescience.

The crime branch also questioned the need for Baby and Kalokhe to store Ajinomoto in such large quantities. The crime branch argued that Baby was a drug peddler, stating, 'She does not conduct any restaurant for using Ajinomoto.' It also claimed that she used Ajinomoto as a 'filler or adulterant' in mephedrone to 'dilute its purity'.

The absence of evidence did not prevent the crime branch from venturing into the realm of pure guesswork. Baby, it argued, had sold Rs 80 lakh worth of gold ornaments to jewellers in Zaveri Bazaar the previous year. Surely she could not have made that kind of money hawking Ajinomoto, which retailed at Rs 40 a kg!

'Thus, it is inferred that the accused is indulging in sale of contraband MD and not sodium glutamate,' the crime branch claimed, 'hence, resampling is necessary.'

The high court agreed with the crime's branch arguments. Justice Prakash D. Naik wrote that the sessions court 'has adopted [a] hyper technical approach' in calculating the fifteen-day deadline for a retest.

'The Special Court has not taken into consideration the entry dated 14th May, 2015 which indicate that the Senior Police Inspector In-charge had received the report on 14th May, 2015,' Justice Naik wrote. He further observed that it was necessary in the interest of justice and for a 'just decision' of the case to permit the crime branch to retest the sample.

He did not comment on whatever motivations Gokhale might have had to draw a 'faulty sample'. The huge quantity of the drug found in Kalokhe's cupboard made this an exceptional case.

Application allowed.

Counsels for Kalokhe, Baby and the five policemen asked that the crime branch draw the samples in their presence for the sake of transparency.

On 28 August 2018, a month after the High Court granted permission for resampling and retesting, the crime branch produced inside courtroom number 44 of the sessions court, the twelve plastic packets found in Kalokhe's police station cupboard. The packets were placed on the wooden table facing the judge's dais where lawyers argued their cases.

In the presence of all the concerned lawyers, the five policemen and court staff, a crime branch officer unsealed each packet. White crystals spilled out on the table every time a packet was unsealed and a uniform sample drawn from it.

After the procedure was concluded, some of the onlookers gathered around the table. The crystals, they thought, looked familiar. There was only one way to say for sure.

They popped some of the spilled crystals into their mouths. Their tongues detected that hard-to-pin-down salty taste of *Indian* Chinese food. An amused whisper filled the courtroom: this is ajinomoto.

The fresh samples were sealed and dispatched by the court to CFSL Chandigarh with a brief description of the case and a request for detailed analysis.

CFSL Chandigarh subjected the samples to exhaustive examinations. The court wanted to know if the samples contained traces of *any* illicit substance.

Between September and December 2018, Dr Deepak Middha, a deputy director at CFSL Chandigarh, subjected the samples to four different physical examinations, nineteen different chemical tests, and two other tests to measure the molecular mass of the samples.

If the samples contained even the most minute traces of amphetamine-type stimulants, barbiturates, benzodiazepines, cannabis products, cocaine, lysergide, mecloqualone, mephedrone, methaqualone and opium derivatives, the tests would find them.

Dr Middha finished his analysis on 11 December 2018 and sent the court his findings: sodium glutamate was detected in all twelve samples!

This time, it *really* was over.

The sessions court received the forensic report on 2 March 2019, a Saturday. It was unsealed in court three days later in the presence of the crime branch, the public prosecutor, the five policemen and their lawyers. Gokhale took an early morning bus from Nashik to reach court on time.

The judge gave the crime branch a month to either file a chargesheet or a closure report citing a lack of evidence to prosecute the policemen.

Now that the case had crumbled, the policemen immediately filed discharge applications. But the court could not pass an order until the crime branch had made a decision.

Unit I had a chargesheet ready. Despite CFSL Chandigarh's report conclusively answering the mephedrone question, Unit I was prepared to persist. There was no doubt that Baby, Kalokhe and Satish had picked up *something* from Samuel at Joshi Vadewale. Baby's CDRs made it clear that the policemen had been in contact with her. Unit I was convinced that its evidence stood a fair chance of surviving a trial.

The crime branch did not honour the sessions court's one-month deadline and requested repeated extensions. It was like a vanquished foe refusing to surrender honourably, determined to stall the victor's march for as long as possible.

No one in Crawford Market wanted to take a decision on the chargesheet. Everything about the case had become a bit of a joke. Internally, the police leadership was candid in admitting that the case was an embarrassment. But no one wanted to be the guy that took the final decision.

In the end, the police arrived at a compromise. Unit I was ordered to drop charges against the policemen. The others would not be spared.

On 17 July, Unit I filed its chargesheet in the sessions court. It had decided to charge Kalokhe, Baby, Satish, Samuel and Padaiyatchi with possessing twenty grams of *charas*, imported liquor and forged documents.

It ceased its quest to prove that the substance in Kalokhe's cupboard was really mephedrone.

'Since sodium glutamate is a white crystalline powder and looks like mephedrone it is mixed into mephedrone by drug peddlers to boost their profits. Since mephedrone is widely consumed we suspect that the seized sodium glutamate had been bought to be mixed into mephedrone,' the crime branch wrote in the chargesheet.

It also admitted defeat in its prosecution against the policemen four years after Kasare had first arrived at that realization. They had maintained contact with Baby before the commission of the alleged offence in her capacity as their informant.

The crime branch further claimed the following:

The arrested policemen were aware that Baby was wanted by the police. Despite being duty-bound to arrest her, they wilfully neglected their duties and remained in constant contact with Baby before and during the commission of the crime. After the crime was committed, the arrested policemen did not arrest her and instead told her to hide and switch off her phone in order to avoid arrest.

In drawing the chapter closed, the crime branch admitted that it had been unable to unearth concrete evidence pointing to the involvement of the policemen in the alleged crime.

'A chargesheet could not be filed against them due to a lack of sufficient evidence. Hence a closure report is being filed.'

The court would take cognizance of the chargesheet on the next hearing of the case, set for 24 July.

Gokhale called me that morning—this time from a number I recognized. He was on a bus to Mumbai. Wind and rain interrupted his speech but he managed to get the message through.

'*Aaj dopahar ko court aa jao. Crime branch ne closure report file kar diya hai* [Come to court in the afternoon. The crime branch has filed a closure report],' he said. Like a man who didn't easily get his hopes up, Gokhale sounded cautious.

He had good reason to be. For unexplained reasons, the court deferred the hearing to 26 July. Gokhale was not crushed. Even in retirement, he stayed occupied. That week, he concluded a two-year-long series of essays on his Facebook page detailing India's drug laws and the dangers of substance abuse. The essays were drawn from his work in the field. His final message to readers was this: 'Be safe, be careful, take care of yourself and your children. I am available 24/7 if you need me.'

Gokhale was back two days later. It was another wet afternoon. The closure report was scheduled to be taken up after the lunch break. But Judge M.S. Mungale regretted that he could not hear the case that day. The court clerk posted the case for 3 August.

Once we were downstairs, Gokhale vented his irritation at another wasted trip. He did not like the idea of another nausea-inducing bus ride to Nashik through the hills of Igatpuri.

'I don't know how I'm going to get home in this rain,' he said as he stepped into the downpour.

It was one of those rare occasions when Gokhale had complained, even though his list of grievances was longer than most.

But he would be back. Vindication was close at hand.

## 27

In truth, the case was doomed to fail the moment Inspectors Ghanvat and Shelke led their convoy out of Khandala police station without a field drug detection kit for mephedrone. A field drug detection kit is not a hundred per cent accurate. Even if the police had one and knew how to use it, there would still be a small margin for error. Used correctly, however, it could at least have told the police that the substance in Kalokhe's travel bags was probably not a drug. But, as already recapped, the Indian police does not have a field detection kit for mephedrone.

The NCB is India's nodal procurement and disbursal agency of drug detection and precursor chemical detection kits to its zonal units, other police organizations and the Indian Coast Guard. It is waiting on a public sector organization in Maharashtra to procure India's first field detection kit for mephedrone.

The answer lies within the corridors of Hindustan Antibiotics Limited (HAL) in Pimpri-Chinchwad, once a hamlet on the outskirts of Pune city and now, a city in its own right.

HAL is a division within the Department of Pharmaceuticals under the Ministry of Chemicals and Fertilizers. For seventy years, it has manufactured bulk medicinal drugs and agricultural products. It is also the exclusive producer of Narcotic Drug Detection Kits, Precursor Chemicals Detection Kits and Ketamine Detection Kits for the NCB.

HAL produced its first field drug detection kit in 1986, precursor detection kit in 1988–89 and a ketamine detection kit in 2011.

The field drug detection kit is a tiffin-box sized rectangular plastic container. Packed inside is a thin rectangular plastic strip with three wells not unlike in a contact lens case, a glass vial, a glass dropper and fifteen labelled glass bottles containing between 10 ml and 20 ml of differently coloured chemicals, called reagents, which are meant to detect cocaine, ephedrine, heroin, marijuana, MDMA, LSD, and other narcotic and psychotropic substances.

The concept is simple. The instruction manual comes printed with a list of drugs, their tailor-made detecting reagents and specific changes in colour that a reaction is expected to produce.

Step-by-step instructions are printed on a flow chart.

For example, when an officer seizes what they suspect to be cocaine, they only need to put a pinch of suspected sample in the well of plastic plate along with the specified reagent provided in the kit. The officer then needs to watch for a change in the colour of the sample. The manual specifies what colour specifies the possible presence of cocaine in the sample. There are only two possible results—positive or negative. The process is the same when the police seizes a drug in liquid form. In such cases, the reaction is conducted in the glass vial.

In 2015, police departments in rural Maharashtra did not have field testing kits and reagents for any drug.

The kits are meant only as a means for rapid and preliminary identification of a suspected drug. Its results are not admissible in court as evidence. Even after the kit detects a drug, the sample still needs to be sent to a forensic lab for confirmatory tests.

As mephedrone became Mumbai's dominant party drug, a new market was emerging for a product over which HAL held a monopoly.

It wrote to the NCB expressing an interest in developing a field detection kit for mephedrone. The Mumbai Police, which was making seizures daily, needed kits urgently.

Government forensic labs in Mumbai and Pune also needed all the help they could get. Performed efficiently, field detection of suspected mephedrone samples could potentially eliminate samples of actual mephedrone from plain cornflour.

The 2015 ban on mephedrone has done little to stanch its production, supply and use. The Mumbai lab continues to receive around fifty suspected mephedrone samples every month. Approximately twenty of twenty-five drug samples received at the Pune lab every month are suspected to be mephedrone. This was before the Mumbai lab sounded an SOS in 2021 and began sending a tenth of its suspected mephedrone samples to Pune.

In 2015, HAL developed a mephedrone field detection kit for the NCB. As per established procedure, the NCB dispatched the kit to the Central Revenues Control

Laboratory (CRCL)—a division of the Central Board of Excise and Customs—for testing. If the kit came through rigorous tests performed by scientists at CRCL, the NCB would place an order with HAL.

It did not.

In the years since, HAL has gone back to the drawing board. In 2022, HAL reopened correspondence with the NCB over a new kit which it plans to submit for testing.

Fingers crossed.

## Inside a forensic lab

The General Analytical and Instrumentation room in a government forensic laboratory buzzes with an incessant mechanical humming. There are banks of tables everywhere—in the centre like a kitchen island and pushed against the walls. The machines that cover every inch of these tables look like nothing a person who isn't a forensic scientist will encounter or even fathom. Blame the obsession of books, TV and cinema with blood spatter analysis and autopsies.

This is the wrong room to look for blood, gore and guns.

The only table that doesn't hold a machine is piled with a sheaf of papers, a landline phone and pens. In drawers where one might expect to find paper clips and sundry staple pins, one would find ziplock plastic pouches of the kind Acid conceals in his phone. Every pouch promises a different treat: chocolatey blobs of *charas*, pungent green clumps of *ganja*, dull white cocaine and brilliant white crystals of pure mephedrone.

The samples arrive at the lab inside sealed envelopes wrapped in a chemical analysis form. A single detail out of place or a signature missing on the form and the envelope is returned to the police constable who comes bearing it.

Whenever possible, the police sends the lab multiple samples from one seizure. The larger the quantity of a substance available to test, the greater the chances of tests detecting traces of a drug or drugs. In any case, scientists prepare homogenous samples for testing by drawing out a pinch from each sample. They have to do this: people dealing in drugs tend to pack the top of stashes with a completely legal adulterant and leave the drug at the bottom.

Analysis of a mephedrone sample begins with testing whether it is soluble in methanol or chloroform. If it is, the scientist proceeds to conduct three colour tests. A good indicator of mephedrone is an orange tinge to the sample when mixed with the Liebermann-Burchard reagent.

The equipment for a colour test in the lab is the same as a field drug detection kit, with only one difference. Instead of a rectangular strip of plastic, the lab uses large blocks of porcelain tiles. The tiles are available in twelve and twenty-four well variants.

Next, the scientist examines a few specimens from the sample under a microscope. Mephedrone crystals are hexagonal.

It is now the turn of the heavy machinery. The sample is tested in the UV-visible spectroscopy machine. This instrument resembles a film projector box. Through a flap on the top of the box, the sample is deposited into a bed illuminated in fluorescent blue light. Once the flap is snapped shut, the instrument exposes the sample to UV light.

Different substances behave differently under UV light to produce distinct and easily identifiable peaks on a graph.

Both in the UV-visible spectroscopy and the High-Performance Thin Layer Chromatography (HPTLC) instrument, the higher the peaks the greater the presence of mephedrone in the sample.

The clincher is the Gas Chromatography-Mass Spectrometry (GC-MS) test, which is conducted inside an instrument the size of a photocopy machine and which groans like a cement mixer. The sample is dissolved in either methanol or chloroform and placed in a glass tube in the instrument's centrifuge. A syringe squirts a reagent into the tube before it spins inside the centrifuge. The GC-MS machine measures the molecular mass of the substance in the tube. Once again, mephedrone is identified by the distinct peaks it leaves on the graph. There is no more accurate test in drug detection. The GC-MS machine is equipped with a library of over two lakh substances. If a sample contains even the most minute traces of mephedrone, a GC-MS test will detect it.

Forensic analysis leaves no room for ambiguity. The tests only report the substances detected in a sample. In samples of mephedrone, the tests usually find baking soda, corn flour, talcum powder or Ajinomoto, which differ only in smell and taste. All these substances are commonly mixed with mephedrone to dilute and cut down its potency. They are also safer to snort than other common adulterants such as turpentine or crushed glass. The human eye has many qualities but telling any of these powders apart with a cursory glance or even a hard stare is not one of them. Unlike a sniffer dog's snout, it cannot be trained either.

The process of communicating results of analysis is also meant to leave no room for ambiguity. Like the station diary at a police station, the Chain of Custody form at a forensic lab maintains precise records of every step the scientist follows, from the time and date a sample enters the lab to the time and date the report is posted to the police. The name of the scientist and duration of every test performed is mentioned on the form. The scientist fills the Chain of Custody form in triplicate: one copy for the lab's records, the second for the police and the third for the court.

Once a report is ready, the dispatch department at the lab takes over from the scientist. Until 2016, government forensic labs in Maharashtra used to send reports in sealed envelopes to the police by Registered AD post. Letters posted by Registered AD typically reach their recipients within a week. But after the police's complaints of delayed reports and allegations of not receiving reports grew unbearable, the labs began dispatching reports by speed post. This alternative gives labs two prongs to refute the police's claims: delivery within two days and live tracking of the letter on the India Post website.

While labs prefer posting the reports, they often find it more convenient to hand them over to the police in person. This is a regular practice in Mumbai, where the volume of drugs seized every day invariably means that at any moment in time, nearly every police station or the ANC is bound to have a sample under analysis. Since a representative of a police station visits the lab with a new sample every few days, it is easier to hand them reports of freshly analysed samples of older cases. The police constable collecting the sample in person is required to sign the Chain of Custody form.

In cases marked priority, the scientist communicates the results of the analysis to the investigation officer by phone as soon as they have finished running all the tests. In urgent cases, the police is known to lean on overworked forensic scientists to prioritize analysis.

A delay of twelve days between analysis being completed and the report reaching the police is possible only if the police delays collecting the report from the lab. A letter dispatched by speed post from Santacruz *will* reach Marine Drive within two working days.

# 28

India's drug prohibition law, the NDPS Act, is a troublesome piece of legislation. It was introduced in the monsoon session of Parliament in 1985 by Janardhana Poojary, the Minister of State for Finance in Rajiv Gandhi's Congress government. A quarter century previously, India had signed the United Nations Single Convention on Narcotic Drugs, 1961. She had had twenty-five years to introduce strong legislation to control the manufacture, supply and consumption of drugs, and discontinue its traditional use of cannabis for anything apart from medical and scientific purposes.

With time running out, US President Ronald Reagan, who had publicly declared a 'war on drugs', exerted tremendous pressure on Gandhi to comply. In the summer of 1985, the NDPS Bill was drafted with minimal consultation with the people it would affect and organizations expected to implement it. Gandhi was determined to pass the Bill in both houses of Parliament and enact it into law before the year ended.

The NDPS Bill proposed rigorous imprisonment for ten years extending to twenty years and a minimum fine of Rs 1 lakh extending to Rs 2 lakh as punishment for drug offences. It proposed to treat drug abusers and drug addicts differently, prescribing a year's imprisonment or a fine or both for consuming or possessing 'hard drugs' like cocaine, morphine or heroin and six months' imprisonment or a fine or both for offences relating to other narcotic drugs and psychotropic substances.

Gandhi's own party colleagues in Parliament had pointed out serious flaws in the Bill.

In the Lok Sabha, Ajay Mushran, the Congress MP from Jabalpur, Madhya Pradesh, said that Section 27, which dealt with small quantities of drugs, was a 'serious lacuna' in the Bill. The NDPS Bill had not defined what amount of a particular drug constituted a small quantity.

'You are opening a Pandora's box for the already corrupt officers ... the definition of the term "small quantity" should not be left to be incorporated in the rules,' warned Mushran, adding that unless the government defined what it meant by a small quantity, there was a high possibility of the law being misused.[81]

He further added:

You are providing for deterrent punishment, but ninety-five per cent of the cases are those where only 13 or 25 grams are found. Your aims and objects are not in conformity with what is provided about the definition of 'small quantity' because ninety-five per cent of cases are going to be left through the mercy of the officers.[82]

Ramashray Prasad Singh, the Communist Party of India's MP from Jahanabad, Bihar, also offered an anecdote to prove his point.

> I saw a tree in the compound of Jahanabad police station. People told me that it was a ganja tree. Now, you may tell us if there would be 30 kg ganja on the tree located in the police station, how [would] the police personnel there, who have to implement the law, implement it? If the police personnel, who have to apprehend the culprits, indulge in such acts, what to say of others?[83]

The government ignored the MPs' pleas to refer the Bill to a select committee for a clause-by-clause analysis and forced it through the monsoon session of Parliament.

The NCB was established a year later as the nodal agency to implement the Act.

The NDPS Act has required amendments to address its many shortcomings. The most significant amendment was made in 2001, when the government defined three different categories of drug quantities—small, commercial and an intermediary one. The severity of punishment was rationalized with the quantity of drugs seized.

---

The NDPS Act is nobody's friend. On one hand, it flips the burden of proof from the police to the person suspected of cultivating, manufacturing, possessing, selling or consuming drugs. A person is presumed to have committed an offence unless and until he can prove the contrary. On the other hand, it provides safeguards to suspects from being falsely implicated. The police can be forgiven for thinking that the Act is stacked in favour of the people they try to prosecute.

It prescribes an exhaustive checklist of steps to be followed by an investigating officer.[84] Neglecting or contravening any of these steps is sufficient grounds for a court to dismiss charges against a suspect before a trial can commence or acquit them after conducting a trial.

Courts insist on strict adherence to all of these provisions. Contravening any of these provisions deprives a person of their fundamental right to life and personal liberty under Article 21 of the Constitution of India.

The case against Samuel and six other men for allegedly smuggling 25 kg of methamphetamine to Mumbai from Punjab in 2009, for instance, collapsed because the NCB did not clearly and unambiguously appraise each suspect of their right to be searched in the presence of a magistrate or gazetted officer. To make matters worse, during the trial at the Mumbai sessions court, the scientist who tested the samples and detected the presence of methamphetamine in them referred to methamphetamine as a narcotic drug instead of a psychotropic drug.

The history books tell of another case from 1994 when the NCB attempted and failed to prosecute nine drug mules from Ethiopia who had flown to Mumbai with capsules of heroin sitting in their stomachs.

The NCB admitted the mules to a hospital and asked a doctor to help them expel the contraband. Every time the mules purged something, a sweeper rummaged through their bed pans for capsules wrapped in black insulation tape. One mule expelled forty-one capsules. The hospital maintained a careful inventory of each capsule expelled by each mule and the NCB tested them with a field drug-detection kit. They indicated the presence of heroin.

That's when the NCB committed the first of its missteps. Its investigating officer took twenty-one days to send the samples to the forensic science laboratory for analysis. An unforgivable delay which raised suspicions that the NCB had tampered with the samples while they were stored in its custody.

When the case went to trial, the NCB did not examine either the sweeper who had cleaned the bed pans or the resident doctor he had shown the recovered capsules to. Instead it examined the doctor in-charge of the ward who had not been present when the mules had expelled their contraband.

The sessions court convicted the mules. The mule who survived after expelling forty-one capsules of heroin from his belly was sentenced to three years in prison. However, the Bombay High Court, where the mule challenged his conviction, did not ignore the NCB's contraventions of the mandatory provisions of the Act. The NCB had not proved that it had separately stored the capsules expelled by each mule. In such a scenario the agency could not prove beyond reasonable doubt that the forty-one capsules had originated from the stomach of the aggrieved mule.

The High Court overturned the conviction. The NCB approached the Supreme Court but did not succeed in its appeal.[85]

## Theories and motives

The cases in Satara and Mumbai would never have gone to trial.

Neither Kasare nor Humbre was able to establish that Baby had obtained her supply from Rukhma Industries in Jalgaon via Samuel. They had both followed up on the lead. But in Jalgaon, they found the facility sealed shut. There was no one to question.

Worse still, drivers Tiwari and Thevar denied knowing Samuel. They did know each other though. Both men had worked a series of daily wage jobs before training as drivers and raising their families above poverty. Tiwari was employed as a driver to the pharmaceuticals executive Vikas Puri. In time, Tiwari saved enough money to set up a used car dealership.

Rukhma Industries director Nitin Chinchole, a friend of Puri, offered Tiwari a side gig. The job was simple: drive to Jalgaon, pick up sacks of chemicals, ask no questions and deliver them to Puri in Mumbai. Puri placed orders of several hundred kilograms at a time. That required more than one car. Tiwari sounded out Thevar. But Thevar wouldn't do long distance trips.

On 13 December 2013, Tiwari drove to Jalgaon with two friends to pick up a consignment from Chinchole. After loading the sacks in the trunk and turning towards Mumbai, the men stopped at a restaurant at 8.30 p.m. Tiwari claims that the DRI arrested him there, denying the agency's claims that it nabbed him in Jalgaon.

The same morning, Thevar left Mumbai on a short trip. He was accompanying a friend to a wedding in Surat, Gujarat. Thevar could not explain to the DRI why he had taken a considerable detour via Dhule in north-east Maharashtra instead of simply hugging the coast and driving north.

At 8.30 p.m., Thevar claimed to have exited a restaurant after dinner when the DRI swooped in on him. Contesting his version, the agency claimed that Thevar too was in Jalgaon that night. Sacks of ketamine were discovered in the car's trunk.

Two years later, a detective from Unit I questioned both men in Jalgaon central prison. They were shown pictures of Baby, Satish, Kalokhe, Samuel and Padaiyatchi. Neither man knew who they were.

Did Puri and/or Chinchole manufacture mephedrone illegally? No, said Tiwari.

This was the second time Samuel had stitched up someone. The Jalgaon connection was the final lead with Unit I. With it went any hope of discovering the origin of the contraband.

In 2019, the Mumbai sessions court convicted Tiwari and Puri and sentenced them to ten and thirteen years imprisonment, respectively. Thevar was acquitted.

There were times in the four years that he waited for his name to be cleared when Gokhale wanted the cases to go to trial just to savour the satisfaction of seeing them collapse spectacularly.

There are discrepancies in the role attributed to him by the Marine Drive police station during the search of Kalokhe's cupboard. While the FIR quotes Gokhale as confirming that the white crystals recovered were mephedrone, he claims that he had only voiced his speculation that the powder could either be mephedrone or Ajinomoto.

The Mumbai sessions court did not venture to speculate why the crime branch arrested Gokhale and the four other policemen on 29 May 2015 despite knowing by then that the substance was not mephedrone. That meant Baby had not committed any crime and the five policemen had not neglected their duties by maintaining contact with her. She was, after all, their informant.

Each policeman has his own theory on why the crime branch delayed ending their ordeal.

The police would also have had a hard time proving that Baby had been in possession of the substance immediately prior to Kalokhe. The travel bags and the cupboard both belonged to Kalokhe. There was no tangible evidence to prove that Baby had ever been in possession of the substance. The police would have had to demonstrate to the court that Baby once had control over the substance and had consciously possessed it.

How does an investigator even go about proving 'conscious possession' of a drug when it is not recovered from the clothes or belongings of a person but those of her accomplice?

The crime branch also did not supply any compelling reasons for not charging Baby's older son Girish and his friend Sachin Dhayalkar for whisking her away from Worli and keeping her hidden for five weeks. Surely they had a much more active role in helping Baby evade arrest than the five policemen?

The crime branch would also have had a hard time proving that it had actually detained Baby at the toll plaza in Panvel after intercepting the bus she was travelling in. The chargesheet it submitted in court does not contain the statement of any witness to the detention. Surely someone among the driver, conductor, passengers and toll plaza employees would have noticed the police unseating four people from the bus and whisking them away in their jeeps?

This leaves us with two questions.

First, did Baby deliberately purchase Ajinomoto from Samuel confident that neither Kalokhe nor the police would be able to identify mephedrone?

And if so, why would she do that?

The first one remains unanswered. No trials mean that the police will never have the opportunity to prove its theories.

As to the second, Baby would never pass on 150 kg of actual mephedrone to Kalokhe while also sending the police to his doorstep. Not only would that make the operation absurdly expensive, but the police would also confiscate and eventually destroy the contraband. No, Baby would never knowingly incur a loss.

She won't admit to anything though. So my guess is as good as anyone else's.

However, I do know this: Baby never forgives an injustice.

# Epilogue

In 2020, when I first mentioned to Baby my idea of writing a book about the case, I had no idea how she would respond. We'd kept in touch intermittently after that first interview in 2015. On the few occasions that she did call in the interim, it was either because she had news to give or needed something done.

Once she asked if I had what it took to go undercover to 'expose' two scandals in her neighbourhood: the sale of drugs outside Worli Dairy and the alleged insurance fraud by a garage owner. *'Tum yeh dono kaam karogey toh tumhara bohot bada naam banega!* [These stories will make you famous!]' On another occasion, she claimed that Kalokhe was operating a matka betting ring in Worli.

I didn't follow up on either lead.

I would have probably not learnt of the Satara sessions court's decision to discharge her from the case as quickly as I did had she not called me that same night. Beating every other reporter to the story the next day felt good.

But the last time we had met was at a *bhel poori* stall outside the sessions court in July 2018. Her face was creased deeper with worry than I'd ever seen.

She had just been to see her lawyer and hadn't come back fortified with good news. Handing Satish, her companion that evening, some money, she sent him out of earshot to another *bhel poori* stall. Then she offered to buy me a plate of geela bhel.

'*Tum bohot patle ho gaye ho. Theek se khaate nahi kya? Ya bimaar ho gaye they?* [You have become very skinny. Do you not eat well? Or were you ill?]' she inquired.

Neither, I told her, but she wasn't really paying attention. She kept wiping her sweaty face with the pallu of her saree while scanning the crowd, street and traffic.

Satish finished his *bhel* and returned to her side. I used that moment to ask Baby how she had been staying busy since her discharge.

'*Maine haapus bechne ka dhanda shuru kiya hai* [I have begun selling alphonso mangoes],' she said.

That wasn't all. She opened the picture gallery on her smartphone and showed me thumbnails of tinier fish.

'*Main WhatsApp pe paplet* [pomfret] *ka order leti hoon* [I take orders for pomfret on WhatsApp],' she said, smiling.

As mother and son hopped into a taxi, something she'd said in 2015 came back to me: *Mereko smartphone chalane ko nahi aata* [I don't know how to use a smartphone].

She had changed her phone number and address by the time I decided to look her up again in the second half of

# Epilogue

2020. The former was easy to acquire. It took a few seconds and many prompts, but she finally placed my voice as that reporter boy. She didn't begin with hello.

'Tell me why my name is on TV these days?' I did not know and did not receive time to respond.

'Why is my name on the news with Rhea Chakraborty? *Yeh log mera naam abhi kyun uchhal rahe hain? Unko pata nahi kya mera case khatam ho gaya hai?* [Why are they bringing my name up again? Don't they know that my case is over?]' she said.

The arrest of the young actor that summer by the NCB on charges of allegedly supplying drugs to her boyfriend, the deceased actor Sushant Singh Rajput, had given a Marathi news channel an excuse to dust off a story on 'Mumbai's Drug Queens' from its archives. Compared with the vilification that Chakraborty had to endure, Baby should count herself lucky. But she wasn't in the mood for small mercies that day. She did, however, agree to meet me a few days later and after some persuasion, agreed with my proposal to write the book. I told her that I would call again soon to arrange for interviews.

Fine, she said. After that, she didn't answer my phone calls for an entire year.

🐱

My best chance was to seek her out in court. That opportunity arrived at the Esplanade Court in the first week of December 2021. She couldn't stay too long to chat that day but promised to continue our conversation later.

'*Tum ko jab mangta hai ghar pe aa jaana. Par pehle phone karna* [Come home whenever you want. But call first],' she had said.

Baby took another month to come good on that offer.

She had moved into a chawl barely five hundred metres away from Siddharth Nagar. I'd first visited her new home in September 2020. Her directions were just as confusing as on that rainy afternoon in Siddharth Nagar five years previously. For some infuriating reason, she wouldn't just tell me the name of her building.

'It's on Worli Naka [junction], right opposite the State Bank of India branch,' she said.

I did not find it.

Baby stayed on the phone while I crossed three of five roads which meet at the junction. '*Arre, mereko tum dikh rahe ho. Thoda peeche aao* [I can see you. Walk back a few paces],' she said.

I stood at the intersection feeling like a lost marionette.

'*Arre, oopar dekho* [Look up]!'

I looked up at a semi-circular chawl building and spotted Baby waving at me from the first floor balcony. A board at the entrance identified it as Bhiwandiwala building.

I had no trouble locating it a year later. The building resembled a smaller version of the curving LIC building in Churchgate. It sat on a boulevard—a road to the working-class BDD chawls on the left and another to Lower Parel railway station on the right. The pavement below the building was a mess of *vada paav*, *pani poori* and sandwich stalls, beggars and squatters. Denim pants, *samosas* and gold jewellery sat on shop displays on the ground floor. I spotted a woman in her fifties, sitting at the entrance hawking vials of lipstick, hair bands, hair clips and cheap jewellery.

There was a curving wooden staircase with uneven and chipped boards leading upstairs. Baby's room was on the first floor. Like all chawl buildings, homes were lined up on the front balcony, overlooking the deafening cacophony below. A one-foot-tall rat-door guarded the threshold of Baby's room. A Wi-Fi router was placed on the door frame. Inside, Baby sat idly on a bed by the right-side wall below large framed pictures of Lord Krishna and of her sons and grandchildren. On a table by the bed was a desktop computer. A wall shelf was drilled into the wall above, and it held a small pile of books.

A flat-screen TV was mounted on the left-side wall painted in aquamarine patterns that could either be waves, moss or cabbages. The only pieces of furniture were a couple of chairs facing the TV, a small chest of drawers besides the door and a cupboard next to the bed.

A foldable wooden staircase at the far end of the room led upstairs to a mezzanine floor where Baby's grandchildren read, slept, or stayed glued to their phones. Below the children's bedroom was the kitchen, separated from the living room by a thick beige screen painted with a flowerpot and floor-length curtains. A barbell and set of dumbbells were stacked at the foot of the screen.

An open door at the rear of the kitchen led to another smaller balcony, which looked down to a spacious tree-lined playground ringed on three sides by rows of cars. They reduced the playground to a box, making overarm cricket impossible. A temple accounted for the rest of the backyard. Baby asked to me to wait for her on a row of benches placed outside the temple's sanctum. But she was in too much pain to climb down the stairs. She asked me to come upstairs instead.

Despite an unusually chilly January evening, Baby was dressed in a nightgown. Oil shone off her limbs. Its vapours cloaked her in a pungent heat shield. Her older son, Girish, roamed around shirtless. A large portrait of his mother covered his left pectoral muscle and another equally large portrait of Lord Krishna covered the right.

In a pan, Dipti was gently frying freshly plucked green peas. Once done, she filled a stainless steel bowl with the oily pods and set down the bowl and an empty polythene bag on the bed between Baby and I. 'Please eat,' she said.

Baby sat at full stretch, with one leg resting on a plastic JOYO ottoman and another tucked beneath her. The ottoman had a white bottom and a bright pink seat. Slowly and painfully she switched one leg on and off the ottoman every few minutes. The smallest movement caused twinges of pain on her face.

Sciatica had severely restricted her movements and activities. Surmounting the staircase was agony; climbing up the hill, inconceivable. Her doctor had advised surgery to alleviate some of the pain, but surgery scared her.

At least thrice a week, Baby visited an Ayurveda practitioner close by for an hour-long *panchakarma* session. The treatment attempts to restore balance to a diseased human body by expelling toxins through every orifice using a series of different oils. For three hours every week, therapeutic oils massaged into her legs coaxed the pain away. It returned the moment she stepped onto the foot of her building staircase.

Baby was desperate for a cure. Before turning to Ayurveda, she had tried electrotherapy treatment. But even zapping her aching nerves with mild electric charges did not give her long-lasting relief. She could no longer walk from the front door to the kitchen without having to sit down to rest.

'*Mereko zyaada time baithne ko nahi hota hai. Aap ko kuch pata hai kya sciatica ka ilaaj?* [I cannot sit down for too long. Do you know any cure?]' she asked me.

# Epilogue

I'd always mixed up sciatica and spondylitis. Naturally, I did not make a suggestion.

'Sorry madam, *par main doctor nahi hoon* [I'm not a doctor],' I replied.

I offered to ask someone who might know better.

The peas, vanishing rapidly, were delicious: a gift from a neighbour's farm. Baby ate them as much on her doctor's advice as for their sweetness.

'*Khao na. Khatam hone ko aaya. Maine hi poora khatam kar diya* [Please eat or they will be over. They're almost gone. I've eaten most of them],' she said.

In between munching on peas, Baby divided her attention between two smartphones. On one, she scrolled through WhatsApp, and on the other she watched a video for a newly-opened saree showroom.

Dipti returned from the kitchen to tip some more fried pods into the bowl. She sat down beside her mother-in-law and for the next quarter hour, the women watched an online recipe for a *chutney* that Baby was craving.

The video ended.

'*Ab poocho tum ko kya poochna hai. Main sab bataungi* [Ask me what you want to. I will tell you everything],' she said.

I ran through some of the allegations in the police's chargesheets.

'*Apan chor hai kya? Apan kuch galat kiye hain kya? Maine ghar powder bech ke nahi banaya. Mereko jagah bechne ka bohot interest hai* [Am I a thief? Have I done anything wrong? I have not built my homes with drug money. I am interested in selling property],' she said, 'I have been very lucky dealing in real estate. *Maine paisa banaya hai. Main nahi bolti ki nahi banaya hai* [I don't deny that I have made money].'

She set the peas and phones aside.

'The police prepared a thirty-year record of my life and did not find a single drug transaction. If I had made my money selling powder, was the police sleeping for thirty years? *Woh kya taali bajaake baithe they?* [Were they clapping their hands?]' Baby smacked her palms together to punctuate her point.

Then, she went back to her bowl of peas.

'*Aap ke family mein koi brahman hai jo kundali banake deta hai? Aap ka koi khaas nahi hai kya? Mummy ka? Papa ka?* [Do you have a priest in your family who prepares horoscopes? Does your mother or father have a priest?]' she asked.

'Why?' I asked.

'*Mereko takleef ho raha hai. Maine socha kundali mein pata chalega itni takleef kyun ho rahi hai aur uska kya ilaaj hai* [I am in constant pain. If I have my horoscope made I will know what is wrong and I can fix it],' she said.

I asked for two days' time.

🐱

Everyone but for Baby and Girish was at a wedding when I visited two days later. Baby could not skip a *panchakarma* session. She rested her massaged legs on the ottoman. Girish lounged in a chair by the bed watching the India Maharajas take on the Asia Lions in the Legends League Cricket 2022 T20 tournament. Baby did not bat an eyelid when Tillakaratne Dilshan middled the first delivery of the innings back at Stuart Binny, who dove to catch the ball without breaking his stride. The camera panned to the captain of the India Maharajas, a delighted Nikhil Chopra.

## Epilogue

I gave Baby the phone number of a priest in Andheri. For her sciatica, I asked if she had tried alternately applying heat and ice packs. She had but that hadn't helped.

'*Tumko jo poochne ka hai poocho* [Ask me what you want],' she said.

Her claim from two days ago of the police not finding a single instance of her selling drugs did not square with her arrest in 2001 for alleged possession of heroin.

'There are people in my family who have always been jealous of me. They framed me. I was called to Worli ANC one day and told that brown sugar was found on me,' she said.

Over time, Baby claimed, she had come to suspect Kalokhe's hand in her arrest.

'*Pyaar mohabbat tha hamara. Abhi peeche se mera baja raha hai mereko kya maloom?* [We were in love. How would I know that he was betraying me?] I didn't know then. I am only now finding out about it,' she said. '*Poocho tum ko jo bhi poochna hai. Main tum ko poora madad karungi* [Ask me what you want. I will help you with everything].'

Baby spoke in uncontrolled torrents but retained enough composure to stop short of saying anything even remotely self-incriminating. In her version of the story, Kalokhe had inserted himself into her road trip in March 2015. She was holidaying in blissful ignorance while Kalokhe plotted behind her back.

'But you see, his plan wasn't successful,' she said.

And what about meeting with Samuel in Pune?

'I don't know who Samuel is. I have nothing to do with Samuel. When I was in the crime branch's custody, I was shown the picture of a man and told that he knows me. I'm sure the police tortured him to say that,' she said.

She answered the question of the mephedrone mystery with a question of her own.

'Why did the police register a case when they didn't have a field testing kit? And then why did they say that they had found Meow Meow? *Bohot bada banaya unhone Baby aur Meow Meow. Arre kaunsa Meow Meow* [They made a deal big of the case. But where was the drug?],' she said.

Baby could afford to say that. The case against her in the Esplanade Court is years away from going to trial. The cases of allegedly supplying mephedrone to students in Worli and Vasai are likely to result in acquittals since they were registered before consuming, possessing and selling the drug became a punishable offence.

All that remained at the time was her appeal before the Appellate Tribunal for Forfeited Property in New Delhi for the return of one car, a dozen homes in Siddharth Nagar and the control of her bank accounts.[86] The holiday home in Malavali was already back with her. But relaxing weekends at the bungalow with her grandchildren felt like pleasant memories from another life.

Now that she rarely left Mumbai anymore, Baby decided to slap on a fresh coat of paint and lease out the bungalow. No self-respecting realtor would allow a property to stay empty.

As I prepared to leave, Baby fretted over an unavoidable trip to Malavali she had to make in two days. '*Poora din baithna padega ek jagah mein* [I will have to sit in one place all day],' she said, her face curling in the anticipation of pain.

Someone would have to supervise the workers and it won't be her sons. Baby only relied on herself to get a job done perfectly. Inflamed nerves wouldn't stop her.

# Epilogue

*Kanheri, seven years later.*

Kalokhe never opened up to me the way Baby did. The closest I ever came to speaking to him was one afternoon in Esplanade Court in December 2021.

I took a seat in courtroom 37 by half past eleven. The lowest rung in the city's criminal justice system has the air of a faded cathedral. The ceiling seems to stretch on forever. The walls are adorned with imposing portraits of bewigged British magistrates who once commanded the bench below. Four rows of twenty-foot-long pew-like benches carved from single logs of wood seat appellants, defendants, police personnel and journalists. Five minutes are enough to cause a sore bottom.

A reverent hush filled the room. A police constable deputed to impose silence flew from his perch by the witness box every time a mobile phone was extracted from a pocket. Anyone who committed the sin of forgetting to switch their phone to silent mode was punished with confiscation.

The cause list pinned to a green baize noticeboard outside the courtroom stated that 'Police Case PW 3700594/2019 DCB CID Unit 1 vs Dharmaraj Baburao Kalokhe' was number 40 on the day's board.

Additional Chief Metropolitan Magistrate Sudhir B. Bhajipale rushed through the first half dozen cases in five minutes. Baby was late. I had no idea if Kalokhe would attend. I took a seat in the middle of the second row, directly in the eyeline of the magistrate.

Around noon, Baby walked in accompanied by a man dressed in a dark blue shirt tucked into a pair of neatly ironed black trousers. They squeezed into the far end of my bench. Baby made a silent gesture of recognition. Kalokhe, who was seated two, perhaps three backpack breadths away from me, remained stock still, his attention focused on the bench.

As the court started to fill so did my end of the bench, which had been empty until then. I kept shuffling to my right to make room for new entrants until I was shoulder to shoulder with the unsmiling man.

The bailiff called out case number 40. Kalokhe and Baby shuffled out of their seats, stood before the bench and raised their hands when the bailiff read out their names. The magistrate nodded in satisfaction and the bailiff nodded in dismissal. No business would be transacted this day.

Afterwards, while Baby and I chatted downstairs, Kalokhe hung around a few feet behind her in stiff formality. He ignored me when I said hello and made no effort to participate in the mostly one-sided conversation—not even when Baby referred repeatedly and agitatedly to him.

'It's bad enough that the police is still harassing me. But how can they continue to harass one of their own?' Baby said.

The look of disinterest on Kalokhe's face didn't change. He came to life when Baby said that she had to go. She had business elsewhere. He walked away to where his silver Royal Enfield Bullet was parked. The engine kick-starting to life momentarily drowned out Baby mid-flow. Kalokhe brought the bike over, refused to make eye contact with me and kept the engine running in wordless impatience.

I asked Baby if she could persuade Kalokhe to speak to me, but she pretended as though she hadn't heard me. She climbed behind Kalokhe and placed one hand on his blue-shirted shoulder. The bike roared away.

#  Epilogue

Only a cold call would do now. Baby wouldn't tell me where Kalokhe was. My friends in the police department weren't sure if he'd retired or not. The only way to know for sure was to go to Kanheri.

In the first week of February I contacted Kalokhe's brother-in-law Popat Veer. Veer confirmed that Kalokhe was in Kanheri. His mother Anusuya, who was in her late eighties, had passed away. Kalokhe had come down to Kanheri for a fortnight with his wife and children.

I hired a car in Pune and drove to Satara one Sunday morning. Veer lives in Sangvi, a village situated amidst sugarcane and jowar fields 4 km off the Mumbai–Bengaluru Highway. The closest town is Shirwal, where buses disgorge tourists by the dozen into Shriram Vada Pav for its eponymous *vada paav*, *missal paav* and *poha*.

Veer was just as friendly as I'd remembered him to be seven years ago. The last time I'd visited Sangvi, locals had readily pointed out the home of the 'arrested policeman's sister'.

Back then, Veer's and his wife Baidabai's faces were lined with worry. For Anusuya, not so much for Kalokhe.

She was found dazed and wandering around Kanheri after the police took Kalokhe away. Veer and Baidabai rushed to Kanheri and ferried her to the nearest hospital. Anusuya's blood pressure had shot up to dangerous levels. The next day, Kalokhe's brother Bhanudas came from Pune and admitted her to an Army hospital there.

When I visited Veer and Baidabai five days later, Zimbabwe's clash with India in the ICC Men's Cricket World Cup was playing on their TV. Veer took the only chair in the living room while Baidabai and her older sister Vimal

Chavan (56) sat on a carpet on the floor. Neither sister could pronounce mephedrone or shed much light on Kalokhe.

'He was always a silent boy, and knowing him, we could never imagine that he would be involved in criminal activities,' Vimal had said.

Kalokhe's visits to Kanheri had become much less frequent after he joined the police department in 1985.

'We do not know much about his wife and children,' she had said.

Veer, who had worked in Mumbai's textile mills in the 1980s and participated in workers' agitations, had been unaware that Kalokhe's chief responsibility in Mumbai was to gather intelligence on protests.

'I have travelled to Mumbai several times but never met him there,' he had said, glancing first at the score and then his wife, before adding, 'It is shameful to admit, but the truth is that members of this family do not stay in touch with each other the way they should.'

Little had changed since then. Veer's communication with Kalokhe was still sporadic.

'Dharma didn't call me after the police arrested him,' Veer said. He had learnt of the arrest from a friend in the police department in Mumbai and rushed to Khandala police station. It was the first time in more than two years that he had heard from or about his brother-in-law.

'Dharma rarely visits. He is never over for Raksha Bandhan or Bhaubeej. He has never brought his wife and children home,' Baidabai said.

Veer attended every hearing in Satara court. He brought him food, a change of clothes and news from home. He liaised with his lawyers. But not once did he receive an explanation from Kalokhe.

## Epilogue

'We do not know what his life in Mumbai is like. We learnt about Baby and Dharma's affair with her only after he was arrested,' he said.

Veer's responsibility ended after Kalokhe was released on bail. He had seen Kalokhe only in intervals of two years since then.

But now he was back.

'I don't have his phone number. But if you go to Kanheri right now you should find him. I met him two days ago,' he said.

We drove past large fields for over a dozen kilometres. Rows of sunflowers winked from the mass of dusty green foliage in bright blurs. A bus stop stood at the mouth of a lane that veered off the main road towards Kanheri.

Once inside, a gradually inclining road to the left led to Kalokhe's home. Just like that last time, everyone I asked for directions in this village of around two thousand inhabitants was helpful.

Seven years ago, the large rectangular house with the signboard reading 'Kalokhe BB' on a window grill, was empty. The front and rear doors were bolted shut and the windows fastened close from the inside with a brown cord. The house stood forlorn in its small yard, ringed off from its neighbour by a waist-high concrete fence.

That morning I had found Jagannath Pawar some distance away from the village, leading his cows to a pasture. He stopped walking when I caught up to him but when I mentioned Kalokhe, he took off again and didn't look back.

The only person willing to speak to me was Kalokhe's drunk neighbour, Ashok Gadhe. His eyes were worryingly bloodshot and speech a little too slurred for that time of day. Gadhe had displayed a fierce loyalty towards Kalokhe that morning. Nearly twenty years ago, Gadhe used to drive an autorickshaw in Mumbai after Kalokhe helped him acquire a driver's licence. Gadhe had given up after eight years in the big city but the sense of indebtedness towards Kalokhe *dada* [older brother] remained.

'Had *dada* asked me to keep his luggage, I would have taken it too—no questions asked,' he told me.

There was no need to seek out Pawar and Gadhe now. Two cars were parked in Kalokhe's front yard and the door was open. His brother Bhanudas, an ex-Army man and retired policeman, came to the front door at the sight of our parked car. The first shoots of grey hair were visible on his bare head. The expression on his face was unfriendly. Bhanudas asked me who I was, where I'd come from and why I was looking for Kalokhe. I told him.

'Dharma has gone to immerse our mother's ashes,' he said.

I asked if I should wait for his return.

'I can't say when he will be back. Could be late evening or night,' Bhanudas said. He wouldn't be any more specific.

I sat on the fence wondering what to do next while Bhanudas retreated to make a phone call. I heard my name and business being whispered in Marathi. The whispering grew clearer as Bhanudas approached the car and reeled off the car's registration number into the phone and hurried inside. The driver discreetly beckoned to me.

'He is clearly suspicious. You told him that you have come from Mumbai but my car has a Pune registration number,' he said.

Bhanudas returned and invited me inside. He sat on a cot below a framed picture of his father, holding a piece of paper and a pen. A set of curtains behind us concealed other rooms and voices.

Bhanudas noted down my name and phone number.

'I will give this to Dharma when he returns and ask him to call you,' he said.

He wouldn't give me a phone number.

'I will ask Dharma to call you,' he repeated, more firmly this time.

I was being dismissed.

Once we had cleared Kanheri, I told the driver what had happened inside the house.

'I don't think he will call you,' he said.

'Why is that?' I asked.

'If he had done nothing wrong, he would have asked to speak to you on the phone. He would want to explain his side of the story. And the brother would have given you the phone number,' he said.

The hostility we had just encountered, the driver continued, was unusual.

'If he has something to hide,' he said, 'he will not call you.'

He was right. The call never came.

---

'*Accha, mereko sun ne mein aaya aap Kalokhe ke ghar me gaye they. Aap mere se bohot kuch baatein chupaate ho. Mereko aap pe gussa aaya bohot. Aap ko kuch batana nahi chahti hai main* [I have heard that you went to Kalokhe's home. You hide a lot of things from me. I was very angry at you. I don't want to tell you anything].'

It had been nearly two months since I'd last met Baby and more than a month since I'd been to Kanheri. It seemed that while I hung around his house, Kalokhe wasn't far away.

'*Usne mereko aap ka photo aur recording bheja. Mereko poocha ki woh kyun aaya tha. Mereko toh pata hi nahi tha ki aap udhar gaye they* [He sent me your photo and recording. He asked me why you had come. I didn't even know that you had gone there],' she said.

'*Kitna ganda ganda gaali diya! Bohot ganda ganda gaali diya! Bacche ke saamne jhooth nahi bolegi main!* [He swore at you a lot! I won't lie in front of my kids!]' she said. Dipti and her children Saurabh and Sayali were in the kitchen. They were out of sight behind the drawn curtains but not out of earshot.

It was impossible to get a word in.

'*Dekho main jitna aap ko support kar rahi hai na woh log utna support nahi karengey.* [He will not cooperate with you as much as I have],' she said.

Baby stopped speaking momentarily when one of her phones rang. Crank call.

'*Udhar jaane ka hi nahi. Mereko accha nahi lagta hai agar kisika bura hua. Aap agar mereko poochte they na toh main aap ko yehi bolti thi ki jao mat udhar* [Do not go there. I do not like to hear anyone being abused. If you had asked me I would have told you not to go there],' she said.

Another phone call, this time from a tenant with a broken water pipe. It was not a long conversation.

'*Main kya baat pe naraaz ho gayi ke aap ne mereko bataya nahi, saamne se aisa woh logo ne mereko bheja, thoda kaharab laga. Baaki kuch nahi* [I was angry that you didn't inform me that and that they sent me your photos. I felt bad, nothing else],' she said.

She was done and returned to her phones. I tried to explain that a part of my job was to contact Kalokhe for a comment. But with a contact list open on one phone and Truecaller on another, she was preoccupied.

That evening, she sat comfortably on a chair by the bed. There was no evidence of even the slightest discomfort nor traces of pungent oils. JOYO, the plastic ottoman, had been banished to a corner of the room. Was her sciatica cured?

She put the phones aside and dropped her voice to a whisper.

'*Dus lakh* [One million rupees].' Baby was barely audible as she uttered these words, as though afraid they might reach listening ears beyond the curtains. She sprang out of the chair and paced around the room in quick, energetic steps until she was almost a blur of purple nightgown.

'*Yeh dekho!* [Look at this!]' she said with every loop.

After four circuits of the room she returned to the chair.

'*Zindagi mein ek vakil, ek baniya, ek baal kaatne waala naai, ek doctor aur ek dost. Zindagi mein paanch aadmi apne ko agar sahi mile na insaan kidhar dhokha nahi khaata hai* [As long as a person has a lawyer, a shopkeeper, hair dresser, doctor and friend by his side, he will never be cheated in his life],' she said.

This time, a friend had helped.

Back when she had nothing, Baby was a housemaid at the Opera House flat of a wealthy doctor. Like Baby's neighbours and friends in Worli, the doctor too had kept her distance after Baby went to jail.

'*Phir sab ko yakeen aa gaya. Abhi sab log "Hi Baby! Hi Baby!" karte hain* [Much later, everyone was convinced that I was innocent. Now they all say hi],' she said.

The doctor came around too. She wrote Baby a referral for Hinduja Hospital in Mahim. Deep tissue laser therapy could help with her sciatic pain. But it wouldn't be cheap.

'The doctor was shocked when I told her how much it would cost,' she said. The doctor was willing to help her out, at the most, with a few thousand rupees.

No need, Baby said. She had it covered.

The pain was excruciating.

'*Laser laganey se nass sunn ho jaata tha par phir bhi kitna dard hua* [The laser deadens sensation in the nerves but the therapy was still very painful],' she said.

'*Ek jhopda becha par mast ho gayi main!* [I had to sell one room but I feel great now!]' she said, '*Abhi main bhaag rahi hoon!* [I am running around now!]'

A blare of motorcycle horns and whooping from the street below caught Baby's attention. It sounded like a procession. She rushed out the door to the balcony while the cheering bikers roared away. Her doctor had advised her three months' bed rest.

'*Hinduja mein yeh pata chala ki woh paise waalo ka hai. Garibon ka nahi hai* [Only the rich can afford treatment at Hinduja Hospital. It is not a place for the poor],' she said.

'*Dus lakh.*'

She opened her mouth once more in silent intonation.

'*Ek hi jhopda bechna pada. Mera pandhra–solah hai* [I only had to sell one room. I have 15–16 more],' she said.

# Acknowledgements

To begin at the beginning, I am grateful to have trained in journalism at *The Indian Express*'s school, Express Institute of Media Studies. The Express way of journalism is a lesson for life. I owe an immense debt of gratitude to N.P. Singh, Shailaja Bajpai and Purnima Singh, the three pillars of the institute and especially to Shailaja ma'am, without whose gentle encouragement none of this would have been possible.

I have to thank the editors during my eight-year stint at the *Express*—Rajkamal Jha, Unni Rajen Shanker, P. Vaidyanathan Iyer, Shaji Vikraman, Sagnik Chowdhury, Shalini Langer, Amrita Dutta, Uma Vishnu, Paromita Chakrabarti, Smita Nair, Kavitha Iyer, Mayura Janwalkar, Nirupama Subramanian and Zeeshan Shaikh. Time and again Nirupama ma'am has provided counsel when I needed to hear it the most. Words cannot express Smita's contributions to my life. She is my idol.

# Acknowledgements

Giving a story the *Express* treatment means going all in. I was fortunate to work on this story alongside ace reporters Gautam Mengle, Megha Sood, Rashmi Rajput, Rohit Alok and Meghana Yelluru. The company of Vasant Prabhu, former chief photographer at the *Express*' Mumbai bureau, while chasing this story in Satara in summer 2015 made for one hell of a road trip. The incredible Shivani Naik, composer of poetic intros, was always available on the other side of the office cubicle.

There are two people who recognized, much before I did, just how remarkable the interview Baby gave to the *Express* in October 2015 was. Kavitha parsed meaning from my garbled and fawning account of that meeting while senior photojournalist Prashant Nadkar captured, what is to me, the defining portrait of Baby. He got her to open up in a way I couldn't have managed on my own.

Mohamed Thaver and Sadaf Modak delivered that crucial initial push. I am fortunate to have had them as sounding boards throughout.

Sagar Rajput was the right man to have in my corner during a few tight spots.

The greatest boost, by far, was my agent Anish Chandy taking a chance on a first-time writer and allowing me the luxury of having to only worry about getting the story right.

I am grateful to Bushra Ahmed, the commissioning editor, and her team at HarperCollins, for their patience and their fantastic work in producing this book.

Nitish Wagle provided a crash-course in the art of structuring stories.

The support of Ardhra Nair, Prateek Goyal and Trupti Abhyankar meant that potentially tricky reporting trips to Pune were a breeze.

## Acknowledgements

The ever-resourceful Shruti Bhiwandiwala solved in a minute a structural issue I had fretted over for weeks.

Several members of the police department extended vital support to this enterprise. Recreating events going back several decades was made possible because these individuals jogged their memories, narrated incidents in graphic detail, chipped in with leads and pointed me in the right direction.

Sunita Gurjar translated an indecipherable document.

I am thankful to Suhas Gokhale, a friend and guide, for permitting me to quote extracts from his memoirs.

I am grateful to every police official, both serving and retired, who chose to speak on the record but more so to those I cannot name. They're the ones who debunked the official version of this case and who went to great lengths to open doors which would have otherwise remained closed to me.

I have to specially mention a few former residents of Siddharth Nagar, who spoke to me on the condition of anonymity and at some personal risk. No one, especially not government employees, is obligated to answer a reporter's questions.

It helped to have documents to refer to at every stage of reporting and writing this story. I am grateful to advocates N.N. Gavankar, Ayaz Khan and Gorakh Liman and fellow reporters, both for readily making documents available and for their time, patience and wisdom.

Access to a forensic laboratory was made possible by a few scientists who don't believe that their work ought to be treated like some state secret.

Through their stories, my former colleague Anish Patil and his mother Manda Patil; and Vijay Worlikar made Worli Koliwada of the last century come alive.

I am thankful to the Psychonaut; to Vijay Surve; and to Acid and Tracksuit for giving me a glimpse into their lives.

My grandmother, Janaki, and mother, Anuradha, single-handedly ensured that I met every deadline. I have tried to meet the standard they expect from books.

The final words of thanks I reserve for Monojit Majumdar, Rakesh Sinha and Muzamil Jaleel of the *Express*: inspirational storytellers and extraordinary teachers.

Now to those persons I was unable to speak with.

I met Atulchandra Kulkarni late in 2021 for his version of events. He said he did not recall details of the case that marked his introduction to the Mumbai Police crime branch. To a specific question on the crime branch's reasons behind the arrest of the five policemen, he said that he didn't remember. I contacted him again in October 2022, asking if he would like to respond. He declined the opportunity.

Of the five arrested policemen, Sudhakar Sarang did not respond despite multiple attempts to seek his comments. Jyotiram Mane declined to comment. Gautam Gaikwad made it clear when I met him in 2021 that he did not wish to participate in the writing of this book. His son Sanket, said that he would meet me to discuss the matter but despite attempting to contact him for over a year, he did not respond.

Gyan Manikkam Samuel did not respond despite multiple attempts to seek his response. Paulraj Padaiyatchi could not be reached for his response.

Rajiv Shah of the Garware Club House declined a request for an interview.

Deputy Superintendent of Police Deepak Humbre could not be reached either on the phone or at his residence. Phone calls and a text message left on his wife's phone also did not elicit a response.

N.D. Chavan, then DCP of the Anti Narcotics Cell, did not respond to requests for an interview.

DCPs Dhananjay Kulkarni and Mohan Dahikar denied being involved in the investigation.

Police constable Madhukar Shingte declined a request for an interview.

Sandeep Bishnoi, Director General (Legal & Technical) of the Maharashtra Police, who heads the Directorate of Forensic Science Laboratories, rejected my request to interview forensic scientists involved in the testing the samples in 2015.

Jagdeo Kalapad, then inspector-in-charge of the Social Service Branch of the Mumbai Police Crime Branch, which was credited with Baby's arrest, would not discuss the case. All he said was, 'There was a lot of pressure on us to find Baby.'

# Notes

**Prologue**

1. European Monitoring Centre for Drugs and Drug Addiction, *Report on the risk assessment of mephedrone in the framework of the Council Decision on new psychoactive substances*, May 2011.
2. Alcohol and Drug Foundation. Website available at https://adf.org.au/drug-facts/khat/
3. European Monitoring Centre for Drugs and Drug Addiction, *Report on the risk assessment of mephedrone in the framework of the Council Decision on new psychoactive substances*, May 2011.
4. *Chemistry World*, 'Wrecked by a high tide', 6 September 2017. Available at https://www.chemistryworld.com/features/the-rising-tide-of-legal-highs/3007738.article
5. Ibid.
6. *Haaretz*, 'A Qat above the rest', 15 October 2004. Available at https://www.haaretz.com/1.4719066

7   *The Guardian*, 'Drug and dance as the Israelis blot out intifada', 4 September 2004. Available at https://www.theguardian.com/world/2004/sep/04/israel
8   *Chemistry World*, 'Wrecked by a high tide', 6 September 2017. Available at https://www.chemistryworld.com/features/the-rising-tide-of-legal-highs/3007738.article

## Chapter One

9   Monosodium Glutamate is most widely available under the trade name Ajinomoto, a Japanese firm founded in 1909 to commercially manufacture the salt of glutamic acid. Special receptors in the human tongue and stomach detect the taste umami, which the acid is responsible for producing, in a variety of foods ranging from meat to eggs. The acid was first discovered by the German chemist Karl Heinrich Ritthausen in 1866. In 1907, the Japanese chemist Kikunae Ikeda identified the taste after experimenting on edible seaweed. A year later, Ikeda patented his discovery and worked with an entrepreneur named Saburosuke Suzuki II to produce it on a commercial scale. Ajinomoto is better known in India for its use in a range of instant soups, *Knorr* Cup Soup.
10   E. Harshbarger, 'The never-ending stories: Inception's Penrose Staircase', *Wired*, 19 August 2010. Available at https://www.wired.com/2010/08/the-never-ending-stories-inceptions-penrose-staircase/
11   Just like the writer William Burroughs' fears for the life of an addicted customer in New York City in the 1940s, an incident he described in his semi-autobiographical novel *Junky: Confessions of an Unredeemed Drug Addict* (1953).

## Chapter Four

12   S.R. Rao and R. Rajput, 2015, 'The Sunday Story: Meow-Meow and Baby', *The Indian Express*, 1 June. Available at https://indianexpress.com/article/india/india-others/the-sunday-story-meow-meow-and-baby/

13  S.R. Rao, 2018, 'Baby's days out: The rise, fall and possible resurrection of a Mumbai drug queen', *The Indian Express*, 15 July. Available at https://indianexpress.com/article/express-sunday-eye/babys-days-out-5258342/

14  S.R. Rao, 2015, 'Mumbai slumlord takes on police, wants to shake off drug queen tag', *The Indian Express*, 26 October. Available at https://indianexpress.com/article/cities/mumbai/mumbai-slumlord-takes-on-police-wants-to-shake-off-drug-queen-tag/

15  S.R. Rao and R. Rajput, 2015, 'The Sunday Story: Meow-Meow and Baby', *The Indian Express*, 1 June. Available at https://indianexpress.com/article/india/india-others/the-sunday-story-meow-meow-and-baby/

16  Ibid.

## Chapter Five

17  S.R. Rao and R. Rajput, 2015, 'The Sunday Story: Meow-Meow and Baby', *The Indian Express*, 1 June. Available at https://indianexpress.com/article/india/india-others/the-sunday-story-meow-meow-and-baby/

## Chapter Six

18  S.R. Rao and R. Rajput, 2015, 'The Sunday Story: Meow-Meow and Baby', *The Indian Express*. 1 June. Available at https://indianexpress.com/article/india/india-others/the-sunday-story-meow-meow-and-baby/

19  Mumbai Mirror, 2011, 'Senior cop held with drugs in police car', *Mumbai Mirror*, 22 February. Available at https://mumbaimirror.indiatimes.com/mumbai/other/senior-cop-held-with-drugs-in-police-car/articleshow/16104253.cms

20  S. Hakim, 2019, 'Cop cleared of drug smuggling charge', *Mumbai Mirror*, 6 September. Available at https://mumbaimirror.indiatimes.com/mumbai/crime/cop-cleared-of-drug-smuggling-charge/articleshow/34084418.cms

## Chapter Seven

21  S.T.B. Sheppard, 2012. *Bombay Place-names and Street-names: An Excursion into the By-Ways of the History of Bombay City.* Ulan Press.
22  Ibid.
23  S.M. Edwardes, 1909. *The Gazetteer of Bombay City and Island Volume 1.* University of Michigan Library.
24  Gillian Tindall, 1982, *City of Gold*, Temple Smith.
25  Ibid.
26  S.M. Edwardes, 1909. *The Gazetteer of Bombay City and Island Volume 3.* University of Michigan Library.
27  S.M. Edwardes, 1902. *The Rise of Bombay: A Retrospect.* Times of India Press.
28  Khorshed Deboo, 2019, 'After Two Years, Century-old Ma Hajiani Dargah Restored to Glory', *The Hindu*, 23 April. Available at https://www.thehindu.com/society/history-and-culture/after-two-years-century-old-ma-hajiani-dargah-restored-to-glory/article26915467.ece
29  S.M. Edwardes, 1909. *The Gazetteer of Bombay City and Island Volume 3.* University of Michigan Library.
30  Ibid.
31  Ibid.
32  Ibid.
33  Ibid.
34  Ibid.
35  Ibid.
36  Ibid.
37  Ibid.
38  Ibid.
39  M. Rahman, 1987. 'PM Rajiv Gandhi's Rs 100 crore gift to Bombay to benefit people of city's largest slum', *India Today*, 31 January. Available at https://www.indiatoday.in/magazine/indiascope/story/19870131-pm-rajiv-gandhis-rs-100-crore-gift-to-bombay-to-benefit-people-of-citys-largest-slum-798486-1987-01-31

## Chapter Eight

40   Press Trust of India, 2014, 'Mumbai: Rakesh Maria takes charge as police commissioner', NDTV.com, 16 February. Available at https://www.ndtv.com/mumbai-news/mumbai-rakesh-maria-takes-charge-as-police-commissioner-550979
41   Correspondent, 2013, 'Top cop Satyapal Singh attracts public ire for his comments during TV interview', *Mid-Day*, 28 August. Available at https://www.mid-day.com/news/india-news/article/top-cop-satyapal-singh-attracts-public-ire-for-his-comments-during-tv-interview-229066
42   R. Maria, 2020. *Let Me Say It Now*. Westland.
43   Press Trust of India, 2014, 'Mumbai: Rakesh Maria takes charge as police commissioner, NDTV.com, 16 February. Available at https://www.ndtv.com/mumbai-news/mumbai-rakesh-maria-takes-charge-as-police-commissioner-550979
44   I.E. Online, 2014, 'Police, narcotics sleuths round up 400 drug addicts in 3 days', *The Indian Express*, 25 February. Available at https://indianexpress.com/article/cities/mumbai/police-narcotics-sleuths-round-up-400-drug-addicts-in-3-days/
45   This table shows drug seizure figures for a two-and-a-half-week-long drive against drug users and peddlers undertaken by the Mumbai Police between February and March 2014.

| Drug | Quantity seized |
|---|---|
| Ganja | 62 kgs |
| Ephedrine | 1.7 kgs |
| Charas | 1.25 kgs |
| Cocaine | 17 grams |
| Amphetamine | 14 grams |

*Source*: Mumbai Police

46   Press Trust of India, 2014, 'Mumbai: Rakesh Maria takes charge as police commissioner', NDTV.com, 16 February. Available at https://www.ndtv.com/mumbai-news/mumbai-rakesh-maria-takes-charge-as-police-commissioner-550979

## Chapter Nine

47  S.R. Rao, 2015, 'Mumbai slumlord takes on police, wants to shake off drug queen tag'. *The Indian Express*, 26 October. Available at https://indianexpress.com/article/cities/mumbai/mumbai-slumlord-takes-on-police-wants-to-shake-off-drug-queen-tag/

## Chapter Ten

48  E.T. Online, 2022, 'From DRI to NCB and back, Sameer Wankhede's controversial run-ins with B-town celebs', *The Economic Times*, 6 January. Available at https://economictimes.indiatimes.com/magazines/panache/from-dri-to-ncb-and-back-sameer-wankhedes-controversial-run-ins-with-b-town-celebs/articleshow/88706124.cms
49  Ibid.
50  Ibid.

## Chapter Twelve

51  P. Thakurdesai, 2012, 'Marine Drive rape case: Sunil Atmaram More sentenced to 12 years imprisonment', *India Today*, 1 March. Available at https://www.indiatoday.in/magazine/indiascope/story/20060417-marine-drive-rape-case-sunil-atmaram-more-sentenced-to-12-years-imprisonment-783339-2006-04-17

## Chapter Thirteen

52  Suhas Gokhale, 2016, *Kaidi Number C-14861* (Marathi), Menaka Prakashan.
53  C. Kapoor, 1984, 'Fury of communal violence burns 80 km stretch from tip of south Bombay to Bhiwandi town', *India Today*, 21 April. Available at https://www.indiatoday.in/magazine/indiascope/story/19840615-fury-of-communal-violence-burns-80-km-stretch-from-tip-of-south-bombay-to-bhiwandi-town-803038-1984-06-15
54  Ibid.

55 C. Kapoor, 1984, 'Fury of communal violence burns 80 km stretch from tip of south Bombay to Bhiwandi town', *India Today*, 21 April. Available at https://www.indiatoday.in/magazine/indiascope/story/19840615-fury-of-communal-violence-burns-80-km-stretch-from-tip-of-south-bombay-to-bhiwandi-town-803038-1984-06-15
56 Suhas Gokhale, 2016, *Kaidi Number C-14861* (Marathi), Menaka Prakashan.

## Chapter Fourteen

57 YouTube, 2015, 'Drug Mafia Baby Patankar lands in police net', 28 April. [Video]. https://www.youtube.com/watch?v=mRvTYMpDVGU
58 Hindustan Times, 2015, 'Will conduct probe in drugs case if need arises: Maharashtra CM Fadnavis', *Hindustan Times*, 28 March. Available at https://www.hindustantimes.com/mumbai/will-conduct-probe-in-drugs-case-if-need-arises-maharashtra-cm-fadnavis/story-2yZOCzSfZiySBDGZstHeTI.html
59 YouTube, 2015, 'Drug don Baby arrested in Panvel', 23 April. [Video]. https://zeenews.india.com/marathi/news/video/drug-smuggler-baby-patankar-caught-by-police-23rd-april-2015/272668
60 YouTube, 2015, 'Mumbai: Property of drugs dealer baby patankar', 23 April. [Video]. https://www.youtube.com/watch?v=4fEpa82RZJM
61 S. Gupta, 2015, 'Too Low? The News Peter, Indrani Mukerjea Sought', NDTV.com, 1 September. Available at https://www.ndtv.com/opinion/too-low-the-news-peter-indrani-mukerjea-sought-1212992

## Chapter Seventeen

62 Prasanna filed a defamation suit against advocates Chomal and Wani before the Chief Metropolitan Magistrate's Court in Mumbai on 17 June 2015.
63 Parte denied these allegations when I interviewed him.
64 Express News Service, 2015, 'Meow meow queen says subjected to obscene gestures in custody, police get a court rap, *The Indian*

*Express*, 28 April. Available at https://indianexpress.com/article/cities/mumbai/meow-meow-queen-says-subjected-to-obscene-gestures-in-custody-police-get-a-court-rap/

## Chapter Nineteen

65  S. Rao, 2015, 'Meow Meow Drug Racket: "Mumbai cops helped Baby evade arrest"', *The Indian Express*, 31 May. Available at https://indianexpress.com/article/india/india-others/meow-meow-drug-racket-mumbai-cops-helped-baby-evade-arrest/
66  Ibid.
67  Ibid.
68  Ibid.

## Chapter Twenty-One

69  S. Hakim, 2019, 'Byculla residents launch night time patrols to combat spread of new killer designer drug', *Mumbai Mirror*, 6 September. Available at https://mumbaimirror.indiatimes.com/mumbai/other/byculla-residents-launch-night-time-patrols-to-combat-spread-of-new-killer-designer-drug/articleshow/45289861.cms

## Chapter Twenty-Two

70  S.R. Rao, 2015, 'Anti-Narcotics Cell to enlist music therapist to wean addicts off drugs', *The Indian Express*, 9 March. Available at https://indianexpress.com/article/cities/mumbai/anti-narcotics-cell-to-enlist-music-therapist-to-wean-addicts-off-drugs/
71  Express News Service, 2015, 'Seven months after request from Mumbai police, Centre bans MEOW MEOW drug', *The Indian Express*, 21 February. Available at https://indianexpress.com/article/cities/mumbai/seven-months-after-request-from-mumbai-police-centre-bans-meow-meow-drug/
72  Hindustan Times Correspondent, 2014, 'CM Fadnavis wants Centre to ban mephedrone', *Hindustan Times*, 13 December. Available at https://www.hindustantimes.com/

india/cm-fadnavis-wants-centre-to-ban-mephedrone/story-KQfUoO01LXthI5XFOspSfO.html
73   Thana Singh vs Central Bureau Of Narcotics, (2013) 2 SCC 590.

## Chapter Twenty-Four

74   S.R. Rao, 2015, 'Meow meow case: "Kalokhe kept changing location of mephedrone before it was seized"', *The Indian Express*, 10 October. Available at https://indianexpress.com/article/cities/mumbai/meow-meow-case-kalokhe-kept-changing-location-of-mephedrone-before-it-was-seized/
75   S.R. Rao, 2015, 'Mumbai slumlord takes on police, wants to shake off drug queen tag', *The Indian Express*, 26 October. Available at https://indianexpress.com/article/cities/mumbai/mumbai-slumlord-takes-on-police-wants-to-shake-off-drug-queen-tag/
76   S. Rao, 2015, 'Sheena Bora Murder: Driver's wife denies police claim, says she last saw him 10 days ago', *The Indian Express*, 27 August. Available at https://indianexpress.com/article/india/india-others/sheena-bora-murder-drivers-wife-denies-police-claim-says-she-last-saw-him-10-days-ago/
77   S.R. Rao, 2015, 'Mumbai slumlord takes on police, wants to shake off drug queen tag', *The Indian Express*, 26 October. Available at https://indianexpress.com/article/cities/mumbai/mumbai-slumlord-takes-on-police-wants-to-shake-off-drug-queen-tag/

## Chapter Twenty-Six

78   M. Plumber, 2015, 'Bombay High Court refuses relief to Baby Patankar, allows her to approach trial court', *DNA India*, 15 December. Available at https://www.dnaindia.com/mumbai/report-bombay-high-court-refuses-relief-to-baby-patankar-allows-her-to-approach-trial-court-2155708
79   Maharashtra Anti Corruption Bureau, 2016, *Statistical Information of cases registered in 2016*. Available at http://acbmaharashtra.gov.in/files/Statistic/79.pdf

80 S. Rajput, 2016, 'Satara DSP held for demanding money from Patankar, Kalokhe', *Hindustan Times*, 7 May. Available at https://www.hindustantimes.com/mumbai/satara-dsp-held-for-demanding-money-from-patankar-kalokhe/story-uggDqAqV3sWDUSICs8MudL.html

# Chapter Twenty-Nine

81 S. Rao, 2021, 'Debating NDPS Act: "A Pandora's box for already corrupt officers …"', Newslaundry, 26 October. Available at https://www.newslaundry.com/2021/10/26/debating-ndps-act-a-pandoras-box-for-already-corrupt-officers
82 Ibid.
83 Ibid.
84 The checklist consists of the following points:
- The investigating officer must record information of a drug case in writing and convey it to their immediate superior officer. They must then plan an operation in the least possible time.
- The officer must head out for a search equipped with an arrest memo, envelopes, official seals, sealing material, chemical analysis forms, paper to write on, a weighing scale, screw drivers, torches, spot lights, mirrors, radios, cameras, binoculars, weapons, vehicles in working condition, and field drug-detection kits and precursor chemical detection kits.
- The officer must make efforts to locate at least two respectable residents in that locality or the adjoining locality to join the search as independent witnesses.
- The officer must seal off entrances and exits of the premises to be searched and ensure that no one is able to escape.
- The officer must inform a suspect that he has the right to be searched in the presence of a magistrate or gazetted officer. If the suspect insists on being searched before a magistrate or gazetted officer, the officer must take the suspect to the nearest such officer.
- A female suspect must be searched by female police personnel. The police personnel conducting the search must respect the suspect's dignity.

- After searching the premises, the officer must prepare a search memo indicating the location and weight of the drug discovered along with the time and date and signatures of the independent witnesses. A separate search memo must be prepared if the drugs are discovered during the personal search of a suspect. The seized substance must be weighed and its weight duly recorded. A copy of the search memo must be provided to the owner of the premises. In case no drugs are recovered during the personal search of the suspect or the premises, the search memo must mention that.
- Representative samples should be drawn from the seized drugs, sealed into envelopes and signed by the officer, independent witnesses, the person from whose possession they are recovered, or the owner of the premises. The samples, a cover letter and a correctly filled chemical analysis form must be deposited in the forensic science laboratory within seventy-two hours of the seizure. The rest of the contraband must be sealed and taken to the police station. Before being deposited in the *maalkhana* of the police station, the contraband must be sealed again in the presence of the investigating officer. The constable in-charge of the *maalkhana* must verify the seals, signatures and weight of the contraband and also record the details in the *maalkhana* register before storing it.

85  Narcotics Control Bureau, Mumbai vs Abdullah Hussain Juma & Anr. (2003). Available at https://indiankanoon.org/doc/141361405/

86  An order is expected to be passed in February 2023.

## About the Author

**Srinath Rao** is a Mumbai-based crime reporter who used to work with *The Indian Express*. He has studied for a diploma in journalism at the Express Institute of Media Studies in Delhi. He is presently an independent journalist.

30 Years *of*

HarperCollins *Publishers* India

At HarperCollins, we believe in telling the best stories and finding the widest possible readership for our books in every format possible. We started publishing 30 years ago; a great deal has changed since then, but what has remained constant is the passion with which our authors write their books, the love with which readers receive them, and the sheer joy and excitement that we as publishers feel in being a part of the publishing process.

Over the years, we've had the pleasure of publishing some of the finest writing from the subcontinent and around the world, and some of the biggest bestsellers in India's publishing history. Our books and authors have won a phenomenal range of awards, and we ourselves have been named Publisher of the Year the greatest number of times. But nothing has meant more to us than the fact that millions of people have read the books we published, and somewhere, a book of ours might have made a difference.

As we step into our fourth decade, we go back to that one word – a word which has been a driving force for us all these years.

Read.

Harper Collins    4th    HARPER PERENNIAL    HARPER BUSINESS    HARPER BLACK    हार्पर हिन्दी

HarperCollins *Children's Books*    HARPER DESIGN    HARPER VANTAGE    Harper Sport